SPECIAL ISSUE
CONSTITUTIONAL POLITICS IN A CONSERVATIVE ERA

STUDIES IN LAW, POLITICS, AND SOCIETY

Series Editor: Austin Sarat

STUDIES IN LAW, POLITICS, AND SOCIETY   VOLUME 44

SPECIAL ISSUE CONSTITUTIONAL POLITICS IN A CONSERVATIVE ERA

EDITED BY

AUSTIN SARAT

Department of Law, Jurisprudence & Social Thought and Political Science, Amherst College, USA

JAI

United Kingdom – North America – Japan
India – Malaysia – China

JAI Press is an imprint of Emerald Group Publishing Limited
Howard House, Wagon Lane, Bingley BD16 1WA, UK

First edition 2008

Copyright © 2008 Emerald Group Publishing Limited

Reprints and permission service
Contact: booksandseries@emeraldinsight.com

British Library Cataloguing in Publication Data
A catalogue record for this book is available from the British Library

ISBN: 978-0-7623-1486-7
ISSN: 1059-4337 (Series)

Printed and Bound in Great Britain by
MPG Books Ltd, Bodmin, Cornwall

Awarded in recognition of
Emerald's production
department's adherence to
quality systems and processes
when preparing scholarly
journals for print

INVESTOR IN PEOPLE

CONTENTS

LIST OF CONTRIBUTORS

Thomas F. Burke   Department of Political Science,
                      Wellesley College, Wellesley, MA, USA

Ronald Kahn   Department of Politics, Oberlin College,
                      OH, USA

Scott E. Lemieux   Department of Political Science,
                      Hunter College, CUNY, New York,
                      NY, USA

George I. Lovell   Department of Political Science,
                      University of Washington, Seattle,
                      WA, USA

Ira L. Strauber   Department of Political Science,
                      Grinnell College, Grinnell, IA, USA

George Thomas   Department of Political Science,
                      Williams College, Williamstown,
                      MA, USA

David A. Yalof   Department of Political Science,
                      University of Connecticut, Storrs,
                      CT, USA

EDITORIAL BOARD

ix

UNDERSTANDING THE IMPACT AND VISIBILITY OF IDEOLOGICAL CHANGE ON THE SUPREME COURT

Scott E. Lemieux and George I. Lovell

ABSTRACT

This chapter offers an explanation for the mixed record of the Supreme Court since the 1960s, and considers the implications of that record for the future. The chapter emphasizes that judicial power is connected to choices made by other political actors. We argue that conventional ways of measuring the impact of Court rulings and the Court's treatment of precedents are misleading. The Court cannot be understood as a counter-majoritarian protector of rights. In both past and future, electoral outcomes determine the policy areas in which the Court will be influential, and also the choices the justices make about how to portray their treatment of law and precedents.

Special Issue: Constitutional Politics in a Conservative Era
Studies in Law, Politics, and Society, Volume 44, 1–33
ISSN: 1059-4337/doi:10.1016/S1059-4337(08)00801-6

INTRODUCTION: RIGHTS, MAJORITIES, AND WARREN COURT HANGOVERS

Earl Warren was Chief Justice for fifteen years, and left the Supreme Court almost forty years ago. Yet the constitutional scholarship inspired by the Warren Court continues to haunt both scholarly and popular under-standings of the Supreme Court. Landmark liberal rulings during Warren's tenure inspired seminal works in constitutional theory that introduced the terminology and theoretical constructs that many scholars continue to use as they try to understand the ongoing role of the Court in the political system. The scholars inspired by Warren's tenure often applauded the liberal direction of the Court and developed faith in the Court as a positive force for social change. However, they also worried that unelected judges were making policy rather than elected officials. Constitutional scholars thus struggled to construct interpretive theories that could reconcile "counter-majoritarian" judicial review with their commitments to representative democracy.[1]

While court scholars took different approaches and reached different conclusions, they shared an underlying understanding of the nature of judicial power and the role of the courts in the political system. First, they understood judicial decisions that struck down state or federal laws as instances where unelected judges established policy outcomes different from the ones preferred by the elected officials. Such rulings appeared to thwart the will of popular majorities, acting through elected representatives. Thus, the power to strike down laws was potentially undemocratic, and in need of special justification.

Second, most scholars understood this power to reverse legislation as a fixed and stable institutional power. Although judicial review was not directly mentioned in the Constitution, they understood the power as firmly established by the Supreme Court in *Marbury v. Madison* (1803).[2] They also saw the institutional capacity of judges to reverse legislative outcomes as the result of permanent features of the Constitution. These included the guarantee of life tenure, which shielded judges from retaliation from both other branches and tides of popular opinion; and the Constitution's cumbersome supermajority requirements for amendment, which meant that judges would allegedly have the final word on constitutional interpretation.

Third, scholars thought that, despite these underlying concerns, judicial review could be a justifiable and attractive component of a liberal democratic state. The seemingly undemocratic nature of judicial review allowed judges to perform an essential role in a constitutional democracy: Preserving the constitutional rights of minorities against the threat of majority tyranny. This view of the Court's role, undoubtedly inspired by several high-profile Warren Court rulings protecting minority rights, meant that scholars could conclude that judicial review could be legitimate in some instances. It also led them to develop methods for distinguishing instances where judges preserved rights or values that were truly part of the Constitution from instances where political or ideological judges abused their power by reading new rights or values into the Constitution.

These basic assumptions about the nature, sources, and role of judicial power have structured both normative and empirical work on the Court. Normative constitutional law scholars tried to evaluate the Court's constitutional rulings by testing whether the Court's justifications were appropriately tethered to constitutional values or constitutional text. Such scholars offered various theories and methods of interpretation for evaluating and perhaps controlling judicial power.[3] Meanwhile many empirical scholars in political science devoted their attention to measuring the extent to which actual judicial decisions could be matched to the legal justifications that judges offered. These scholars delighted in challenging normative scholars by showing that judicial rulings could be predicted by looking at the political ideology of judges, and without paying much attention to legal or constitutional criteria (e.g., Segal & Spaeth, 2002; for an overview of this literature, see Baum, 1997). Despite their differences in approach and conclusions, the more empirically minded political scientists (like the constitutional theorists) understood judicial power as fixed by constitutional guarantees and thus unconstrained by ordinary democratic processes.

The recasting of the Court in the role of protector of minorities was a tempting move by scholars trying to explain or justify an atypically liberal Court. The model's persistence as a general model of how the Court works is, however, rather puzzling, given both the Court's history before Warren and the changes that the Court has experienced since Warren's departure. Before World War II, the Court openly clashed with elected officials much less frequently. Moreover, the cases where earlier Courts did succeed in reversing determined elected officials in the national government do not match the Warren Court's reputation as a "counter-majoritarian" protector of the rights of discrete and insular minorities (Dahl, 1957). Earlier confrontations with the Court involved decisions protecting the interests of numeric minorities who were less attractive to liberal scholars, including slave owners, proprietary capitalists, factory owners who wanted to employ children, and corporate opponents of labor organizations and economic regulation (Ross, 1994; Paul, 1960).

While the counter-majoritarian model may not fit well for the years before Warren, scholars could still make a powerful case for the model if it continued to fit the Court in the post-Warren years. Since Warren's departure, twelve of fourteen new justices have been appointed by Republican presidents. Each of those Republican presidents had attacked liberal court decisions while campaigning, and had also promised to appoint new justices who would reverse the rights-protecting proclivities of the Court. The results of these efforts to remake the Court could provide a good test of the counter-majoritarian model. If the Court has somehow remained a counter-majoritarian rights protector despite the determined efforts of elected officials to change the Court, the models developed to explain or justify the Warren Court would still provide a useful framework for understanding the Supreme Court as an ongoing institution. If, however, the Court's role changed (or returned to normal) in response to these outside pressures and events, the counter-majoritarian model might simply be a particularized description of an unusual Court that existed during an unusual period of American history.

Unfortunately, the record of the post-Warren Court does not make it easy to decide whether the counter-majoritarian model has passed this test. The Court has produced a mixed record that confounds easy assessment, and the model itself does not provide good tools for evaluating that mixed record. The case in favor of the counter-majoritarian model can be made on the basis of some surprising Burger and Rehnquist Court rulings that confounded expectations about what Republican appointees would do. Liberal rulings following closely on Warren's departure struck down the death penalty (*Furman v. Georgia*, 1972) and state laws banning abortion (*Roe v. Wade*, 1973). Even after 1975, when the fifth new Republican nominee (a Court majority) took his seat, the Court did not stop protecting the rights of disfavored minorities. The Court attracted a great deal of attention and criticism when it struck down both state and federal laws targeting flag burning (*Texas v. Johnson*, 1989; *United States v. Eichman*, 1990). Much more recently, after several more Republican appointments, the Court struck down a Nebraska law banning a late-term abortion procedure (*Stenberg v. Carhart*, 2000), and Texas law criminalizing same-sex sodomy (*Lawrence v. Texas*, 2003). The Court has also recently placed at least some obstacles in the path of George W. Bush's policies for detaining alleged terrorists (*Rasul v. Bush*, 2004; *Hamdi v. Rumsfeld*, 2004; *Hamdan v. Rumsfeld*, 2006). In addition to these rulings striking down laws or blocking executive actions, the Court has also defied expectations by declining to overturn notorious liberal precedents on criminal justice, affirmative action, and, most famously of all, abortion.[4] This record has led many observers to conclude that the Court, while tilting to the right, has remained a centrist institution and thus survived political attacks and efforts to remake the Court (Savage, 1992; Simon, 1995; Kahn, 1994, 1999; Rosen, 2006).

Cases like these help to explain the puzzling persistence of the model of the Court as a counter-majoritarian protector of rights. They are not, however, the entire story. As we explain below, some of the high-profile rulings announcing decisions to "reaffirm" liberal precedents have actually drained those precedents of any bite. In addition, numerous scholars and other observers have begun to call attention to other lines of cases that reveal a substantial conservative shift on the Burger and Rehnquist Courts (Spann, 1993; Tushnet, 1999; Keck, 2004; Noonan, 2004). After the Court's suspect involvement in the 2000 presidential election, Balkin and Levinson (2001) argued that a string of recent rulings suggested that the United States was on the brink of a "constitutional revolution." The rulings that reveal these conservative shifts have not always attracted as much attention as more "centrist" rulings like the flag burning case. The conservative rulings have taken on technical issues like the scope of federal regulatory power and state government immunity from lawsuits, and many have come in statutory rather than constitutional cases. However, the cases that reveal the more conservative trend have significant implications for minority rights, and also seem to turn the Warren Court-era understanding of the Court completely on its head: Some of the most important doctrinal innovations of the Rehnquist Court have come in cases where the Court has reversed or limited efforts by legislative *majorities* to protect the rights of minorities.

The Court's mixed record makes it difficult to assess whether the models inspired by the Warren Court remain relevant and useful. The competing trends cry out for some measure of the relative significance of different cases and the relative degree to which different judicial rulings act as a continuing constraint on elected officials. Unfortunately, however, theoretical constructs like the "counter-majoritarian difficulty" are not refined enough to facilitate such comparisons. For reasons explained below, instances where the Court strikes down a law do not all constitute the same sort of counter-majoritarian interference with majorities. Simply counting and comparing the number of statutes struck down or precedents reversed in different eras will not provide a very accurate picture of the extent to which the Court has constrained majorities or protected minority rights. More importantly, the conventional model's assumptions about the sources and constraints on judicial power distort the Court's record by masking some of the most important ways that judicial rulings – and judicial choices about how to characterize rulings – can impact political outcomes and policymaking processes.

The current stage in the Court's history is a particularly good time to reassess both the Court and the theoretical constructs that scholars use for understanding the Court. The appointments of John Roberts and Samuel Alito as replacements for Chief Justice Rehnquist and Justice O'Connor create the possibility of a considerably different (and more conservative) Supreme Court jurisprudence. In this chapter, we attempt to provide a foundation for assessing the Court's recent record and for understanding future developments. Our account rejects the counter-majoritarian under-standing because we find it to be too simplistic and reductionist in its understanding of the way underlying political dynamics create and constrain opportunities for judges to exercise power. Our account builds on a variety of recent and innovative scholarship that challenges the view that judges who strike down laws necessarily thwart the will of majorities by exercising fixed institutional powers. We draw in part on work by historical institutionalist political scientists who have looked at how judicial power evolves over time. Far from being impermeable to political influence and permanently established by *Marbury v. Madison*, judicial roles and capacities have changed considerably. While judges have always been important policymakers in the United States (Horwitz, 1977; Orren, 1991) the institutional and procedural mechanisms that allow judges to make policy are always changing. The institutional capacities and jurisdiction of federal courts have expanded considerably, but that expansion has occurred because judges have proven effective (if sometimes inadvertent) servants for the interests of powerful actors in other branches (Graber, 1993, 1996, 1998, 1999; Gillman, 2002; Lovell, 2003; Whittington, 2005; see also Dahl, 1957; Melnick, 1983, 1994; Miller & Barnes, 2004). We are also inspired by rational choice scholars who have illuminated some of the incentives that elected official have for tolerating or expanding judicial power (Shipan, 1997; Rogers, 2001; Ginsburg, 2003). Scholarship in both the historical and rational choice traditions has shown that elected officials have a variety of incentives to expand judicial power. Legislators might expand judicial offices or jurisdiction in order to protect immediate electoral gains from subsequent losses (Gillman, 2002; Ginsburg, 2003; Hirschl, 2004); or try to shift blame for resolving controversial or cross cutting issues (Graber, 1993; Lovell, 2003). At the same time, this scholarship suggests that judicial power is more fragile and more dependent upon the actions of other branches than the counter-majoritarian model assumes.

While no single, unified theory of judicial power has emerged from these often disparate sources, the scholarship presents numerous challenges to more conventional views of judicial power. In particular, such work suggests that interaction between judges and other political actors cannot be understood as a zero-sum struggle where each branch tries to minimize the influence of other branches in order to have a direct and final say over policy. Such scholarship also challenges some seemingly straightforward assumptions about how to interpret evidence. The conditions that give elected officials incentives to create or tolerate expansions of judicial power also lead those officials to disguise both their motives and the nature of the choices that they are making. Moreover, in many cases the real impact of a court ruling is not the immediate effect it has on policy outcomes, but the way the ruling changes the political dynamics surrounding an issue. As a result, scholars have to be very careful about how they interpret evidence. Appearances of both judicial usurpation and legislative acquiescence are often quite deceiving.

We do not try to sketch a complete alternative theoretical account in this chapter. Our more modest goal is to offer an explanation and interpretation of the seemingly mixed record of the post-Warren Court, and to draw out some of the implications of that record for the future. In the final section, we offer some predictions about what might happen under the new Roberts Court. Our predictions are contingent upon various possible political outcomes in the other branches. The predictions are contingent not because we want to hedge our bets, but because we want to reinforce an important substantive point at the heart of our account: Both the ideological direction that the Court takes and the degree to which that direction will be easily observable in the Court's rulings *always* depends on the opportunities created by institutions and events outside the judiciary.

The core of the chapter consists of sketching out some do's and don'ts regarding how to evaluate the ideological shifts on the Court and the degree to which the Court at any particular time is constraining elected officials or clashing with outside political actors. Our analysis shows how conventional ways of assessing ideological shifts on the Court or the political impact of court decisions can be misleading. The discussion also suggests that the model of the Court as the counter-majoritarian protector of constitutional rights is not a very useful tool for evaluating the Court's complex record since Warren's departure.

Our concluding section takes the analysis into the future and looks at how electoral outcomes will shape ideological shifts, the policy areas in which the justices will assert themselves, and the choices that the justices make about how they portray their treatments of precedents. The ideological trajectory of the Roberts Court and the extent to which it will clash with the other branches will depend on political outcomes in other branches. Thus, instead of offering unequivocal predictions, we detail some alternative scenarios that serve to illuminate the significance of the premises outlined in the second section.

FIVE DO'S AND DON'TS FOR ASSESSING IDEOLOGICAL SHIFT ON THE COURT AND THE IMPACT OF JUDICIAL RULINGS ON DEMOCRATIC POLITICS

Don't Assume that When a Court Strikes Down a Law, it is Necessarily Thwarting the Will or Expectations of Majorities of the Population or of Elected Officials

Bickel's claim that the judicial review created a "counter-majoritarian" difficulty in a democratic system has been influential because his terminology succinctly expressed the concerns that scholars felt about instances where judges reversed choices made by more directly accountable officials. Unfortunately, the phrase "counter-majoritarian" is also very misleading, as is the implicit account of underlying political processes that the phrase is meant to capture. In many plausible circumstances, a judicial ruling striking down a law will come much closer to the wishes of majorities than the law that is struck down. Grouping together all cases where judges strike down laws as posing the same "counter-majoritarian" difficulty hides enormous differences in the way that different kinds of judicial reversals impact ongoing democratic processes.

The most fundamental problem is that there is no guarantee that any particular law on some statute book is supported by contemporary popular or legislative majorities. The 2006 vote in South Dakota to repeal a recently passed ban on abortion (Davey, 2006) provides one powerful example. Outcomes in legislative bodies depend not just on the expressed will of the majority, but also on the way entrenched interests are able to take advantage of particular elements of the political process; including the rules that determine how legislative districts are drawn, electoral campaigns are funded, who gets party nominations, and who gets to vote (see Ely, 1980). At the federal level, several core features of the "elected" branches are non-majoritarian, most notably the Electoral College and the gross malapportionment of the Senate (Levinson, 2006). More generally, the American public simply does not participate in electoral politics in sufficient numbers, or pay attention to politics with sufficient intensity, to guarantee even awareness of most legislative policies, let alone approval (Zaller, 2005; Campbell et al., 1960). Attention to factors like these can make it difficult to say that some legislative outcomes are majoritarian or even democratic. For example, noticing that very large numbers of citizens living in Southern states in 1954 were unable to participate in electoral politics makes it much more difficult to say that the statutes that the Court invalidated in *Brown* were the outcomes of a "democratic" process.

Even laying these issues of legislative responsiveness to the public aside, there is no guarantee that even a majority of *legislators* support a law that is struck down by the Court. Legislative processes in both Congress and the state legislatures quite often give minority factions power to veto changes in the law (Tsebelis, 2002). Among other things, this means that anachronistic laws do not automatically disappear from the statute books as soon as they fall out of favor. The Court's decision to strike down a Connecticut law banning birth control in *Griswold v. Connecticut* (1965) came about only because a single legislative faction was able to prevent repeal of a silly law (Garrow, 1994). The Court did not thwart some majority of Connecticut citizens that was determined to imprison married couples who used birth control.

It is also easy to exaggerate the effects of largely symbolic rulings where the court strikes down laws that are not being systematically enforced. For example, rulings in *Griswold v. Connecticut* and *Lawrence v. Texas* forced a very small number of recalcitrant states into line with a broader national movement to successfully repeal outmoded laws.[5] Supreme Court rulings that accelerate or nationalize an ongoing repeal process in the states have a very different impact than rulings that thwart a budding popular movement by striking down a novel state legislative reform that might otherwise have been adopted in all fifty states. The Court's impact in the second type of case is much more consequential, but the difference cannot be captured by simply counting how many existing state statutes were invalidated by a ruling.

In many instances, the characterization of a ruling as "counter-majoritarian" depends entirely on which geographic unit the alleged majority is being drawn from. For example, in *Romer v. Evans* (1996), the Court struck down a Colorado statewide initiative the targeted efforts by elected local officials to add protections for gay and lesbian rights to civil rights laws. The Court had to choose which majority of which unit to side with, not between a majority and a minority. More generally, many Court decisions force outlying states or regions to fall into line with positions favored by national majorities. Many of the Warren Court's controversial "counter-majoritarian" decisions were supported by political elites in control of the national government, the American public as a whole, or both.[6] For example, the Court's decision in *Brown* was unpopular with many Southern whites, but was viewed favorably in national opinion surveys and supported in the amicus briefs filed by the Eisenhower administration (Balkin, 2004, pp. 1539–1540). *Brown* reflected a growing national consensus that segregation had to be dismantled, both for reasons of internal economic development and international pressures related to the cold war (Dudziak, 2002; Klarman, 2004; McMahon, 2004; Bell, 1980).

The idea that any decision that strikes down a law is a "counter-majoritarian" reversal of the preferences of elected officials is further challenged by recent studies that show that elected officials sometimes deliberately invite judges to reverse their announced policies. Elected officials have incentives to allow or invite judicial "interference" when the appearance of judicial usurpation can help those officials to manage certain types of political conflicts. For example, Mark Graber (1993) has shown that party leaders sometimes try to maintain otherwise divided coalitions by encouraging judges to resolve contentious and cross-cutting policy issues. More generally, Lovell (2003) has shown how legislators sometimes use deliberate statutory ambiguity to shift blame for difficult decisions to the courts, and to navigate and manipulate political pressures from interest groups. Of course, elected officials who engineer such blame-shifting strategies will take steps to hide the fact that they are trying to shift responsibility to less accountable officials. The possibility of deception is particularly important to pay attention to because scholars can otherwise mistake instances of deliberate deference to the courts as instances where judges thwart elected officials. Significantly, both Graber's and Lovell's studies of legislative deference focused on cases that more conventional frameworks have identified as instances where judges usurped democratic processes with counter-majoritarian rulings. The lesson is that scholars need to make inquiries into the underlying political conditions, and pay careful attention to the reasons particular issues end up in courts, before classifying any instance of judicial review as an instance of judicial usurpation of the democratic process.

Do Remember that Elected Officials Have Numerous Available Weapons for Limiting the Impact of Judicial Rulings. Always Ask Why Such Weapons Were Not Utilized Before Concluding that Judges Successfully Thwarted the Collective Wishes of Elected Officials

One way for scholars to develop more accurate assessments of the degree to which judicial decisions thwart the will of elected officials is to pay careful attention the way elected officials respond to judicial rulings. Contrary to Bickel's solemn concerns about "finality" of the Supreme Court's constitutional holdings, there is no institutional reason why judges have to have the "final" word on any policy outcome. Legislators have numerous weapons for limiting the reach of judicial rulings. While constitutional amendments require supermajorities for enactment, legislators can deploy other weapons through much simpler and routine legislative processes.

Scholars need to take the existence of such weapons into account when making claims about judicial rulings thwarting or reversing democratic processes. Some scholars who chronicle the important influence that courts play in a variety of policy areas are quite comfortable assuming that mere existence of such judicial influence makes the Court's "dangerous" and "activist" usurpers of powers that properly (and traditionally) belong to others (see, e.g., Powers & Rothman, 2002). However, the fact that judges make an enormous amount of policy does not, by itself, make such claims credible. Much more attention has to be paid to the fact that many policy controversies are resolved by judges only because legislators have themselves chosen to structure administrative processes to empower judges to review agency decisions and to make it easier for aggrieved parties to bring their complaints to court.[7] The rules that give access to the Courts and structure judicial review in the United States can be modified by elected officials who would genuinely prefer less judicial oversight of regulatory agencies. In addition, legislators who prefer to restrict judicial review of rulings by individual agencies can (and sometimes do) craft statutory language that protects agency discretion or that makes it more difficult for potential litigants to establish standing (Lovell, 2003, Chapter 6).

When legislators fail to take preemptive steps to keep issues out of the Courts, they can still reverse, or at least limit the effects of judicial rulings after the fact. Legislators can, and often do, reverse statutory rulings by passing new statutes.[8] Reversing the effects of judicial rulings in constitutional cases can be more difficult, but still does not always require constitutional amendment. In many constitutional cases, legislators will have available alternative legislative strategies that can produce very similar outcomes on the ground while sidestepping the Court's expressed constitutional objections.[9]

Even when the Court articulates a relatively impermeable constitutional barrier, the Constitution still leaves elected officials with numerous means of escape. For example, the Constitution allows legislators to expand the size of the Supreme Court by statute, and invites legislators to make "exceptions" to the jurisdiction of federal courts. These more dramatic weapons are used only rarely, and perhaps with some reluctance, by elected official who might fear that direct attacks on the Court will create a backlash. Nevertheless, the fact that the weapons are not used often does not in any way diminish their significance. The weapons still exist and can be used at any time. Moreover, they have been used more often and with more consequence that many scholars recognize (Lovell, 2003, Chapter 5). The decision by Congress in 2006 to strip the federal courts of jurisdiction to hear *habeas* petitions from most of the prisoners being held at Guantanamo Bay provides a useful reminder of the ability of willing legislators to revoke court jurisdiction. Congress passed the Military Commissions Act (MCA) in 2006 after the Court refused to retroactively apply the Detainee Treatment Act of 2005 in *Hamdan v. Rumsfeld.* The jurisdiction stripping provisions of the MCA are particularly instructive because they show that it does not necessarily take much direct interference from the Court to trigger such a dramatic form of legislative retaliation. In contrast to Roosevelt's notorious court-packing plan, the MCA was not prompted by stark confrontations in which justices repeatedly reversed popular policies chosen by elected officials. The Supreme Court's rulings on President Bush's detainee policies rebuked the president's efforts to conduct programs that contradicted existing law without clear congressional authorization. But instead of creating impenetrable barriers to the president's programs, the rulings invited Congress to correct a statutory problem by revising existing statutes and making the president's policies legal. And while elements of the Court's rulings hinted that there may be a constitutional need for at least some judicial safeguards on detainee policies, the Court did not directly thwart any effort to detain and punish suspects.[10] Nothing in the Court's rulings has suggested, for example, that the Court was prepared to order the release of suspected terrorists. Nevertheless, the Court's minor procedural rebukes and open invitations to legislate were enough to prompt Congress to take the dramatic step of overturning the Court by stripping all federal courts of power to hear *habeas* appeals from detainees designated as enemy combatants.

Although powers like jurisdiction stripping are not used often, their existence makes it difficult to distinguishing cases of judicial usurpation from cases of legislative acquiescence. When legislators decline to take easy steps to limit judicial power, what looks like usurpation might actually be a case of willful acquiescence in an outcome that legislators do not object to, and/or a case where legislators are happy to have judges assume responsibility, and thus blame, for some contentious issue. On the other hand, the failure of legislators to respond aggressively is never enough by itself to prove willful acquiescence. Small factions can sometimes block a majority of elected officials from reversing an unpopular judicial ruling, particularly during periods of divided government. Nevertheless, when legislators allow easily contained judicial rulings to stand unchallenged for many years, and across numerous turnovers in partisan control, it becomes much more difficult to attribute policy outcomes to some fixed ability of the Supreme Court to have the final say, thwart determined majorities, and protect minority rights. At the same time, however, scholars should not measure legislators' unhappiness with the Court by counting how many times individual legislators have introduced jurisdiction-stripping legislation in response to Court rulings. Legislation without the backing of Congressional leaders (and hence with no chance of moving to a successful floor vote) is another form of symbolic politics. Court-curbing proposals that are obviously doomed to failure can allow individual legislators to express opposition to certain constituencies without taking responsibility for actually changing the policy.

Don't Let an Obsession with Judicial Review Lead to Overlooking Other Ways Judges Shape Policy, Influence Political Outcomes, and Register Shifts in Ideological Direction

Instances where judges strike down laws on constitutional grounds provide the starkest illustrations of judicial power to alter policies. However, judges more routinely shape policy through their powers to interpret statutes and review decisions made by administrative agencies. Nevertheless, scholars interested in understanding how severely judicial rulings interfere with outcomes produced by elected officials tend to pay far more attention to constitutional rulings than to statutory interpretation.

The tendency to focus on judicial review reflects the (often mistaken) belief that Supreme Court rulings give judges a final say on policy, while statutory rulings can be more easily overturned by statute. There is also a more practical reason for the focus on constitutional cases. Cases involving judicial review are more tractable methodologically because those cases seem to present clear and easily interpreted instances of interbranch conflict. Whether or not they find a particular constitutional ruling to be correct, scholars feel comfortable interpreting *any* instance where judges strike down a statute as an instance where judges thwart the will of elected officials. (As already noted, this assumption is false in some cases.) In comparison, there is no neutral and uncontroversial way to identify and quantify precisely which statutory rulings thwart the will of Congress. In statutory cases, a scholar's assessment of whether the judiciary thwarted the will of elected officials will depend on whether that scholar thinks a court made the correct decision about the meaning or intent of the statute. Unfortunately, most statutory cases, particularly among those that make it as far as the Supreme Court, involve a difficult choice between two or more plausible interpretations of an open-ended statutory provision. Such cases usually end up in court precisely because elected officials did not express their will clearly (or because a statute contained strategically vague language to paper over fractures within a legislative majority).

Despite these important differences, focusing too narrowly on constitutional cases can mask some important trends in the ideological direction and significance of Supreme Court rulings. Consider, for example, the core question of whether the Court should be understood as an institution that protects the rights of minorities. As already noted, the Rehnquist Court's constitutional rulings on issues like flag burning, late-term abortions, and sodomy gave credence to the view that the Court has remained a counter-majoritarian rights protector. Meanwhile, its ruling striking down the Religious Freedom Restoration Act (RFRA) (*City of Boerne v. Flores,* 1997) and the civil remedy provision of the Violence Against Women Act (*United States v. Morrison,* 2000), as well as rulings that immunize states from some federal civil rights standards (e.g., *Board of Trustees v. Garrett,* 2001),[11] indicate a quite different trend toward limiting the power of majorities to protect minority rights. Judgments about which of these competing trends is more significant will be much more accurate if the Court's constitutional rulings limiting rights protections are grouped together with *statutory* rulings that illustrate the same trend. Once attention is expanded to cover statutory cases, the Court's hostility to efforts by majorities to expand rights protection is more apparent very early in Rehnquist's tenure as Chief Justice. In the 1980s, the sharpest conflicts between the Court and Congress were over Court interpretations of civil rights laws that made it much more difficult to bring cases challenging race and sex discrimination. Congress eventually overturned the conservative justices' narrow readings of civil rights laws with the Civil Rights Act of 1991 (Yarbrough, 2000, p. 250; Barnes, 2004, pp. 12–13). More recently, the Court has made a series of decisions interpreting the Americans with Disabilities Act (ADA). That statute, passed by overwhelming majorities in Congress in 1990, is arguably the most important and far ranging civil rights law passed since the Johnson administration. While the Court has not struck down the law, its rulings have done much to shape the development of the law. Importantly, the Rehnquist Court has been, with rare exceptions, "very grudging in its interpretation of the ADA," thus considerably limiting its reach (Tushnet, 2005, p. 343).

When these statutory rulings are considered alongside the Court's federalism and sovereign immunity decisions, they seem to dwarf the Court's more symbolic rulings protecting rights. The statutory and constitutional rulings on the ADA, for example, have taken millions of potential cases outside of the reach of the ADA (Noonan, 2002, pp. 113–119). Those rulings also mean that states can choose to avoid the potentially high costs of accommodating disabled employees under the federal ADA standards and avoid the need to adjust a wide range of other policies to accommodate religious liberty under the RFRA. In contrast, rulings on such rare practices as flag burning, late term abortions, or systematically unenforced sodomy statutes have considerably less practical impact on the ground.

Don't Try to Measure Ideological Shifts on the Court by Counting How Many Times the Justices Have Chosen to Identify One of Their Rulings as "Overruling" an Earlier Decision

The view that the Supreme Court has remained a centrist, rights-protecting institution is based in part on several high profile cases where the Court declined opportunities to formally overturn notorious liberal precedents. The precedents in question were targeted both by conservative activists and by Republican presidential candidates who later made appointments to the Court. The most famous of these cases is *Planned Parenthood v. Casey* (1992). With two new Republican appointees (Thomas and Souter) on the Court as replacements for two liberal supporters of *Roe* (Marshall and Brennan), many observers expected the Court to finally overrule *Roe* in *Casey*. Thus, the Court's dramatic decision to say that it was reaffirming *Roe v. Wade* was a surprise (Keck, 2004, pp. 173–174). *Casey* has quite often been Exhibit A for the claim that the post-Warren Supreme Court has remained a centrist protector of rights, whether the explanation for that centrism is the continuing influence of legal standards and precedent (Kahn, 1994, pp. 255–257) or the centrist policy preferences and/or political savvy of the Republican appointees (Savage, 1994; O'Brien, 2005; Rosen, 2006).

Such readings of *Casey* are misleading. Rather than demonstrating the Court's centrism, the case actually provides a very good example of why justices' choices about how to characterize their treatment of precedents are poor indicators of whether a Court is adhering to principles espoused by prior courts. The "joint opinion" produced by three judges at the center of the Court did include a lengthy discussion of the importance of adhering to precedents like *Roe*, as well as the statement that *Roe* was being affirmed. Nevertheless, the joint opinion also rejected many core elements of *Roe*, including the trimester framework for evaluating abortion regulations. The joint opinion also formally overruled two earlier cases that had applied *Roe* more rigorously and struck down abortion restrictions. Most importantly and tellingly, the Court ended up upholding almost all the restrictive provisions in Pennsylvania's abortion law. Given that *Casey*'s messages about both precedents and abortion rights are, at best, mixed, it is a mistake to put too much weight on the Court's claim that it was not overturning *Roe*.

To understand the degree to which the Court protected abortion rights in *Casey*, it is much more important to look at what the Court actually *did* to the Pennsylvania statute than what the Court *said* about *Roe*. To evaluate whether the Court was protecting abortion rights against "majorities" who might otherwise curtail those rights, it is most important to understand what signals the Court was sending to state legislators through its rulings, and whether those signals are the reason elected state legislators have not successfully created additional restrictions on abortion.

Casey was a challenge to a Pennsylvania statute that contained numerous provisions that were designed to make it much more difficult for women to obtain abortions. Because the provisions applied throughout the pregnancy rather than after the end of the first trimester, all the restrictions would have been unconstitutional under *Roe*'s announced standard (at least as the Court had previously applied that standard in *Akron v. Akron Center for Reproductive Health*, 1983). Nevertheless, the Court upheld every provision of the law except for one. The upheld provisions included two that were nearly identical to provisions that the Court had struck down in earlier cases. To uphold those provisions, the Court had to formally overturn two recent cases (Akron, 1983 and *Thornburgh v. American College of Obstetricians and Gynecologists*, 1986). Another provision upheld by the Court made it *impossible* for at least some women to obtain legal abortions

(Silverstein, 1999). While the Court did strike down a provision mandating that married women notify their spouses before obtaining an abortion, the Court did nothing else to stop Pennsylvania from restricting abortion rights.

Of course, it might be argued that the real impact of the Court's ruling going forward was that the statement reaffirming *Roe* inhibited state legislators who might otherwise gone even further than Pennsylvania and created more stringent restrictions on abortion. Such inhibiting effects are difficult to pinpoint, however, and very easy to exaggerate. Certainly, the Court's relatively clear rulings in *Akron* and *Thornburgh* did not inhibit Pennsylvania legislators from passing laws that were clearly unconstitutional under the standards announced in those cases. Why would a case abandoning *Roe*'s trimester framework and upholding numerous new restrictions on abortion be more inhibiting?

A realistic picture of the inhibiting effects of *Casey* can emerge only after comparing the signal sent by the Court's ruling with the actual response made by elected officials since the decision was made. That response makes it difficult to believe that *Casey*'s reaffirmation of *Roe* is the main reason majorities have not enacted more stringent abortion regulations. It is common for scholars to assume that the continued availability of abortions in the United States is the result of some lingering effect of *Roe*. At some point, however, scholars have to contend with the possibility that at least part of the reason abortion remains available to some women is the fact that majorities of the population support abortion rights.[12] The task of sorting out the relative contribution of judicial rulings and political factors is never the straightforward one suggested by the counter-majoritarian model.

To understand the degree to which rulings like *Casey* protect abortion rights by preventing legislators from enacting restrictions, it is useful to consider the reaction of a hypothetical state legislator who was determined to reduce the availability of abortion. What would such a legislator have learned from the ruling in *Casey*? He would have learned that the Court would strike down statutes requiring spousal notification, as well as any other provisions that five justices determined would create an "undue burden" to a women's right to obtain an abortion. However, the legislator would also learn that the mysterious undue burden standard did not create a particularly high barrier. The Court showed that it would uphold a range of abortion restrictions under that standard, including provisions designed to make it very difficult (and in some instances impossible) for women to obtain abortions, as well as provisions nearly identical to ones that the Court had just recently struck down.

Given that set of signals, how plausible is it to claim that a counter-majoritarian ruling in *Casey* is the primary reason for the continued availability of abortions in the United States? It seems difficult to believe that such a legislator would read the Court's ruling as a warning from a determined Court that was poised to strike down any state regulation that took even a small step beyond what Pennsylvania had done. It is far more reasonable for the legislator to read the ruling as invitation to experiment with novel abortion regulations designed, like Pennsylvania's, to make it very difficult for some women (particularly classes of women with the fewest resources and the least political power) to obtain abortions. While our hypothetical legislator could not have known precisely how far his state could go under the Delphic "undue burden" standard, the best, and only way to find out would be to enact new legislation that either pushed on the limits that the Court upheld (e.g., longer waiting periods, more cumbersome, costly, or time-consuming informed consent and reporting requirements), or that created novel obstacles for women or abortion clinics.

The question to turn to now is whether the actual response of state legislatures to these signals in *Casey* indicates that the Supreme Court inhibited democratic processes that would otherwise have produced sharper reductions in the availability of abortion. The record, it turns out, is quite mixed. Many states have enacted laws with restrictions that mirror the ones upheld in *Casey*. A much smaller number of states have engaged in more aggressive experimentation (Rose, 2006, pp. 102–155). Ohio, for example, took a novel approach with a law requiring abortion clinics to obtain a "written transfer agreement" with hospitals in case of emergencies, and attempted to close a clinic when it failed to obtain a waiver. The Sixth Circuit Court of Appeals prevented the state from closing the clinic on narrow procedural grounds, but held that the written transfer requirement did not constitute an "undue burden" even if it forced the clinic to close (*Women's Medical Professional Corp. v. Baird*, 2006). A Supreme Court ruling upholding such mandatory transfer agreements could have a significant effect on abortion access. Nebraska passed a complete ban on a late term abortion procedure that was struck down by the Supreme Court in *Stenberg v. Carhart* (2000). While Nebraska's experiment failed to survive a court challenge, it did help legislators and other observers to locate another limit under the "undue burden" standard. (This limit, however, has quickly vanished under the Roberts Court.)[13] A few states have recently pushed even harder by enacting laws with sweeping criminal bans on abortion. For example, South Dakota's legislature recently passed an outright ban on abortion, but the law was overturned by popular referendum before it went into effect (Davey, 2006). Louisiana passed a similarly stringent restriction in 2006 (Alford, 2006).

The restrictions enacted by some states since *Casey* have significantly curtailed access to abortion, particularly in rural states and for poor women. Interestingly, regulations permitted by the Court under *Casey* like mandatory waiting periods, parental notification and consent requirements, and regulations that make it more difficult or costly for clinics to operate are all most likely to make it impossible for poor women to get abortions. At the same time, the two types of regulation that the Court has struck down, spousal notification requirements and (some) bans on late term abortion procedures, are more likely to create decisive obstacles for relatively affluent women. This pattern may be a coincidence, but it is worth pointing out because it means that abortion regulation today is not all that much different on the ground than it was in the years before *Roe*. Numerous scholars have shown that even in the days when the statute books contained restrictive bans on abortion, affluent women generally had access to safe abortions (Graber, 1996; Reagan, 1998). Thus, in both the pre-*Roe* and post-*Casey* periods, women with the right resources or the right connections have access to safe abortions while poor women (especially those in rural areas) face much greater constraints.

The states that have passed abortion regulations like the ones upheld in *Casey* have sharply curtailed access to abortion for a significant number of women (Rose, 2006). It is difficult, however, to read the regulations that have already been enacted as evidence that there is a great deal of pent-up demand among majorities of elected officials for even more stringent restrictions on abortion, demand that would be acted upon if not for the Court's courageous adherence to *Roe* in *Casey*. The overall record across the United States does not support such a conclusion. While many states have enacted *Casey*-style standards, and a few states have gone even further, there are still many states that have not gone even as far as the Court allowed Pennsylvania to go two decades ago. Moreover, counting the *number* of states that have passed restrictions is misleading because some of those states are quite small. More telling is the fact that two-thirds of the U.S. population lives in states that have ignored the Court's invitation in *Casey* and declined, for fifteen years, to enact the full range of restrictions that the Court upheld.[14] The continued availability of abortion for women in those states reflects the popularity of abortion rights in most of the country, not the fact that the Supreme Court has continued to act as a bulwark against majority sentiment nationwide.

Seen in this light, the Court's announcement that it was upholding *Roe* no longer provides an example to illustrate how a centrist Court continues to play the role of protector of rights against majority tyranny. *Casey* is much better understood as a significant retreat from protecting rights, a retreat that has allowed some states to enact policies that are considerably more restrictive than national majorities would support. The parts of the *Roe* ruling that the Court abandoned in *Casey* would have prevented elected officials from enacting most of the restrictive abortion laws that are in effect today. In comparison, the parts of *Roe* that the Court retained in *Casey* appear to inhibit very little legislative activity. Only in the relatively smaller number of outlier states whose legislators and citizens would tolerate enactment of absolute bans on abortion or abortion procedures can the Court plausibly be credited (or blamed) for inhibiting democratic activity that would have curtailed abortion rights. Thus, rather than demonstrating that Court's respect for precedent or persistent centrism, *Casey* is instead emblematic of the broad and underappreciated rightward shift on the Court.

Beyond abortion, there are numerous other areas where the more conservative Court's failure to overturn liberal precedents masks considerable shifts in doctrine and policy results. Consider, for example, *Brown v. Board of Education*, the most famous and celebrated Warren Court decision, and the case that inspired the generation of constitutional scholarship focused on the counter-majoritarian problem. *Brown* has not been challenged in the same way as *Roe*. No President has ever urged its reversal and no Supreme Court justice has ever written an opinion urging that *Brown* be overruled. Once again, however, the failure to officially overrule the precedent does not mean that *Brown* has not been considerably eroded. The Burger Court famously disappointed Nixon's expressed intentions by issuing a ruling upholding a school busing plan in 1971, although the Court also emphasized that federal courts were not *required* to create such plans (*Swann v. Charlotte-Mecklenberg Board of Education*, 1971; Brest, 1983, pp. 116–117). However, very soon afterward, the Court chose to read *Brown* as a narrow set of protections against de jure segregation, while ignoring other language in the opinion that articulated a much broader constitutional principle of equality of educational opportunity.[15] The Court used its narrow reading to justify a 1973 decision that rejected efforts to force states to provide adequate funding to schools serving minority populations (*San Antonio v. Rodriguez*), and a 1974 decision that sharply limited remedies for racial segregation in the North (*Milliken v. Bradley*). The result, quite predictably, was that, contrary to the promises of *Brown*, very large numbers of minority students attended schools that were largely separate and entirely unequal (Kozol, 1991, 2006). More recently, a series of Rehnquist Court decisions, often on obscure and technical issues, have allowed Southern school districts to escape federal court supervision. Those rulings were followed by a pronounced trend toward re-segregation in the South (Orfield & Eaton, 1996).

None of this is meant to suggest that Court's choices about how to characterize its treatment of precedent are meaningless. The decision to characterize its ruling on the Pennsylvania law as "reaffirming" *Roe* undoubtedly had considerable *political* significance, particularly coming on the eve of a close Presidential election in which a Republican candidate could only win reelection if he received support from a substantial number of pro-choice voters. A ruling where recent Bush appointees Thomas and Souter provided the decisive votes to formally overturn *Roe* would have had a significant impact on that election, likely increasing Clinton's margin of victory. The decisions in *Rodriguez* and *Milliken* would certainly have touched off a different sort of political reaction had the Court acknowledged that it was abandoning *Brown*'s equality of educational opportunity principle instead of pretending that the principle was not articulated in *Brown*. Nevertheless, the fact that judicial characterizations of rulings have such political effects is another very important reason *not* to take those characterizations at face value. Once it is recognized that judges' characterizations have these radiating political effects, it must also be recognized that judges have incentives to exaggerate some rulings while soft-pedaling others, depending on the likely popularity of the rulings. These incentives should be clear in light of our above discussion of the tactics that other officials can use to reverse judicial decisions or retaliate against the Court. Thus, our point here is not that scholars should not pay attention to the political dynamics set off by judges' choices about how to characterize their rulings. Rather, it is that the significance of any professed change or stability in precedent can only be gauged by evaluating what judges say in light of a better understanding of the underlying political dynamics.

Do Not Assume that Ideological Shifts in the Broader Population can be Estimated or Matched to Ideological Shifts on the Court, Particularly During Times of Closely Contested Partisan Control in the Other Branches of Government

In his seminal 1957 article on the role of the courts in the political system, Robert Dahl noted that the Supreme Court tends to follow the will of ruling partisan regimes because the appointment process leads to the selection of justices who share the values of the people in power. Dahl used that observation to explain why the Court so rarely strikes down important laws on which there is continued national consensus. The primary exception to that pattern occurred during the New Deal, an unusual period when the Court remained out of step after a major and sudden political realignment. Dahl's article was written, however, at the end of several long periods of relatively stable party control over government that were punctuated by regular and identifiable moments of partisan realignment. In the years since Earl Warren's departure, periods of divided government have become the norm rather than the exception. No dominant regime or alignment has emerged that has been able to control both Congress and the presidency for even two presidential election cycles.

This point is worth mentioning because there is an almost reflexive tendency to think that the Republican Party's ability to nominate so many justices is a reflection of Republican success at the polls or the popularity of the conservative policies.[16] Such assumptions do not, however, stand up. Since *Roe* was decided, there have been eight presidential elections. Democrats and Republicans have each won the popular vote four times. There have been 17 Congressional elections. Democrats have emerged with control of the House after eleven of those elections, Republicans in just six. The less representative Senate has been evenly split with each party winning control over eight elections. (We count the 2000 election as a tie because of Sen. Jeffords' switch.) During this period, there have been very few elections that have given one party a decisive victory. In only five of those seventeen election cycles has one party emerged control of the presidency and both houses of Congress (1976, 1992, 2000, 2002, 2004). Thus, the period since *Roe* has been an unprecedented period of divided party control and party turnover, where neither party has been able to establish a stable ruling regime.

During that period of very close competition and divided government, Republicans managed to completely dominate the Supreme Court nomination process: Republican presidents have nominated seven Supreme Court justices and Democrats only two. This unprecedented gap between winning elections and controlling Supreme Court appointments is the result of accidents, strategic retirements, and the counter-majoritarian combination of the Electoral College and the failure of Florida to hold a fair contest for its presidential electors in 2000. It is not a result of the popular will registered through elections. The trend is even more disturbing when looked at in light of evidence that the limited success of the Republican Party is not the result of the popularity of Republican policies but instead the result of undemocratic structural conditions that favor the Republicans (Hacker and Pierson, 2005). The fact that American Supreme Court vacancies – unlike in countries with fixed, non-renewable terms – will continue to occur at "random" intervals creates the potential for further gaps between the composition of the Court and the political branches. There is certainly no guarantee that the ideological composition of the Supreme Court will come into line with majority sentiment during periods of divided government. The potential for disjuncture between the Court and the political branches challenges those defenders of the Court who claim that the politicized appointment process ensures that the Court is unlikely to stray far from the values of the other branches (Dahl, 1957; Peretti, 1999; Rosen, 2006). As Keith Whittington (2007) notes, the Court has often "been active during times of relative electoral stability, when the judiciary should be firmly under the control of the dominant coalition and presumably passively endorsing the work of its coalition partners in Congress" (pp. 42–43; see also Casper, 1976). The fact that the Court both overreached and capitulated quickly during the New Deal constitutional crisis does not make such a result *inevitable* should similar ideological clashes occur in the future.

FUTURE DIRECTIONS OF THE COURT

What does the analysis presented here mean for assessing future develop-ments of the Court? Should the Court be expected to simply continue its quiet conservative drift under Chief Justice Roberts? More generally, what is the best way of predicting which direction the Court will take and measuring any changes as they occur? Will excavations of a new appointee's prior voting record, or repeated questions from senators about whether a nominee wants to "overturn" *Roe v. Wade* provide the information needed to answer these questions?

We believe that the theoretical purchase growing out of the above discussion is that judicial power cannot be understood as some fixed star of the constitutional system. The Supreme Court rarely, if ever, wins momentous power struggles with other branches if actors in those branches are committed to creating policies at odds with Court pronouncements. The institutional capacities of the courts evolve over time in response to outside political and institutional changes, changes that can themselves be affected by the choices that judges and elected officials make. Most importantly for purposes of prediction, the opportunities for judges to exercise power, and the appearance of ideological shift that results from those opportunities, is always dependent on actions taken by other political actors outside the courts. These observations mean that the Court should not be expected to play the same role in the constitutional system across different periods. The Warren Court's active role as a seemingly counter-majoritarian rights protector and force for progressive social change is not the inevitable result of life tenure or *Marbury v. Madison*. Moreover, calling the Warren Court's jurisprudence "counter-majoritarian" is in many respects misleading. The Warren Court existed during a period when Lyndon Johnson shepherded dramatic civil rights reforms through Congress, won a historic landslide electoral victory while advocating a dramatically expanded welfare state, successfully implemented new social welfare programs, and made Ramsey Clark the Attorney General of the United States. We live in a different world today, so it should be no surprise that we have a very different Court.

Given our claims so far, it should come as no surprise that we cannot offer unequivocal predictions about what future direction the Court will take or whether the Court will hide or call attention to changes in its ideology or role. Outcomes will continue to depend on broader political trends outside the Court. We thus offer three somewhat stylized scenarios and some broad sketches about what might under each of them. The starting point under each scenario is the current Court, dominated by Republican appointees and tilting conservatively on many issues. (The replacement of O'Connor with Samuel Alito has made the Roberts Court more conservative that the late Rehnquist Court.) However, the future personnel changes will be affected over time by the different political conditions of each scenario.

A first scenario is that the electoral shift of 2006 accelerates. The Democratic Party makes gains and retains control Congress and the White House for the next several election cycles, and also makes considerable gains in state legislatures. This scenario is the one most likely to produce heightened conflicts between the Court's conservatives and the national government, particularly if the Democrats who gain office are committed to an activist regulatory or civil rights agenda rather than being centrists like Bill Clinton. The passage of an active and liberal legislative agenda would produce conflicts if conservative Supreme Court justices read new economic regulations narrowly in statutory cases, exercised aggressive oversight of enforcement decisions made by the regulatory agencies like the EPA, or discovered additional limits on Congress's enumerated power to protect the civil rights of minorities in the penumbras of the 11th or 14th amendments. Such conflicts could be overt and sometimes dramatic, particularly if retirement patterns delayed Democratic Party efforts to shift the ideological balance on the Court. However, over time, history suggests that the conservatives would either have to moderate their interference with federal policies, or face retaliation from politically strong Democrats. On regulatory oversight and statutory issues, it would be relatively easy for a Democratic majority to enact measures reducing interference from the Courts.

With respect to the issue of abortion, Democratic gains would make passage of state laws limiting abortion less likely, but some states might continue to experiment with novel laws making it harder for at least some women to get abortions. (The states most likely to ban abortion access are the states least likely to fall into the control of pro-choice Democrats.) Under this first scenario, it seems exceedingly unlikely that the Court would formally overturn *Roe*. Even after the replacement of O'Connor with the more conservative Alito, there are still five justices on the Court who are on record as opponents of formally overturning *Roe*. Since, under this first scenario at least, it is unlikely that one of the five remaining supporters of *Roe* would be replaced by a *Roe* opponent, *Roe*, or at least what is left of *Roe*, would be safe. Nevertheless, many state and local regulations might be upheld by the current Court under the malleable "undue burden" standard of *Casey*. The Court would only be forced to decide whether to announce the demise of *Roe* if the Court decided to take a case challenging a state that passed an absolute ban on nearly all abortions. It might also be worth noting, however, that a conservative justice who hated *Roe* but also wanted to see Republican fortunes improve at the polls would not want to create national headlines announcing the end of the popular *Roe* precedent.[17] The Court's recent decision upholding the Federal Partial Birth Abortion Ban Act (*Gonzales v. Carhart* 2007) provides strong evidence that the Roberts Court will go out of its way to avoid announcing any departures from precedent in abortion cases. Consistently with the strategies discussed above, the Court rather implausibly claimed that its ruling was consistent with its earlier ruling in *Stenberg v. Carhart*. Under this first scenario, Congress is unlikely to exercise the additional power that the Court supported in *Gonzales v. Carhart*. Nevertheless, the powers of the states (including states conservative enough to defy a general progressive shift, which are of course the states most likely to regulate abortion in the first place) would also be expanded without necessarily attracting a powerful response from potential opponents in Congress.

A second scenario is the reverse of the first: The Republican Party instead ends up in control of Congress and the White House while making gains in state legislatures. Under such a scenario, the Court would be able to move boldly to the right, but the Court would also have fewer opportunities to register that shift through decisions striking down federal statutes. This is because the Court would have fewer opportunities to narrow or overturn new economic, environmental, or civil rights legislation because such laws would not be enacted, and because the executive's enforcement policies for existing laws would be much less likely to conflict with the preferences of the Court. The same justices who would appear to be activist enemies of progressive causes under the first scenario would appear quite restrained and centrist in the second, but only because they had fewer opportunities to reverse decisions by other officials. As a result, conventional scholars might continue to puzzle at the Court's lack of more aggressive conservatism and continue to be haunted by Earl Warren's ghost. However, Republican control would also mean that there would likely be noteworthy constitutional tests of new criminal justice policies and practices, including more punitive state criminal justice policies and expanded federal policies in the "wars" on drugs and terrorism. New faith-based initiatives might also produce policies that present opportunities for the Court to announce additional retreats from Warren Court rulings on the separation of church and state. Republican gains in state legislatures would likely mean that the Court would confront aggressive efforts by some states to restrict abortion. *Roe* would be much more likely to officially fall. Nevertheless, the popularity of abortion rights means that there is still no guarantee that the Court would go out of its way to trumpet the end of *Roe*. Regardless of what might happen, the degree to which the Court allowed abortion restrictions at the federal and state level to go into effect would continue to be much more important than anything the Court decided to say about whether or not it was "overturning" *Roe*.

A third scenario is that control of government remains divided. Neither party is able to win decisive victories at the polls, and there continues to be fairly frequent turnover of party control of Congress and the presidency, and state governments continue to reflect sharp regional variation in party strength. This scenario presents the most complicated strategic terrain for the Court to negotiate, and in some respects maximizes the Court's policymaking discretion. Federal policies on economic regulation, civil rights, criminal justice, and internal security would likely be more moderate because each party would have some veto power. Thus, the opportunity for the court to make novel rulings on economic regulation, criminal justice, and the separation of church and state would diminish. At the same time, a period of close party competition and divided government is more likely to produce compromise legislation that leaves key policy controversies unresolved, thus giving the federal courts numerous opportunities to shape policies through interpretive rulings on ambiguous statutes. Divided government would also make it more difficult for elected officials to coordinate an effective response to unpopular judicial rulings. No matter which way the Court ruled on the meaning of an ambiguous regulatory law, the Court would, under this third scenario, have an ideological ally at one of the veto points in the divided government (Tushnet, 2003, p. 33). Thus, the currently conservative court would likely have numerous opportunities to push, or at least nudge, new economic, environmental, and civil rights regulations in a conservative direction.

Under this scenario, states would produce a range of outcomes pointing in different ideological directions; from localized attempts at more aggressive environmental and economic regulation in the blue states to aggressive regulation of abortion in the red states. As a result, state laws would be more likely than federal statutes to give the Court opportunity to make dramatic rulings striking down laws or reversing well-known precedents. However, the willingness of the Court to pursue an activist agenda (and to frame its rulings in ways that called attention to that activism) might be tempered by the justices' awareness of the intense level of party competition. Conservative justices who wanted the Court to remain conservative would still have incentives to frame rulings gutting popular precedents like *Roe* as narrowly as possible. (The two new conservative appointees both seem to prefer careful, "minimalist" rulings to the broad holdings often favored by their colleagues Justices Scalia and Thomas (Sunstein, 2005)). The Court might be more willing to choose bolder pronouncements when ruling on issues where the conservative position is more popular, such as the separation of church and state and criminal procedure (i.e., the areas where Warren Court rulings can be plausibly described as "counter-majoritarian"). However, it is also important not to exaggerate the extent to which justices are politically savvy, or the extent to which political motivations produce a reliable account of judicial behavior. For example, the Warren Court pushed ahead with criminal procedure rulings that were almost certainly damaging to the Democratic electoral coalition, and had Ronald Reagan been able to get Robert Bork confirmed, *Roe* would almost certainly have been formally overturned despite the negative effects such a ruling would have had on some Republican candidates. Note also that outcomes are particularly difficult to predict over the long term under this third scenario. Another extended period of close party competition and frequent turnover in the White House will mean that future ideological shifts on the Court will depend, as they have for the past 30 years, on which party gets "lucky" on the timing of retirements.

In conclusion, we note that the uncertainty and contingency of our predictions matches the uncertainty about the future of the closely divided American polity itself. The power of judiciary is simply not fixed under a separation-of-powers system. At least two things are certain, however. First, scholars will not be able to understand changes on the Court and the impact of Court rulings if they focus narrowly on counting the number of cases where the Court itself chooses to make stark announcements of changes in legislation or precedents. Second, in cases where the Court really does manage to have significant effects on policy outcomes or thwart the will of majorities, the Court's success will not simply be the result of fixed institutional powers that make other political actors helpless spectators. Rather, the Court will be able to exercise power because a particular configuration of political conditions, and an identifiable set of choices by outside actors, create opportunities for the Court to act.

NOTES

1. For an overview that links the development of constitutional theory to the Warren Court, see Kalman (1996), Ward and Castillo (2005). Alexander Bickel (1962), and Herbert Wechsler (1959) each produced influential works that were obviously animated by concerns about *Brown v. Board of Education*. John Hart Ely (1980) dedicated his landmark effort to reconcile Warren Court landmarks with the Constitution's commitment to representative government to his "hero" Earl Warren.

2. Scholars as different as Bickel (1962, pp. 1–11) and Segal and Spaeth (2002, pp. 21–24) begin their theoretical accounts of judicial power with *Marbury v. Madison* and suggest that the case settled the question of judicial supremacy once and for all.

3. For an overview of such interpretive theories, see Whittington (2001, pp. 18–34) and Bobbitt (1982).

4. *Dickerson v. United States* (2000), *Grutter v. Bollinger* (2003), and *Planned Parenthood v. Casey* (1992).

5. Other examples are recent cases preventing states from executing minors and mentally handicapped prisoners (*Atkins v. Virginia,* 2002; *Roper v. Simmons,* 2005).

6. See Powe (2000, Chapter 19). The exceptions are primarily criminal procedure decisions made during the period when the Court had a majority of liberals (1963–1968).

7. See Shapiro (1988) and Strauss (2002) for overviews of the role of judges in administrative processes. See also Shipan (1997), on the efforts of legislators to structure judicial power to review administrative decisions.

8. On legislative overrides, see Barnes (2004) and Eskridge (1991). Of course, the committee structure of Congress and informational constraints mean that legislators

will not succeed in reversing judges in a large number of cases where judges choose interpretations of statutes that are opposed by a majority of legislators (Segal, 1997).

9. Compare, e.g., *RAV v. St Paul* to *Wisconsin v. Mitchell*. See also Hiebert (2002), which details how the Canadian Parliament addressed its policy concerns in response to judicial overrulings without using its formal override powers.

10. See especially *Hamdi v. Rumsfeld* (2004, O'Connor, J.).

11. On the "sovereign immunity" cases generally, see Noonan (2002) and Manning (2004).

12. A CNN/Opinion Research poll conducted in January 2007 found that 62% of the people surveyed "would not" overturn *Roe v. Wade*, while only 29% "would." This is broadly consistent with most public opinion surveys about Roe, which generally show it supported by roughly 2-to-1 margins. See http://www.pollingreport.com/abortion.htm, last accessed February 27, 2007. More generally, see Cook et al. (1992).

13. *Gonzales v. Carhart* (2007). See Lemieux (2006).

14. This claim is based on state-by-state information on abortion regulation available at http://www.naral.org. The following states have informed consent, waiting period, and parental consent restrictions that go as far or further than *Casey* and that have not been invalidated by state courts on state constitutional grounds: Alabama, Georgia, Indiana, Louisiana, Mississippi, North Dakota, Ohio, Oklahoma, Pennsylvania, South Carolina, Texas, Utah, Virginia, and Wisconsin. Based on 2000 census figures, those states have a combined population of 93,293,911, or 33% of the U.S. total.

15. On the equality of educational opportunity principle in *Brown*, see Fiss (1965). Scholars who insist that Brown only addressed *de facto* segregation, or that the constitutional principle in the case rested on a citation to social science evidence, provide a good illustration of Donald Kingsbury's adage that "Law is what is read, not what is written" (Kingsbury quoted in Bonsignore, et al., 2001, p. 21).

16. For an example of this tendency, see Balkin and Levinson (2005, pp. 1075–1076).

17. It is clear that Court appointees are sensitive to these political dynamics. Even when Republicans have controlled the Senate, every Republican nominee since Robert Bork has scrupulously avoided taking a stance on *Roe v. Wade* during confirmation hearings. Meanwhile Democratic nominees have felt free to state or imply that the popular case was correctly decided and should not be overturned.

REFERENCES

Alford, J. (2006). Louisiana governor plans to sign anti-abortion law. *New York Times* (June 7).

Balkin, J. (2004). What Brown teaches us about constitutional theory. *Virginia Law Review, 90,* 1537–1577.

Balkin, J., & Levinson, S. (2001). Understanding the constitutional revolution. *Virginia Law Review, 85,* 1045–1109.

Barnes, J. (2004). *Overruled? Legislative overrides, pluralism, and contemporary court-congress relations.* Palo Alto: Stanford University Press.

Baum, L. (1997). *The puzzle of judicial behavior.* Ann Arbor MI: University of Michigan Press.

Bell, D. A., Jr. (1980). Brown v. Board of Education and the interest-convergence dilemma. *Harvard Law Review, 93*, 518.

Bobbitt, P. (1982). *Constitutional fate: Theory of the constitution*. New York: Oxford University Press.

Bonsignore, J. J., Katsh, E., d'Errico, P., Pipkin, R., Arons, S., & Rifkin, J. (2001). *Before the law: An introduction to the legal process* (7th ed.). Boston: Houghton Mifflin Company.

Brest, P. (1983). Race discrimination. In: V. Blasi (Ed.), *The Burger Court: The counter-revolution that wasn't*. New Haven: Yale University Press.

Campbell, A., Converse, P. E., Miller, W. E., & Stokes, D. E. (1960). *The American voter*. New York: John Wiley.

Casper, J. (1976). The Supreme Court and national policy making. *American Political Science Review, 70*, 50–63.

Dahl, R. A. (1957). Decision-making in a democracy: The Supreme Court as a national policy-maker. *Journal of Public Law, 6*, 279–295.

Davey, M. (2006). South Dakotans reject sweeping abortion ban. *New York Times* (November 8).

Ely, J. H. (1980). *Democracy and distrust: A theory of judicial review*. Cambridge: Harvard University Press.

Eskridge, W. N. (1991). Overriding Supreme Court statutory decisions. *Yale Law Journal, 101*, 331–455.

Fiss, O. (1965). Racial imbalance the public schools: The constitutional concepts. *Harvard Law Review, 78*, 564.

Garrow, D. J. (1994). *Liberty and sexuality: The right to privacy and the making of Roe v. Wade*. New York: Macmillan.

Gillman, H. (2002). How political parties can use the courts to advance their agendas: Federal courts in the United States, 1875–1891. *American Political Science Review, 96*, 381–394.

Ginsburg, T. B. (2003). *Judicial review in new democracies*. New York: Cambridge University Press.

Graber, M. A. (1993). The non-majoritarian difficulty: Legislative deference to the judiciary. *Studies in American Political Development, 7*, 35–73.

Graber, M. A. (1996). *Rethinking abortion: Equal choice, the constitution, and reproductive politics*. Princeton: Princeton University Press.

Graber, M. A. (1998). Establishing judicial review? *Schooner Peggy* and the early Marshall Court. *Political Research Quarterly, 51*, 7–25.

Graber, M. A. (1999). The problematic establishment of judicial review. In: H. Gillman & C. Clayton (Eds), *The Supreme Court in American Politics: New institutionalist interpretations* (pp. 28–42). Lawrence, KS: University Press of Kansas.

Hacker, J. S., & Pierson, P. (2005). *Off center: The Republican revolution and the erosion of American democracy*. New Haven: Yale University Press.

Hiebert, J. (2002). *Charter conflicts: What is Parliament's role?*. Montreal: McGill/Queens University Press.

Hirschl, R. (2004). *Towards juristocracy: The origins and consequences of the new constitutionalism*. Cambridge: Harvard University Press.

Horwitz, M. (1977). *The transformation of American law, 1780–1860*. Cambridge, MA: Cambridge University Press.

Kahn, R. (1994). *The Supreme Court and constitutional theory, 1953–1993*. Lawrence KS: University Press of Kansas.

Kahn, R. (1999). Institutional norms and Supreme Court decision making: The Rehnquist Court on privacy and religion. In: W. C. Cornell & H. Gillman (Eds), *Supreme Court decision making: New institutionalist approaches*. Chicago: University of Chicago Press.

Kalman, L. (1996). *The strange career of legal liberalism*. New Haven: Yale University Press.

Keck, T. (2004). *The most activist Supreme Court in history*. Chicago: University of Chicago Press.

Klarman, M. J. (2004). *From Jim Crow to civil rights: The Supreme Court and the struggle for racial equality*. New York: Oxford University Press.

Kozol, J. (1991). *Savage inequalities: Children in America's schools*. New York: Crown Publishers.

Kozol, J. (2006). *The shame of a nation: The restoration of apartheid schooling in America*. New York: Crown Publishers.

Lemieux, S. (2006). Partial-Birth's Trojan Horse. *American Prospect Online*, November 20. Available at http://www.prospect.org/web/page.ww?section = root&name = ViewWeb &articleId = 12252

Levinson, S. (2006). *Our undemocratic constitution: Where the constitution goes wrong (and how we the people can correct it)*. New York: Oxford University Press.

Lovell, G. I. (2003). *Legislative deferrals: Statutory ambiguity, judicial power, and American democracy*. New York: Cambridge University Press.

Manning, J. F. (2004). The Eleventh Amendment and the reading of precise constitutional texts. *Yale Law Journal, 113*, 1663.

McMahon, K. J. (2004). *Reconsidering Roosevelt on race: How the presidency paved the road to Brown*. Chicago: University of Chicago Press.

Melnick, R. S. (1983). *Regulation and the courts: The case of the Clean Air Act*. Washington, DC: Brookings Institution.

Melnick, R. S. (1994). *Between the lines: Interpreting welfare rights*. Washington, DC: Brookings Institution.

Miller, M. C., & Barnes, J. (2004). *Making policy, making law: An interbranch perspective*. Washington, DC: Georgetown University Press.

Noonan, J. T. (2002). *Narrowing the nation's power: The Supreme Court sides with the states*. Berkeley: University of California Press.

Orfield, G., & Eaton, S. (1996). *Dismantling desegregation*. New York: New Press.

Orren, K. (1991). *Belated feudalism: Labor, the law, and liberal development in the United States*. New York: Cambridge University Press.

Paul, A. M. (1960). *The conservative crisis and the rule of law*. Ithaca, NY: Cornell University Press.

Peretti, T. J. (1999). *In defense of a political court*. Princeton NJ: Princeton University Press.

Powe, L. A. (2000). *The Warren Court and American politics*. Cambridge, MA: Harvard University Press.

Powers, S., & Rothman, S. (2002). *The least dangerous branch? Consequences of judicial activism*. Westport, CT: Praeger.

Reagan, L. (1998). *When abortion was a crime: Women, medicine, and law in the United States, 1867–1973*. Berkeley: University of California Press.

Rogers, J. R. (2001). Information and judicial review: A signaling game of legislative–judicial interaction. *American Journal of Political Science, 45*(1), 84–99.

Rose, M. (2006). *Safe, legal, and unavailable? Abortion politics in the United States*. Washington: CQ Press.

Rosen, J. (2006). *The most democratic branch: How the courts serve America*. New York: Oxford University Press.

Ross, W. G. (1994). *A muted fury: Progressives and labor unions confront the courts: 1890–1937*. Princeton: Princeton University Press.

Savage, D. G. (1992). *Turning right: The making of the Rehnquist Supreme Court*. New York: Wiley.

Segal, J. A. (1997). Separation of powers games in the positive theory of Congress and courts. *American Political Science Review, 91*, 28–44.

Segal, J. A., & Spaeth, H. J. (2002). *The Supreme Court and the attitudinal model revisited*. Cambridge; New York: Cambridge University Press.

Shapiro, M. (1988). *Who guards the guardians? Judicial control of administration*. Athens: University of Georgia Press.

Shipan, C. R. (1997). *Designing judicial review*. Ann Arbor: University of Michigan Press.

Silverstein, H. (1999). Road closed: Evaluating the judicial bypass provision of the Pennsylvania Abortion Control Act. *Law & Social Inquiry, 24*, 73–96.

Simon, J. F. (1995). *The center holds: The power struggle inside the Rehnquist Court*. New York: Simon and Schuster.

Spann, G. (1993). *Race against the Court: The Supreme Court and minorities in contemporary America*. New York: New York University Press.

Strauss, P. L. (2002). *An introduction to administrative justice in the United States* (2nd ed.). Durham, NC: Carolina Academic Press.

Sunstein, C. (2005). On the contrary. *The Washington Post* (January 11), p. A25.

Tsebelis, G. (2002). *Veto players: How political institutions work*. Princeton: Princeton University Press.

Tushnet, M. (1999). *Taking the Constitution away from the Courts*. Princeton: Princeton University Press.

Tushnet, M. V. (2003). *The new constitutional order*. Princeton: Princeton University Press.

Tushnet, M. V. (2005). *A court divided: The Rehnquist Court and the future of constitutional law*. W.W. Norton.

Ward, K., & Castillo, C. (Eds). (2005). *The judiciary in American democracy: Alexander Bickel, the countermajoritarian difficulty, and contemporary constitutional theory*. Albany: SUNY Press.

Whittington, K. E. (2001). *Constitutional interpretation*. Lawrence, KS: University Press of Kansas.

Whittington, K. E. (2005). Interpose your friendly hand: Political supports for the exercise of judicial review by the United States Supreme Court. *American Political Science Review, 99*, 583–596.

Whittington, K. E. (2007). *Political foundations of judicial supremacy: The presidency, the Supreme Court, and constitutional leadership in U.S. history*. Princeton: Princeton University Press.

Yarbrough, T. (2000). *The Rehnquist Court and the constitution*. New York: Oxford University Press.

Zaller, J. R. (2005). *The nature and origins of mass opinion*. New York: Cambridge University Press.

CASES CITED

Akron v. Akron Center for Reproductive Health, 462 U.S. 616 (1983).
Atkins v. Virginia, 536 U.S. 304 (2002).
Brown v. Board of Education, 347 U.S. 483 (1954).
City of Boerne v. Flores, 521 U.S. 507 (1997).
Dickerson v. United States, 530 U.S. 428 (2000).
Furman v. Georgia, 408 U.S. 238 (1972).
Gonzales v. Carhart, 550 U.S. 238 (2007).
Griswold v. Connecticut, 381 U.S. 479 (1965).
Grutter v. Bollinger, 539 U.S. 306 (2003).
Hamdan v. Rumsfeld, 126 S. Ct. 2749 (2006).
Hamdi v. Rumsfeld, 542 U.S. 507 (2004).
Lawrence v. Texas, 539 U.S. 123 (2003).
Marbury v. Madison, 1 CR. (5 U.S.) 137 (1803).
Milliken v. Bradley, 418 U.S. 717 (1974).
Rasul v. Bush, 542 U.S. 466 (2004).
R.A.V. v. St. Paul, 505 U.S. 377 (1992).
Roe v. Wade, 410 U.S. 113 (1973).
Romer v. Evans, 517 U.S. 116 (1996).
Roper v. Simmons, 543 U.S. 551 (2005).
San Antonio Independent School District v. Rodriguez, 411 U.S. 1 (1973).
Stenberg v. Carhart, 530 U.S. 914 (2000).
Swann v. Charlotte Mecklenberg Board of Education, 402 U.S. 1 (1971).
Texas v. Johnson, 491 U.S. 397 (1989).
Thornburgh v. American College of Obstetricians & Gynecologists, 476 U.S. 747 (1986).
United States v. Eichman, 496 U.S. 310 (1990).
United States v. Morrison, 529 U.S. 598 (2000).
Wisconsin v. Mitchell, 508 U.S. 476 (1993).
Women's Medical Professional Corp. v. Baird, 438 F. 3d. 595, 6th Cir. (2006).

AN INDIFFERENCE THESIS: CONSTITUTIONAL LAW AND POLITICS IN AN ERA OF "CONSERVATIVE DOMINATION" OF THE JUDICIARY

Ira L. Strauber

INTRODUCTION: AN INDIFFERENCE THESIS ABOUT COMMENTARY

This chapter addresses commentary about constitutional law and politics in this current era of a conservative domination of the judiciary.[1] Its primary concern is the different ways in which a working majority on the Court and its judiciary of appointees by Presidents Reagan, George H. W. Bush, and George W. Bush might be conservative,[2] and the different ways in which domination might take place.[3] The frame for the chapter is what I call an "indifference thesis" for analyzing constitutional law and politics. Stated boldly, the thesis is that there should be a commentary distinguished by an interpretive attitude that distrusts, and intentionally resists, analysis based on preconceived notions about the strengths and weaknesses of any constitutional law and politics, be it conservative or left-liberal.[4] Perhaps, to many readers, an indifference thesis for commentary appears

Special Issue: Constitutional Politics in a Conservative Era
Studies in Law, Politics, and Society, Volume 44, 35–71
Copyright © 2008 by Emerald Group Publishing Limited
All rights of reproduction in any form reserved
ISSN: 1059-4337/doi:10.1016/S1059-4337(08)00802-8

methodologically odd, if not politically perverse. Therefore, the first order of business is to try to make the thesis less odd and perverse by explaining its provenance and attributes.[5]

The indifference thesis is inspired by a meld of premises extrapolated or interpolated from Benjamin Cardozo's realist jurisprudence about the common law in *The Nature of the Judicial Process* Cardozo (1921, 1974), suitably qualified and amended by more contemporary premises from the New Institutionalism's constitutive approach to analysis of the Supreme Court (McCann, 1999, pp. 78–91) and a version of a pragmatic approach to inquiry about law and politics.[6] Specifically, the indifference thesis picks up from Cardozo's classic text four premises to be associated with constitutional law and politics. The first premise is the law's indeterminacy. In working with the law

> for every tendency, one seems to see a counter-tendency; for every rule its antinomy. Nothing is stable. Nothing absolute. All is fluid and changeable. There is an endless "becoming." (Cardozo, 1921, 1974, p. 28)

Second, in the midst of indeterminacy, judicial activism is inevitable: "judges must and do legislate" (Cardozo, 1921, 1974, p. 69), primarily because factors such as fact- and rule-freedom associated with indeterminacy make judge-made law inescapable (Cardozo, 1921, 1974, pp. 98–102). Yet, inevitable as indeterminacy and activism are, the presumption is that the law's material (especially the use of legal rules, principles, and precedent) and expectations about judging ordinarily limit activism "from molar to molecular motions" (Cardozo, 1921, 1974, p. 69), but in rare instances the law might move significantly beyond these motions in a short period of time (Cardozo, 1921, 1974, p. 49).

Third, because judges can be expected to disagree about what indeterminacy and activism require, accretions in the law that accompany the judicial process often make the law appear to be unstable, if not downright confused and purposeless (Cardozo, 1921, 1974, p. 176). But, in the long term, the premise is that the judicial process is subject to inescapable pressures of dominant practices, interests, and values of the polity. These pressures require balancing competing conceptions of what is "right" (or principle) and "useful" (or practical), and what emerges from balancing in the judicial process comes to be understood as "the social welfare of the polity" (Cardozo, 1921, 1974, pp. 71–72, 105–106, 178–179).

Fourth, because competing conceptions of what is right and useful are persistently changing, the judicial process is an "endless process of testing and re-testing" (Cardozo, 1921, 1974, p. 179). (Hence the endless becoming of the law.) Naturally, in the process of testing and re-testing, there will be (intense) disagreements about whether the law is falling short or even downright mistaken about the balance between what is right and useful. Nevertheless, in the short term it is prudent to be cautious about making too much of what might otherwise appear to be the advantages or disadvantages of the law (as construed from the perspective of competing conceptions of what is right and useful). Caution is prudent because the law is the law, and in a pluralist polity, the pressures of a judicial process of testing and re-testing tend to balance out short-term benefits and shortcomings (Cardozo, 1921, 1974, p. 179).

These premises about indeterminacy, activism, a balance between what is right and useful, and a judicial process of trial and error virtually cry out for amendments and qualifications to accommodate contemporary scholarship. I have two such amendments and qualifications in mind. For one, there is Cardozo's focus on the law's indeterminacy and activism solely in terms of the judge's role in the judicial process. From the perspective of the constitutive branch of the New Institutionalism, indeterminacy and activism are diffused throughout the political culture. Actors in institutions and social processes outside of courts interpret and adapt the material of the law (e.g., its language, norms, and symbolic connotations) as a means of shaping conceptions of their political and legal identity, interests, aspirations about what is right and expedient, and strategies for achieving those aspirations. Thus, permeation of the material of the law throughout society entails that law simultaneously shapes and is shaped by activities in and outside of courts (McCann, 1999, pp. 78–81). The diffusion of the law thus makes

> all members of a polity *at once* subjects of the law and, at least potentially, also active "mobilizers" of law's indeterminacy in their everyday social and political interaction. (McCann, 1999, p. 80)[7]

Accordingly, activism and indeterminacy are factors that play a role in law and politics inside and outside of courts.

For another, there is Cardozo's confidence in a judicial process of trial and error as a means to balance what is right and useful for the social welfare of the polity. In contrast to this confidence, research under the umbrella of a constitutive approach to law and politics suggests being skeptical of such confidence in the judicial process. Hence, the indifference thesis is driven by two crucial questions about the judicial process: (1) to what extent does the process (even) have the capacity to be a force, in and of itself, for shaping the social welfare of the polity and (2) to what extent is the judicial process actually a means for justifying and stabilizing the existing distribution of resources and power relations in the polity rather than a means of articulating a balance between various conservative and left-liberal conceptions of the social welfare of the polity (McCann, 1999, pp. 64, 89)?

Note that the first question raises the second question (of whether a conservative judiciary can dominate the polity) and the second question complicates analysis of *conservative* domination of the judiciary by forcing the distinction between two kinds of conservatism. It is certain that answers to these questions are impacted by conceptual, ideological, and factual disputes among scholars, and therefore those answers are essentially contestable. It is questions like these and their answers that instigate an interpretive attitude distrustful of analysis based on preconceived notions, or blanket conceptual and normative generalizations, about constitutional law and politics, as, for example, for what counts as *domination* by a judiciary.

The kind of distrustful analysis that I have in mind is pragmatic in that it leans heavily on "facts and consequences *rather* [italics added] than ... conceptualisms, generalities, pieties, and slogans" (Posner, 2003, p. 3).[8] Put differently, this pragmatic analysis is distrustful of logical, prescriptive, and theoretical claims that are not qualified, even to the point of being destabilized, by the details of contextual and circumstantial considerations. For better or worse, this kind of pragmatic analysis requires lots of moving parts. Hence, when it comes to analysis of conservative domination of the judiciary, pragmatic conclusions are untidy and indefinite rather than neat and unambiguous (Michelman, 1989, p. 313). Although such analysis is undoubtedly odd or perverse from an ideological or partisan perspective, indifference thesis analysis is satisfied to stand by qualified conclusions (Dewey, 1935, p. 78) or "shafts of light" (Zuckerman, 1991, p. 72) when it comes to empirical and normative claims about constitutional law and politics. This is so because the thesis makes it difficult to be confident about the extent to which "conservative domination" of the judiciary (variously conceived) is a good thing, bad thing, or more of much ado about nothing.

In the first section of this chapter I present four hypotheses for understanding "domination" by the judiciary; the second section presents four conceptions of what counts as a "conservative" judiciary. The third and fourth sections use this material, first tacitly and then explicitly, in an indifference thesis case study of "conservative domination of the judiciary," Commerce Clause federalism, and water environmental policy and law. Commerce Clause federalism is a particularly appropriate choice for a case study because of its central role in conservative politics and law since the Nixon Administration. Of course, a single case study casts no more than a shaft of light on indifference analysis of "conservative judicial domination," but that should be sufficient to warrant the concluding section's few words about the strengths and weaknesses of indifference analysis.

HYPOTHESES FOR LOCATING "DOMINATION" OF THE JUDICIARY

In indifference analysis, questions about judicial domination, or the extent to which activism matters, relate to the extent to which the Court's cultural authority and power, its bureaucracy, and the indeterminate material of the law enjoy efficacious command and control over other institutions, political and social practices, and beliefs of elites and masses. The authority and power of the Court can be connected to each of the four hypotheses about judicial domination.[9] The first (most radical) hypothesis is the hegemonic hypothesis: the Court, judiciary, and the law are, for all intents and purposes, always efficacious because they are companions of systemic politics that maintain the existing and persistent unequal distributions of resources and power in the polity, as well as imparting legitimacy to and producing acceptance of the system (McCann, 1999, pp. 87–88).[10]

In the hegemonic hypothesis, indeterminacy, activism in and outside of courts, and the trial and error of the judicial process are all at work, but, at bottom, all of the activity associated with them serves solely to adjust structures, processes, and policies so that the advantages of the "haves" over those of the "have-nots" are never fundamentally threatened (McCann, 1999, pp. 88–89). Hegemony therefore tolerates challenges to its legitimacy and acceptance, but only to the extent that it provides the kinds and degrees of conservation and change necessary for the system to sustain itself.

To illustrate (and to over-simplify for the moment) conventionally the Warren Court is identified with left-liberal judicial domination (conceived loosely), whereas the Burger, Rehnquist, and Roberts Courts are identified with conservative judicial domination. Also, the conventional understanding of the Burger Court is that it did not constitute a counter-revolution against the Warren Court, but put a conservative stamp on Warren Court's jurisprudence and policies, but also, in some instances, expanded Warren Court left-liberal jurisprudence. Arguably, the Rehnquist Court reinforced and expanded the Burger Court's conservative stamp, but it did not constitute a counter-revolution against Warren Court jurisprudence or policies. From the hegemonic perspective, this pattern is beside the point.

All there is to the judicial process is change and conservation which solidifies the legitimacy of politics-as-usual by normalizing constructions of the social welfare compatible with "prevailing power relations" (McCann, 1999, p. 89). What this means is that the judiciary by and large justifies the existing structures and authority patterns of the polity and discourages serious challenges to them. Thus, in the hegemonic hypothesis, not very much is to be made of short-term advantages or disadvantages of the law (as construed from the perspective of competing left-liberal and conservative conceptions of what is right and useful) because, in a pluralist polity, the social welfare is a chimera and the pressures of a judicial process of testing and re-testing simply serves up the interests of those who benefit from hegemony.

In contrast, in the cultural efficacy hypothesis, activism, indeterminacy, and the judicial process are more complex and unpredictable than they are in the hegemonic hypothesis because pluralism is not a chimera. It is reasonable to hypothesize that the judiciary has the capacity, in and of itself, to organize boundaries for what is reasonable and likely to be effective in pursuing constitutional agendas and political conflicts about what is right and useful. But activism and the rest of it are such that the law is

> subject to multiple constructions and contestation over time by differently situated ... actors. (McCann, 1999, p. 79)

Therefore, in effect, there is, within those boundaries, ample opportunities for significant tugs-of-war of unpredictable outcomes within the Court, between the Court and its bureaucracy, between federal and state courts, and outside of courts over the meaning of the social welfare.

In these tugs-of-war, the Court and judiciary have significant cultural and political advantages, most notably to the extent that they are viewed as the "authoritative" voice for the meaning of the Constitution, and the Court in particular to the extent it is accepted as the "last say" over what counts as efficacious constitutional arguments. But, even these advantages can be uncertain given the constellation of social, political, and economic factors that surround the judicial process. The history of constitutional conflict is replete with dramatic examples of challenges to these advantages – in the 19th century there were contests over whether the due process clause included freedom of contract (which an earlier judiciary "lost") and in the 20th century over the significance of the de jure/de facto distinction for desegregation of schools (a closer call, but where the earlier judiciary also "lost"). Tugs-of-war like this make it apparent that what counts as persuasive, authoritative, or politically adequate policies (Foster & Leeson,

1992, 1998, p. 3) is always a matter of dispute that the judiciary cannot altogether control.

Therefore, the premise is that judicial cultural efficacy has "normatively ambiguous ... implications for the advancement of social justice" (McCann, 1999, pp. 64–65) because the dynamics of shifting struggles over what is right and expedient creates a "feedback" effect (Canon & Johnson, 1998, p. 26) that has the judiciary both shaping and being shaped by how the material of law is used. Consequently, in the short term one must be cautious about over-emphasizing what could be seen as the law's advantages or disadvantages because it is so difficult to predict the judiciary's long-term cultural efficacy in patrolling its boundaries.

It bears reiterating, that (conservative) domination (activism) of the judiciary could help build constitutional margins that advance conservative jurisprudence and policies. What a judiciary builds will be tested and re-tested, and in some instances destabilized; the success of destabilization varies with the issue and the power of groups and interests to work the permeable boundaries of (conservative) jurisprudence and policies, in and outside courts. Back around to the starting point, certainly the advantages in testing and re-testing the law are on the side of those with a greater share of the unequal distribution of material, political, cultural, and symbolic resources in the polity. Yet, the law's malleable material suggests that challenges to conservative jurisprudence and policies in and outside of courts should not be underestimated.

The implementation hypothesis also focuses on tugs-of-war among the Court, other institutions, and actors along the lines indicated above, but it emphasizes the dynamics of power relations and processes more than it does the law's malleability. In that respect, *domination* of the judiciary is a misnomer to the extent that it refers to anything more than the internal dynamics of the Court and its majority, concurring, and dissenting opinions. What really matters when it comes to the nature and extent of the judiciary's power over the shape of the social welfare of the polity are partisan, ideological, institutional, and policy strategies (activism) of other (Federal and State) courts, governmental institutions, interest groups, and political actors. Second, what also might matter is the mass media's impact on public opinion as it bears on the Court's institutional legitimacy, its specific policies, and the role of the judiciary in executing those policies.[11] The implementation hypothesis also presumes the dynamics of a neo-pluralist polity such that some groups have inordinate control over some tugs-of-war over policies, but no one group or constellation of groups controls all policy results.

Consequently, not too much should be made of perceived short-term shortcomings and mistakes in law (be they conservative or left-liberal) because, in the long term, what operates is a political process wherein the Court, in and of itself, is a relatively weak player. Put somewhat differently,

> when the Court does decide major questions of public policy, its rulings decide only the instant case and not the larger surrounding political controversies. (O'Brien, 2005, p. 198)

It is, then, the dynamics of prevailing power relations, as reflected in the testing and re-testing of rulings during implementation and compliance with the judiciary, that shapes the efficaciousness of a conservative Court (Baum, 2007, p. 225; McCann, 1999, pp. 69–75). Because activism and testing and re-testing of law and politics are diffused throughout the polity, the judiciary's impact "is complex, highly variable, and ... difficult to measure" (Baum, 2007, p. 218), and is significantly constrained by the dynamics of "checking and balancing interplay among various institutions ..." (McCann, 1999, p. 68), political processes, and actors.

The electoral competition hypothesis focuses on how systemic dynamics shape and constrain a Court and the judiciary. The electoral hypothesis differs from the implementation hypothesis primarily in relation to the level of analysis for understanding systemic constraints on judicial activism. Where the implementation hypothesis directs attention primarily to micro-level (or issue-by-issue) tugs-of-war, the electoral competition hypothesis presumes that the distribution of power in the polity is shaped primarily by the shifting dynamics of Federal and State political party competition and electoral politics. Within this context, the outstanding initial question is whether party competition and electoral politics characteristically produces unitary or divided governments.[12]

For the last 40 or so years, the answer to that question has been divided government for national and most state governments (Adamany & Meinhold, 2003, p. 371; Fiorina, 1992; Hershey, 2007, p. 246).[13] At the national level, the upshot of this is the tendency toward Republican Presidents, a Democratic House, and the Senate to be something of a toss-up. At the state level, the trend is that a

> governor will face an opposition party majority in at least one of the two houses, and it is not unusual for the governor to find both houses under the control of the opposition party. (Keefe & Ogul, 1997, p. 118)

Associated with divided government is a tangled web of party competition and electoral trends: (a) the incumbency effect (the overwhelming extent to which legislative incumbents are likely to win re-election);[14] (b) terms limits at the State level which perhaps increase executive and decrease legislative control over policy agendas – as well as perhaps increasing the impact of interest groups in the policy-making process (to the extent that they are the source of future job opportunities or a means of promoting issues useful for seeking other political offices) (Fiorina, 1992, pp. 56–57; Tushnet, 2003, pp. 28–30); (c) a steady decline in voter party identification and "voters more likely to respond to attractive candidates and issues of the other party" (Fiorina, 1992, p. 13); (d) increasingly partisan and ideological party competition – and, at the national level in particular, parties that "have become more distinctive in their stands on important policy questions ..." with the Democratic Party becoming more liberal and the Republican Party more conservative (Hershey, 2007, p. 287); (e) and increasing numbers of voters casting split ballots (Fiorina, 1992, pp. 13–14).

This list of ancillary trends is just a sketch and is meant to suggest the tangled web of factors that enter into the electoral hypothesis' considerations of activism and tugs-of-war over the social welfare. For example, say that a pattern of divided governments at either the Federal or State levels (with its interceding instances of unitary governments) makes it more difficult for political party factions and coalitions to enjoy the fruits of electoral victories by implementing their (and companion interest group) policy agendas. Perhaps a bind ensues? Legislative agendas and results are shaped by the necessity of seeking policy compromises (Hershey, 2007, p. 246), and the tangled web of ancillary trends makes compromise complicated (Fiorina, 1992, pp. 95–96) because political actors are uncertain what the best strategy is to insure their policy preferences (Whittington, 2005, p. 594). Perhaps, the results are an admixture of some ideological and partisan successes for electoral winners alongside compromises with losers that may or may not be acceptable to party coalitions and factions in either camp?

In the electoral competition hypothesis, these results are a backdrop for the transformation of political conflicts into legal ones by those who see a potentially sympathetic ally in the judiciary. In the tugs-of-war of divided governments, tactical advantages can be found in anticipating that a sympathetic (conservative) judiciary would intercede with jurisprudence and policies that would be efficacious, not necessarily in setting the boundaries of conflicts but in policing boundaries constituted by legislative and executive action or inaction. Thus, the judiciary acts either in harmony with (conservative) partisan or ideological causes or in disharmony with forced compromises or legislative defeats (Graber, 1999, p. 41; Hirschl, 2004, pp. 38–44; Tushnet, 2006a, 2006b, p. 117; Whittington, 2005, p. 584).

More specifically, consider three possible structural roles that a judiciary might play along these lines. Role one: Judicial activism could help preserve (conservative) facets of policies in compromises that might suffer, or have suffered, the vicissitudes of divided government. Two: Activism could help obstruct or limit the impact of compromises that have emerged out of those vicissitudes that are seen to be antagonistic to (conservative) partisan and ideological interests (Gillman, 2006; Tushnet, 2006a, 2006b; Whittington, 2005). Three: Activism arises from delegations of power to the judiciary by legislative or executive actors seeking to promote (conservative) policies which (conservative) political coalitions and factions could not achieve, or could not achieve sufficiently on their own (Gillman, 2006, pp. 140, 144; Graber, 1993; Lovell, 2003; Whittington, 2005, pp. 584–585, 589, 593).

Certainly a judiciary is not a mere handmaiden for these structural roles, and the judiciary can be an independent messenger about the shape of the social welfare of the polity in the process of testing and re-testing the law. "Pure" jurisprudential commitments; political socialization that leads judges to meld jurisprudential commitments with their sense of "goals and tensions within the broader political regime" (Whittington, 2005, p. 584); the reality of the molecular motion of the law, the constraints of the law's materials (like precedent) (Fish, 1999, pp. 152, 156), and the fact that the judiciary views itself as the steward of its own institutional legitimacy; all mean that not every political claim has a legal remedy (Graber, 2006a, 2006b, p. 684) and that the judiciary's structural roles might be more limited than those who anticipate them (Graber, 2006a, 2006b, p. 687). Consequently, not too much is to be made of perceived short-term advantages or disadvantages in the law independent of the dynamics of electoral politics and party competition that channel activism.

More could and should be said to substantiate these hypotheses, but enough has been said to see that they can be related to one another in various combinations which would give one or another more or less analytic weight. Perhaps at some grand theoretical level, for those who think in those terms, the four hypotheses should be seen as parts of some whole. On the other hand, competing methodological commitments, empirical findings, to say nothing of explicit or tacit partisan and ideological preferences, suggest that no single hypothesis is the best way to get at the implications of conservative judicial domination. Apropos of the indifference analysis though, the point being made here is that the four hypotheses justify skepticism about blanket generalizations of what counts as judicial *domination.* In the next section, I seek to justify this point with regard to a *conservative* era of the judiciary.

CONCEPTS OF A "CONSERVATIVE" JUDICIARY

Consider four versions of what counts as a "conservative" era, each of which has been foreshadowed in the previous discussion of judicial domination. One version of "conservative" relates solely to hegemony; the other three, inter-related, versions of "conservative" connect to the three other hypotheses, but only in a minor, or trivial, way to the hegemonic hypothesis because of its view of long-term domination. These versions do not exhaust what could count as "conservative," but they should be sufficient to represent the extent to which conservatives can take different positions on various issues, in part because there are disagreements among conservatives over what is an appropriate "conservative" policy, approach to constitutional interpretation, and the role of courts in the polity.

The first version of "conservative" as hegemonic is straightforward. In the long term, every era of the judiciary is conservative in that the judiciary is always part of politics and the process for maintaining the prevailing and systemic unequal distribution of resources and power relations. In the short term, a conservative era of the judiciary is simply the testing and re-testing of the Republican Party and/or contemporary conservative agendas as they relate to maintaining the more "right-wing" side of systemic inequality. But the details of short-term conservativism do not really matter that much in light of the long-term arc of the systemic conservation of inequalities.

The second version of a "conservative" era refers to the Court's institutional accomplishments. Recall the patterns of continuities and discontinuities between and among the Warren–Rehnquist courts mentioned above. The hub of institutional accomplishments relates to discontinuities with Warren Court jurisprudential and instrumental activism related to such "hot button" issues as equal protection and due process doctrines constituting individual and minority group rights; First Amendment doctrines expanding political participation and electoral representation; reform of basic political institutions; deference to Congressional Commerce Clause and 14th Section 5 regulatory power as a means of managing social, economic, and political problems; and the premise that the Court is and ought to be the last word in interpreting the Constitution and the first word for progressive social change (Belknap, 2005, pp. 306–320). Opposition to these institutional benchmarks is a significant part of gauging a conservative era of the judiciary. So, from an institutional perspective, a subsequent Court can be more or less "conservative" (in opposition to Warren Court jurisprudence and instrumentalism) depending upon which benchmark is under consideration.

Benchmark considerations are relatively easy to make on a results-oriented basis (e.g., for or against this or that party or policy), but that basis misses details that usually complicate matters. Consequently, consider a third and fourth version of a "conservative" era. The third version of conservative is jurisprudential and refers to the commitment to legal criteria that are used to indicate what counts as authoritative and persuasive constitutional arguments. These criteria include commitments to the plain or original meaning of legal texts (statutes and the Constitution); the original intention embedded in legal texts; deference to legislative majorities and executive discretion; the values of dual Federalism and separation of powers; stricter adherence to precedent; natural law philosophy; (at the margins) economic analysis of rights (Gerhardt, Rowe, Brown, & Spann, 2000, pp. 183–285); and conceptions of courts as venues for dispute resolution rather than as agencies of social policy formation. While not exhaustive this list is sufficient to indicate that conservative jurisprudence is not uncomplicated, and that conservative jurisprudes can, and do, disagree with one another over what counts as authoritative and persuasive conservative commitments.

At a lower level of generality, a conservative jurisprudence could tend, for example, toward more restrictive or narrow interpretations of the scope of the equal protections clause in relation to claims about race, gender, and sexual discrimination; more narrow equal protection and due process adjudication in relation to claims about rights of criminal defendant and privacy claims; broader interpretations of Fifth Amendment property rights and takings clause claims; lesser deference to Congressional Commerce Clause power; more sympathy for Tenth and Eleventh Amendments in relation to reserved power and sovereignty of States; and sympathies for Article II executive branch authority. But, differences over more abstract conservativism can lead conservative jurisprudes to take different sides at a lower level of generality. Also, complicating how conservative jurisprudes come down at this lower level of generality are instrumental considerations.

Hence, the fourth version of "conservative" refers to instrumental goals related to contemporary conservative ideology or judges' personal policy preferences, and/or the Republican Party and its Presidential Administrations' agendas, and/or values and attitudes associated with political socialization and professional experiences at odds with either the Warren Court or contemporary liberal welfare state politics and policies. Instrumental and jurisprudential conservatism have a complicated relationship with each other. Sometimes they can be in tandem and therefore reinforce one another. Sometimes they can be at odds with one another in familiar ways such that a jurisprudential commitment could appear to have been sacrificed for the sake of instrumental ones. In that case, we routinely (if not necessarily correctly) think of conservative jurisprudence as being unprincipled. Or apparently conservative instrumental concerns could trump conservative jurisprudential commitments, in which case we routinely say that conservative jurisprudence is principled. Accordingly, analysis must contend with the extent to which conservative jurisprudence has a comparatively significant, insignificant, or ambiguous instrumental impact compared to Warren Court jurisprudence and instrumentalism.

To illustrate indifference thesis benchmark analysis using the four hypotheses for domination and versions of conservatism, I offer the following case study of a Roberts Court Commerce Clause federalism case, one *Rapanos et. ux., et al. v. United States* (2006). The next section, the background for *Rapanos*, uses the hypotheses and versions tacitly; the case-law analysis that follows uses them explicitly, thereby providing a fuller sense of what indifference thesis commentary aims for.

THE BENCHMARKS: A TANGLED POLITICAL AND JUDICIAL WEB

The consolidated case of *Rapanos v. United States* (with *Carabell v. United States Corps of Engineers*, excluded in this case study) narrowed the reach of environmental regulations under the Clean Water Act 1977 (Federal Water Pollution Control Act Amendments) and the discretion of the Army Corps of Engineers (as representative of the Environmental Protection Agency (EPA)). The goal of the next two sections is (1) to illustrate why and how those competing hypotheses about judicial domination and versions of conservatism yield, in at least this instance, competing reasonable interpretations of conservative judicial "domination," in narrowing environmental regulations and, thereby (2) to provide some evidence for the plausibility of the indifference analysis as a way of approaching conservative judicial domination.

The appropriate place to begin is *Rapanos*' broader context in the politics and constitutional law of federalism and Commerce Clause jurisprudence and instrumentalism. Federalism emerged as a central theme with the Nixon Administration (1969–1974). By the late 60s to early 70s, for a variety of ideological, partisan, electoral, and policy reasons,[15] the Republican Party took issue with what scholars call cooperative federalism. Cooperative federalism refers to the promised partnership between the national and state governments whereby the latter would cede power to the Federal government for the sake of alleviating joint social, economic, and political problems. For all intents and purposes, the promise of partnership between the governments fell into the inertia of national command and control, leaving little room for the role of States and localities over joint problems and a lot for the Nixon Administration to object to about the erosion of State and local discretion (Strauber, 2002, p. 135).

In the midst of divided government, the principle behind the Administration's New Federalism was to initiate a range of funding and bureaucratic reforms that would reduce the national government's role and revive State and local governments authority and power. In practice, the New Federalism did spur some significant degree of State and local policy innovations, but even it did relatively little to decrease federal domestic expenditures or the political and bureaucratic inertia of national command and control (Strauber, 2002, p. 135). On the whole, post-Nixon Republican Party reactions to the inertia of command and control have been characterized by inconstant rhetorical variations on the New Federalism, and a more constant rhetoric about strict construction (Clayton & Pickerill, 2004, pp. 95–101; Hensley, Hale, & Snook, 2006, pp. 281–282).

For example (and the rhetoric of strict construction aside), the Reagan Administration (1981–1989) (also amidst divided government) articulated a less pragmatic and more ideological version of federalism. Its rhetoric conveyed the message that the goal was to shrink, if not hollow out, the federal government's role in inter-governmental relations, but also curtail State and local governmental policy making, and deregulate and privatize as much as possible. Although these goals did not necessarily result in corresponding reductions in governmental services at the national level (not in the least because federalism claims rarely are allowed to interfere with partisan politics), but did encourage some measure of State and local policy shrinkage, they did convey the electoral message that the polity's social welfare ought not be pursued as business as usual. That message resonated with elite antagonisms to governments and cross sections of the voting public regardless of party affiliation (Strauber, 2002, pp. 135–136).

The George H. W. Bush Presidency adds little to this political story. But the Clinton Administration (1993–2001) – a unitary government that succumbed to divided government and the Gingrich "revolution" as heir to the Reagan years – learned the electoral lessons of not pursuing the social welfare as business as usual. It tore a page from the Nixon Administration's New Federalism script, and melded it with Democratic Party goals to advance ideas about broad bureaucratic and budget reforms that were to facilitate re-organizing inter-governmental relations for the sake of political and economic innovation.

The Clinton (or Clinton–Gore) approach to federalism was designed to promote policy partnerships that would decrease national command and control and would encourage state and local power in order to make room for policy initiatives and experiments (Strauber, 2002, pp. 146, 149). The Administration's rhetoric initially attracted some measure of bi-partisan support, but was ultimately seen by Republicans as a covert path to more command and control and an attempt to undo a Reagan Administration-like approach to federal power. As for the current George W. Bush Administration, for the last seven years, other than casual rhetoric about too much governmental power, budget cuts in specific areas, and attempts to deal with the political embarrassments over Hurricane Katrina relief, federalism has not been a high priority issue (although strict construction rhetoric continues unabated). This patchwork quilt of federalism initiatives since the Nixon Administration has had a greater impact in some policy areas than others, making some dents in the overall inertia toward political centralization along the way and encouraging (or compelling) States and localities to pursue policy innovation (within budgetary constraints), but overall the inertia of command and control continues.

There is a companion legal side to this see-saw politics. A Republican Party shibboleth since the Nixon Administration is "strict construction" of the Constitution. The rhetoric of strict construction has been diffuse because it is deployed to serve changing electoral functions. Initially, in the Nixon Administration strict construction was primarily related to the Republican Party's Southern Strategy to carve out an electoral base out of what had been the Democratic Party's stranglehold in the South. Hence, the rhetoric was used to signal objections to specific Warren Court desegregation policies, reform of the criminal justice system, the use of the Fourteenth Amendment to incorporate the Bill of Rights, and to generalized objections to national government versus "states' rights."

After the Nixon Administration, the rhetoric continued to signal such objections, but it also signaled generalized opposition to the New Deal and the Johnson Administration Great Society welfare state (no matter the Nixon Administration contributions to the latter) as well as support for the stance that good judging was less-constrained judging, the implication being that if judges adhered to the text and structure of the Constitution then the judiciary would manifest requisite judicial deference to the decision-making discretion of political bodies. At a sophisticated level, in regard to federalism in particular, strict construction rhetoric eventually trumpeted the Tenth Amendment as a potential limit on the reach of Article I, Section 8 Congressional Commerce Clause power for the sake of powers reserved to States. Yet it takes some effort to draw tight linkages between strict construction and Burger–Roberts Court jurisprudence and instrumentalism, and the latter are equally well thought about in relation to

> political changes initiated within the electoral political system and advanced by the political parties. (Clayton & Pickerill, 2004, p. 112)

That said, in 1976, at the tail end of the Ford Administration and eight years of Republican domination of the Presidency (but divided government), the Burger Court, in a 5-4 decision (the majority consisting of five post-Warren Court Republican appointees and one Warren Court Republican appointee), rediscovered the moribund Tenth Amendment principle that "powers not delegated to the United States, nor prohibited by it to the States, are reserved to the States respectively, or the people." *National League of Cities v. Usery* (1976), authored by then Justice William Rehnquist, used the Tenth Amendment to linch the holding that a 1974 statutory provision extending maximum hours and minimum wage provisions of the Fair Labor Standards Act (1938) to state governments and their political subdivisions was unconstitutional.

Using the Tenth Amendment was a remarkable stroke of judicial activism because ever since the *Darby* Court[16] the Tenth Amendment had been rendered virtually irrelevant as a jurisprudential check on national power in general, and on Congress's commerce power in particular. Nevertheless, one of Rehnquist's core arguments in *National League of Cities* was that the Tenth Amendment *required* judicial recognition of the extent to which traditional State governmental functions, related to such duties as police protection and public health services, have attached to them attributes of sovereignty of States as States. These attributes render States immune to the otherwise extensive command and control of Congress and national power (Strauber, 2002, p. 130). Thus, at the time, *National League of Cities* appeared to write a potentially generous promissory note for a Republican Party New Federalism politics, policies, and jurisprudence.

But the maturity date of that note has ultimately become uncertain and ambiguous. After about nine years, a Burger Court decision signaled that line drawing between national power and the sovereignty of States as States had proven to be a futile jurisprudential task, conservative politics of Federal–State relations notwithstanding (Strauber, 2002, p. 130). In 1985, in the midst of the Reagan Administration and divided government, *National*

League of Cities, and, for all intents and purposes, Tenth Amendment jurisprudence, appeared to get scuttled. In *Garcia v. San Antonio Metropolitan Transit Authority* (1985), the Burger Court revisited the Fair Labor Standards Act, writing for the majority, Justice Harry Blackmun (a Republican appointee), who had concurred in *National League of Cities*, held for a 5-4 Court (two Democratic and one Republican Warren Court appointees in the majority, joined by two post-Warren Court Republican appointees[17]) that the protection of State power in Federal–State relations was not a matter for the judiciary but for the political process to manage. Thus, *Garcia* appeared to write a close-call promissory note for conventional Democratic Party command and control politics, policies, and jurisprudence and a Democratic, not Republican, view of the role of courts in Federal–State relations (Clayton & Pickerill, 2004, p. 101).

With Federalism doctrine hinging on a single vote, it could be said, "the Rehnquist Court thus inherited a most ambiguous legacy of federalism jurisprudence" (Hensley et al., 2006, p. 281). And, in 1992, during the Bush Administration and divided government, the Rehnquist Court, in *New York v. United States* (1992), appeared to make things more hazy by reiterating judicial oversight of Congressional action and Tenth Amendment activism on behalf of States. Justice Sandra Day O'Connor's opinion in *New York* held the "title provision" of the Low-Level Radioactive Waste Policy Amendments Act of 1985 unconstitutional because its provision that States either comply with Congressional waste disposal instructions or "take title" of the waste was a coercive alternative that violated the Tenth Amendment's umbrella of protection of the States' "residual and inviolable sovereignty" (*New York v. United States*, 1992, p. 188).

Coincidental or not, in the same year, the Republican Party also "specifically cited the Tenth Amendment as a constitutional limit on federal power" in their party platform by declaring that

> We will not initiate any federal activity that can be conducted better on the state or local level. In doing so, we reassert the crucial importance of the 10th Amendment. (Clayton & Pickerill, 2004, p. 102)

But the *New York* decision was not a mirror image of Republican commitments. *New York* was a 6-3 decision, and although the majority comprised six Republican appointees, a concurring opinion was filed by one Warren Court Democratic appointee and two post-Warren Court Republican appointees; an opinion concurring in part and dissenting in part was signed by the Democratic appointee joined by two post-Warren Court Republican appointees; and a separate opinion concurring in part and dissenting in part was posted by the post-Warren Court Republican appointee. In the midst of all those opinions, it was difficult to tell from *New York* just how the Tenth Amendment limited Federal power, if it actually did do so.

Nonetheless, the Republican Party's commitment to federalism politics and jurisprudence appeared to receive a clearer, and major, doctrinal boost in 1995. In *United States v. Lopez* (1995), the Rehnquist Court, in yet another in the string of 5-4 decisions (with five post-Warren Court Republican appointees in the majority) held an act of Congress unconstitutional for the first time in over half a century. The Gun-Free School Zones Act (1990), a product of the Bush I Administration and divided government, prohibited possession of a gun within 1,000 feet of a school, and *Lopez* held that the law failed to satisfy the substantive effects test for the reach of Congress's Commerce Clause authority, i.e., an activity, taken alone or in its aggregate consequences, must have a substantial impact on economic enterprises or market activities involving interstate commerce to be regulated by Congress.

Lopez thus reinforced the impression that there was a Rehnquist Court majority prepared to draw lines to limit national power and protect traditional State governmental functions. Nevertheless, doctrinal ambiguity remained because the *Lopez* Court used a threefold version of the conventional substantive effects test,[18] making no reference to the Tenth Amendment, and therefore depended on constitutional law and Congressional fact-freedom deferential to national power (Strauber, 2002, pp. 130–131). Even so, apparent commitments to restrict Federal power were buttressed twice more, with remaining ambiguities about the Tenth Amendment, by the Rehnquist Court, in two significant cases in 1997 and 2000.

In *Printz v. United States* (1997) the Lopez majority, yet again by a 5-4 decision, held that the Brady Handgun Violence Prevention Act (1993), a product of the Clinton Administration and unitary government, violated the reach of the Commerce Clause when State officers were commanded to perform background checks on potential handgun purchasers. Justice Antonin Scalia's majority opinion linked Tenth Amendment jurisprudence, textual and structural considerations of the Commerce Clause, and the Necessary and Proper Clause to warrant the claim that Congressional action violated the principle of dual sovereignty and the inviolable residual power retained by States (Strauber, 2002, p. 131).

The 2000 decision was *United States v. Morrison* (2000). Chief Justice Rehnquist, for the *Lopez* majority against its four dissenters, held that the portion of the Violence Against Women Act (1994) (a Clinton Administration unitary government legislation) providing a federal civil remedy for victims of gender-motivated violence, was unconstitutional. But the Tenth Amendment faded out again as a significant jurisprudential element, as the Court looked not there but to the *Lopez* decision's Commerce Clause distinction between national and police powers and its reading of the limits on Congressional Section 5 Fourteenth Amendment power in relation to state authority as a boundary for Congressional authority (Strauber, 2002, p. 131).

After *Morrison*, it appeared that the Rehnquist Court conservative majority was poised to cash in on some kind of federalism promissory note by constructing some sort of doctrinal change in federalism and Commerce Clause, if not Tenth Amendment, jurisprudence and policy instrumentalism compatible with some facet of Republican Party ideology and agendas. Put in different words, if it was apparent that there was a dominant conservative majority sympathetic to Commerce Clause federalism, the jurisprudence for it was far less apparent. Then, in the midst of this confusion about what was apparent and not apparent (and the five-year stretch of unitary government of the Bush II Presidency, 2002–2007), the Court, in *Gonzales v. Raich* (2005) in a 6-3 decision (with two of the Lopez majority migrating over to sustain federal power), sustained Congress's Commerce Clause power by holding unconstitutional California's Compassionate Use Act (1996) permitting medicinal uses of marijuana. The 1970 Controlled Substances Act classified marijuana in that class of drugs that has a

> high potential for abuse, no accepted medical use, and no accepted safety for use in medically supervised treatment. This classification renders the manufacture, distribution, or possession of marijuana a criminal offense.

Justice John Paul Stevens' decision held that California's Compassionate Use Act (based on positive medical claims about doctor-supervised marijuana use for serious medical conditions) was an intrastate activity that was rationally related to economic activities that have a sufficient substantive impact on commerce that Congress has the plenary power to regulate it.

Although *Raich* was a *potential* instrumental and jurisprudential federalism victory, it proved to be a *kinetic* rejection of Commerce Clause federalism. The use of the rational basis test signals maximum deference to Congressional power over specific policies (in this case drugs); it also eclipses altogether a State's attempt to assert its autonomy and sovereignty to pass an innovative medical policy between its borders. Accordingly, taking into consideration the jurisprudential confusion that preceded it, and the instrumental factor of drug policy, *Raich* only obscures further what it means to have a conservative majority on the Court deliver on its promise to allow "state governments adopt and implement policies that diverge from one another and from the national government," considering that such "divergence is a precondition of state experimentation and accommodation of diverse preferences?" (Young, 2005, p. 23).

The see-saw of the *Lopez–Morrison* line and then the *Raich* decision mark our turning point into the narrower matters of direct concern: the Clean Water Act (CWA), wetlands, and federalism. The CWA was prompted by what had become widespread recognition of the critical conditions of water pollution in the United States and the corresponding need for a cooperative federalism approach to linking Federal and State policy-making solutions.

True to cooperative federalism principles, the CWA was designed to promote and preserve state regulatory power, but, over time, inertia of command and control set in, particularly in regard to regulations over what counts as "navigable waters" and "waters of the United States," not in the least because it appeared, especially to the EPA, the Corps, and environmental interests, that only national command and control, rather than state regulatory power, could be efficacious in restoring the integrity of the nation's water resources and supplies. It should be said that from the beginning the CWA reflected comparatively widespread, and politically bi-partisan, recognition of not only ecological imperatives but also a range of economic, business, and social imperatives behind the need for water regulations. These imperatives include degradation of water resources and supplies effects: the status of "commercial fisheries," "recreational fishing and hunting," "water-based recreation," "wetlands … as rich areas that support … wildlife … seafood" as well as "flood control, increases in land values, pollution reduction, water supply, recreation, and aesthetics," "the quality of drinking water," and the use of water to "irrigate crops, forests, and other lands." (Adler, Landman, & Cameron, 1993, pp. 88–102).

Wetland protection, under Section 404, was one of the unique facets of the Act, giving the Army Corps of Engineers and the EPA joint responsibility for wetland security (originally characterized by the issuance of permits for discharging materials into the waters of the nation, but later expanded to protect wetlands and its habitats from the impact of commercial development) (Andreen, 2004, p. 538, footnote 8). By and large, as the situation is now, Congress and most commentators view the CWA and its subsequent revisions as a command and control success story. This story includes wetlands policy, at least with regard to reducing the rate at which wetlands continue to be degraded (Andreen, 2004, p. 542). Naturally, there are those who object to command and control wetlands regulations based on what they see as the CWA's impact on their individual property interests, or its negative consequences for commercial, real estate, and development activities. These objections are not simply self-interested, they can include trenchant public policy questions about when the costs of (wetland implementation) policies outweigh their putative benefits. On the other hand, supporters of wetland regulations pushed such questions aside. They contend that wetlands degradation requires even more command and control to protect them from persistent threats of pollutants, dredging, draining, agricultural, residential development, highway and bridge construction, and the like (Andreen, 2004, p. 585). By way of one summary, it is fair to conclude that wetlands policies today, like most complex policies, are frustrating for all parties involved (Flournoy, 2004, p. 609).

One way to cut into these complexities is to trace back to the Reagan Administration. It encouraged the Army Corps of Engineers to reduce the impact of its wetland regulations, which put the Corps at odds with both the EPA and Congress. Initially the Bush I Administration appeared to break with the previous administration and commit itself not to retreat from CWA regulations. But opposing interests about "wetlands" regulations prompted a Democratic Congress to legislate that the Corps follow the previous Administration's narrower approach to wetlands. The Bush Administration eventually came around to Congress's point of view, and the result was that the EPA vacillated between more and less expansive wetland policies. The Clinton Administration's response, in accord with its approach to federalism, was to recommend a policy of flexible balancing of interests of competing parties and institutions (Bergeson, 1993; Flournoy, 2004, pp. 611–614; Quade, 1982). This is the situation the Bush II Administration inherited.

Then the Rehnquist Court enters the story with *Solid Waste Agency of Northern Cook County v. United States Army Corps of Engineers* (2001). In *SWANCC*, the *Lopez* 5-4 majority, remarkably, with hardly a nod to either *Lopez* or *United States v. Morrison*, held that the CWA and the Commerce Clause do not extend to non-navigable, isolated, intrastate waters. In formalistic terms, the opinion applied only to the regulation of migratory birds, but the EPA and most federal courts treated *SWANCC* as a general judicial challenge to the Corps discretion versus the more expansive view of navigable waters in the Burger Court's *United States v. Riverside Bayview Homes, Inc.* (1985) (Strauber, 2002, p. 143).

In 2003, the Bush II Administration responded by giving notice that it read *SWANCC* to require the EPA and Army Corps of Engineers to pull back from enforcing CWA regulations related to "isolated" waters and non-navigable waters because they were outside the character of "waters of the

United States" as understood by reading the CWA. Initially the EPA responded accordingly, and

> one analysis of a leaked version of the agencies' proposed rule suggested that it would exclude a fifth of remaining wetlands and dramatically reduce protection in the arid West and Southwest, eliminating protection of 80–90% of the streams in the Southwest. When public outcry opposing this outcome ensued, the EPA and Corps backed away from the proposed rule and announced that they were abandoning plans to narrow protection ... . (Flournoy, 2004, p. 614)

As a consequence, the GAO reported that the Corps would proceed district-by-district, and case-by-case in determining which waters and wetlands were subject to CWA jurisdiction (Parenteau, 2004/2005, p. 36).

The lesson here is that the see-saw of the politics, policies, and jurisprudence of federalism, juxtaposed to wetlands constitutional politics and law, can hardly be anything but confusion and frustration. That sentence foreshadows the Roberts Court. There we find four justices (John Paul Stevens, Ruth Bader Ginsburg, David Souter, and Stephen Breyer) on the *Raich* side of things in support of national command and control and environmental regulations. There are three justices (Antonin Scalia, Clarence Thomas, and Anthony Kennedy) on the *Lopez* side of things as advocates for some form of federalism instrumentalism and jurisprudence, at least two of whom (Justices Scalia and Thomas) are not disposed (for different reasons) toward expanding national or state environmental regulations, leaving Justice Kennedy, as is frequently the case, something of a wild card. Lastly, Justice Samuel Alito voted with Scalia in *Rapanos*, and Chief Justice Roberts provided a brief concurring opinion in *Rapanos* (appearing to concede that Congress should resolve the wetlands controversy); but it is too early to say where to put either of them in relation to the 4-3 split described above.[19] Enter *Rapanos*.

RAPANOS AND "CONSERVATIVE DOMINATION OF THE JUDICIARY"

Land developer John A. Rapanos owned three separate parcels of land (totaling 230 acres) in Midland, Michigan which are not directly adjacent to any navigable waters (Mikalonis, 2006) and are some 11–20 miles from Saginaw Bay and Lake Huron (Buchwalter, 2006).

After a heavy rain, water from the fields owned by Rapanos makes its way in to a man-made ditch. It flows to a small creek and then to a river that empties into ... Saginaw Bay. (Savage, 2006, p. 18)

In 1988, Rapanos wanted to fill the land to build a shopping center and requested approval to proceed from the Michigan Department of Natural Resource. Michigan authorities repeatedly advised him that he could proceed with his plans if he secured a permit, and that he should not proceed with any construction without it. Mr. Rapanos refused to secure a permit, contended that neither state nor federal regulations applied to his land, and continued to work it (Buchwalter, 2006).

The EPA proceeded to file criminal and civil charges against Rapanos, resulting in 18 years of litigation and accumulated fines and fees of 13 million dollars. In 2006, the Supreme Court heard Rapanos' appeal of what had been until then a losing cause. The heart of his litigation was to challenge the EPA and Corps assertion, backed by the Sixth Circuit's ruling, that the proper reading of the CWA gives the EPA and Corps jurisdiction over inland "waters of the United States" (which includes wetlands) that are non-navigable and not directly adjacent to navigable waters. "About seventy-five percent of ... wetlands are on private property, and many of those acres are dry much of the year" (Savage, 2006, p. 18). This litigation challenged decades of EPA and Corps discretion (Barringer, 2006). It also boldly underlined the tensions between property rights activists on the one hand and, on the other hand, environmental regulators (Tupi, 2006). And it brought Solicitor General Paul Clement to argue in support of decades-long EPA and Corps discretion. (Perhaps the Solicitor General's role in *Rapanos* is an example of the Bush II Administrations lack of concern with federalism, at least in regard to water policy.)

Rapanos thus represents a conservative Administration defending command and control environmental institutions and regulations against property interests before a conservative Supreme Court working with Commerce Clause federalism precedents which have reflected earlier sharply divided decisions! It is worth noting that all but two States submitted amicus briefs backing the government. But one of the two dissenting states was Alaska which has most of the nation's wetlands, over half of which would be subject to CWA regulatory power if the Court sustained the government's view. The Roberts Court response, apropos of confusion and frustration, was a 4-1-4 plurality that remanded the case back to the District Court. *Rapanos* held that statutory interpretation of the CWA, controlling precedents (*SWANCC* in particular), and state regulatory power required the conclusion that the EPA and Corps' approach to the wetlands under review was inappropriate. But Justice Scalia (joined by Justices Thomas and Alito), with the Chief Justice and Justice Kennedy, concurring, made it uncertain what the standard should or would be with regard to remand and future environmental controls over remote waters. (To complicate things further, one news story suggested that Justice Scalia's opinion had originally been a dissent until Justice Kennedy shifted his vote and wrote a concurring opinion recommending a different standard for remote water regulations than the one recommended by Justice Scalia.)[20]

As a first impression, *Rapanos* is another contribution to the see-saw that keeps alive confusion over Commerce Clause federalism activism, judicial control over the EPA, the Corps and lower courts, and it has the potential to add fuel to the sometimes intense partisan and ideological fires in and out of government at the State and Federal levels over how environmental protection law and politics should proceed.[21] Details about *Rapanos* reinforce this impression. Justice Scalia's contribution begins with his portrayal of the Corps as "an enlightened despot" (*Rapanos*, 2006, p. 2) that abuses its discretion over economic, aesthetic, recreational considerations, and, more generally, over the social welfare of the polity, in order to vastly expand CWA regulatory power to the furthermost ambit of Commerce Clause power. Scalia acknowledges that post-*Riverside Bayview Homes, Inc.* lower court decisions might appear to justify Corp discretion. But he rejects the Sixth Circuit's finding that regulatory discretion extended to wetlands that are merely "adjacent" to navigable waters. Via textual analysis of the CWA, and what he referred to as the "natural definitions" of terms such as "waters," "source points" of pollution, and the distinction between "navigable" and "non-navigable waters," Scalia concludes that

> the CWA phrase "the waters of the United States" includes only those relatively permanent, standing or continuously flowing bodies of water "forming geographic features" that are described in ordinary parlance as "streams[,] ... oceans, rivers, [and] lakes." (*Rapanos*, 2006, p. 20)

Scalia relies heavily on *SWANCC* in order to characterize what counts as "relatively permanent" and "open waters" within the context of concerns over "impingement of the States' traditional and primary power over land and water use" as "a quintessential state and local power" (*Rapanos*, 2006, p. 20). His statutory interpretation and reading of *SWANCC*, balanced against *Riverside Bayview's* apparent grant of discretion to the Corps to use ecological criteria to determine what counts as wetlands, led Scalia to reject the "extensive federal jurisdiction urged by the Government." Despite the preferences of the majority of the States and lower courts to defer to the

Corps, Scalia finds that judicial deference "would authorize the Corps to function as a de facto regulator of immense stretches of intrastate land" without an unequivocal Congressional mandate to intrude "into traditional state authority" (*Rapanos*, 2006, p. 19).

In sharp contrast, Justice Kennedy rejects virtually every element of Scalia's textualist reasoning, which he characterized as "inconsistent with [the Act's] text, structure and purpose" (*Rapanos*, 2006, p. 19) and controlling precedents. The counterpoint to Scalia's portrayal of the Corps is Kennedy's portrayal of Rapanos as, in effect, a criminal for proceeding with his wetlands project without proper authorization and in the face of cease-and-desist orders. On the legal side, Kennedy cites what he finds to be precedents for the Corps discretion to make ecological judgments about what "waters" and "wetlands" should be subject to CWA regulations. Most significant, and in contrast to Scalia's emphasis on the relative permanence and connection of waters, Kennedy leans heavily on *Riverside Bayview* and *SWANCC* to indicate that the Corps discretion and lower court litigation have always depended on fact considerations about whether remote waters and wetlands "possess a significant nexus to other waters that are or were navigable in fact or that could reasonably be so made" (*Rapanos*, 2006, p. 1). At bottom, Kennedy holds that the significant nexus test alone is sufficient to satisfy "the evident breadth of congressional concern for protection of water quality and aquatic ecosystems" (*Rapanos*, 2006, p. 1). Furthermore, it is "important public interests ... served by the CWA in general and by the protection of wetlands in particular" (*Rapanos*, 2006, p. 20) that determine State rights and responsibilities regarding its waters.

It is worth noting that *Rapanos* not only provides two competing approaches to determining Corps discretion (via statutory interpretation versus a fact-finding rule), but the significant nexus fact-finding rule can cut two ways. A Scalia-informed reading of the rule would provide a more narrow scope for understanding Corps fact-finding and lower court oversight regarding remote and non-navigable waters, whereas Kennedy's remarks about the breadth of Congressional concerns for protecting water supplies implies a wider scope for Corps discretion and judicial oversight. So, if the Kennedy reading guides future EPA, Corps, and lower court instrumentalism, but it is the Scalia opinion which drives the significant nexus test, then policy results could still be closer to the Scalia reading of the CWA and precedents. Of course, if the Corps and lower courts proceed on a case-by-case basis, then there could be some Scalia-like decisions, some narrow, Scalia-like significant nexus findings, and some broader significant nexus findings. Coincidentally, in 2005, Democrats in the Senate (with one independent) and in the House (with a handful of Republicans) appeared not to want to take any chances, and introduced, but could not pass, the Clean Water Authority Restoration Act, to replace references to non-navigable waters with "waters of the United States," and to include "intrastate" and "intermittent" waters within the ambit of "waters of the United States."

Whether a subsequent Congress will amend the CWA, or lower courts adopt Scalia's or Kennedy's approach to the Corps and lower court discretion, or any of the rest of it, is, of course almost entirely sound and fury signifying little from the perspective of the hegemonic hypothesis. Conservative domination of the judiciary necessitates the conclusion that the to and fro of Commerce Clause federalism and the wake of *Rapanos* only obscures the lack of a genuine controversy over national power or environmental regulations. What there has been and will continue to be is judicial activism, politics, and policies protecting "private property interests and capitalism's economic growth and business interests" that balances centralization of power

> with just sufficient autonomy remaining to the states and local governments to keep the system from disasters of too much command and control. (Strauber, 2002, p. 107)

Accordingly, indeterminacy is an instrument of hegemonic balancing. And, in spite of everything that might be said about CWA regulations by those who are opposing it, much of it is meant to and does, on balance, at the macro-level, protect property interests and capitalism's economic growth and business interests. Conservative domination of the judiciary guarantees that the testing and re-testing of the judicial process and the social welfare of the polity wind up there (either by intention or tacit cultural constraints).

For example, the hegemonic prediction is that judicial conservative domination will not interfere, by and large, with interest in Alaska to maximize private property interests, statewide economic development, and that exploitation of natural resources will be abetted by the inertia of political culture and national judicial and political power (Nagel, 2001; Tushnet, 1985). There will be jurisprudential and policy trade-offs between rankly partisan or ideological conservative and left-liberal conceptions of those interests and public goods; and some trade-offs will not be reducible to those factors and will include apparently genuine concerns with scientific risk assessments, risk management policies, and considerations of ecosystem sustainability (Strauber, 2002, pp. 135–136, 149). But a conservative judiciary's part is to insure that these trade-offs

> rarely alter, and in fact often only reinforce, the overall patterns of social hierarchy and group power relations within society. (McCann, 1999, p. 88)

Alternatively, if the reference point for domination is cultural efficacy, then *Rapanos* could have some significant non-hegemonic consequences, notwithstanding the inertia of political command and control. *Rapanos* does seem to send a signal that there is a Roberts Court majority inclined to police Rehnquist Court jurisprudential and instrumental boundaries. But within the Court, differences between Scalia's statutory textualism and Kennedy's instrumentalism, uncertainties about Chief Justice Roberts and Justice Alito's jurisprudence and instrumentalism, and unknowns about how and why *Rapanos* might be re-tested make *Rapanos* an uncertain institutional benchmark for the contours of conservative domination.

Further, the Court's reaction to *Rapanos* will be shaped in part by the lower court discretion and indeterminacy constituted by differences between Scalia's textualism and Kennedy's nexus test. These differences provide opportunities for lower court activism, testing and re-testing in *Rapanos*, a process fashioned partly by judges' competing commitments to various facets of conservative and left-liberal jurisprudence and instrumentalism about what is right and expedient regarding the CWA. It is to be expected that this process will have normatively ambiguous implications for the efficacy of *Rapanos* and compliance with the CWA.

Outside of court, *Rapanos* is fodder for multiple and diverse reactions that could give rise to their own uncertainties about Roberts Court domination. For example, indeterminacy, concerns about activism, testing and re-testing, and their consequences for the CWA could explain Congress's reaction to *Rapanos*. In addition, *Rapanos'* cultural efficacy over adjacent wetlands is ripe for challenges from the EPA, the Corps, States, environmentalists, and landowners. All of these potential, uncertain ramifications of the cultural efficacy of Roberts Court domination over the CWA are important in and of themselves, and justify hesitancy exaggerating conservative domination of the judiciary. What is more, these considerations of activities in and outside of courts prompt thinking more along the lines of the dynamics of power relations and processes rather than lines associated with the Roberts Court and the law's malleability.

To illustrate, if a subsequent Congress should succeed in amending the CWA to consolidate EPA and Corps discretion, then Roberts Court conservative jurisprudence and instrumentalism would be muted, if not silenced, hemmed in by explicit Congressional statutory intent regarding remote waters. But, if Congress does not act, then *Rapanos'* indeterminacy leaves the EPA and Corps free to patrol their own jurisdictional boundaries. (More of this shortly.) Inaction could energize both pro- and anti-regulatory forces to initiate legal challenges to the Corps and EPA's actions (whichever direction those decisions go in), using *Rapanos* ambiguities and Congressional inaction as material to capitalize on their vested interests via the Court's 4-1-4 split. The indeterminacy of *Rapanos* might also energize States to pursue their own oversight over wetlands development as individual and corporate landowners accelerate their personal and commercial plans for their property in the midst of *Rapanos* uncertainties. Thus, *Rapanos'* significance could be more heavily influenced by tugs-of-war outside rather than inside the judiciary.

Of course, such tugs-of-war would enter the feedback loop back into lower courts and, probably, back to the Court itself. What scant evidence there is now suggests that inside courts, *Rapanos* looks like another motion of the see-saw. Consider three cases as if they were part of a pattern. In *Northern California River Watch v. City of Healdsburg* (2006), the Ninth Circuit Appeals decision applied the significant nexus test and held that the adjacent wetlands under review fell within CWA's jurisdiction. And a Seventh Appeals Court decision, *United States v. Gerke Excavating, Inc.* (2006), on remand from the Supreme Court, sent its case back to the District Court to make findings consistent with the significant nexus test. But in *United States v. Chevron Pipe Line Co.* (2006), the Fifth Circuit read *SWANCC* narrowly and adopted Scalia's reading of the CWA on point sources to hold that the waters under review were not "navigable" and therefore did not fall within the CWA's jurisdiction (Mikalonis, 2006).

Even if CWA command and control inertia appears to favor the significant nexus test over Scalia's version, these three cases still indicate considerable potential for diverse lower court implementation of *Rapanos.* Three cases are insufficient to make informed guesses about what to expect of conservative lower court jurisprudence and instrumentalism. Moreover, as of this writing, the EPA and the Corps, in consultation with the Department of Justice's Environmental and Natural Resources Division, appear to be taking a case-by-case approach to jurisdiction over adjacent waters. How this process will work itself out is unknown. Therefore, the safest presumption to make about post-*Rapanos* implementation is that its implementation will be determined by how various actors test and re-test it, correlated with how the Army Corps proceeds on a case-by-case basis, and how that process works itself out in the lower courts, until, and unless, either Congress and/or the Court should intervene.

Then again, perhaps all of the above leans much too heavily on the legal and judicial process side of things. Perhaps *Rapanos* indeterminacy will be channeled into symbolic and rhetorical tugs-of-war between President Bush and Congress, quite apart from any material changes in CWA policies.

In light of the forthcoming Presidential election, divided government, instabilities associated with Democratic control of the legislature, and the global warming dimension of cultural politics, there is potential for broad-spectrum environmental issues to become part of ongoing partisan and ideological debates between Republicans and Democrats over the social welfare, the role of the judiciary, and public policy formation and implementation.

We are now in the narrative arc of electoral and party competition conjectures. Recall the possibility of some (marginally) bi-partisan Congressional action being successful in either promulgating CWA revisions denoting wider conceptions of "navigable waters" and "waters of the United States" and/or reinforcing Corps decision-making discretion over adjacent waters. If President Bush should find strategic electoral advantages in signing such legislation (e.g., to solidify what might remain of his base for the sake of party and electoral goals), then that would be an impetus to command and control inertia, rendering conservative activism and domination virtually toothless.

Consequently, for conservative domination of the judiciary to be efficacious in this controversy, it is essential that either (a) Congressional Republicans not cooperate with the Democrats; or (b) if they do cooperate for electoral reasons, then for President Bush to veto CWA legislation. Either non-cooperation or a presidential veto is the functional equivalent of a legislative or executive delegation of power to a sympathetic conservative judiciary. The judiciary could then promote deregulatory policies which conservative coalitions and factions in the legislative and executive branch could not achieve on their own. Specifically, judicial activism in the midst of *Rapanos* indeterminacy could help preserve some measure of conservative jurisprudence and policies during *Rapanos* testing and re-testing. It could do this by obstructing compromises that the EPA and Corps make on their case-by-case jurisdiction over wetlands; or, most aggressively, it could promote a narrower reading of the CWA than Republican Administrations have unsuccessfully urged on the EPA or Corps. Lastly, electoral and party competition and delegation to the judiciary could further encourage anti-regulatory groups to pursue litigation in the hope of solidifying, if not expanding narrow *Rapanos* implementation.

Certainly not every anti-regulatory claim will be sustained. Prominently, there is the inertia of CWA command and control jurisprudence and instrumentalism, and the uncertainties of an evolving Roberts Court version of a conservative majority. Nevertheless, within these parameters, the molar and molecular motions of a conservative judiciary with delegated power could contribute significantly to making a dent in EPA and Corps policies, with the potential to carry over into other regulatory policies as well. And very shortly, there will be those elections. Health and age make two of the dissenting Justices of the divided *Rapanos* Court likely to be replaced, and, if so, they will be replaced by a yet to be decided Administration and Congress. It goes without saying that a Republican Presidential victory, and/or Congressional realignment, would have a significant impact on both the nature of the Court's conservative jurisprudence and instrumentalism.

To illustrate the uncertain implications that follow from instances where anti-regulatory claims are not sustained, consider *Massachusetts et al. v. Environmental Protection Agency et al.* (2007). This case was decided too late to receive the detailed attention it deserves, but what follows should be sufficient to indicate the complexities of the law and politics of federalism jurisprudence and the EPA. In the 2007 case, Justice Kennedy provided the fifth vote to sustain an environmental interest group challenge, with amicus support by States, of a Circuit Court holding that the Clean Air Act did not authorize or require the EPA to address the impact of automobile gasoline emissions and their global climate implications. Significantly, rather than joining Chief Justice Roberts' dissenting opinion for the minority rejecting the suit as non-justiciable (Justice Scalia provided a separate textualist defense of EPA's discretion and the lack of statutory justification for regulating gasoline emissions), Justice Kennedy signed on to Justice Stevens' majority opinion – an opinion that arguably can be read to endorse a bold approach to statutory interpretation for the sake of judicial activism and an expanding role for national regulatory command and control.

It will be interesting to learn whether, or to what extent, Justice Kennedy's vote foreshadows a significant step forward in his, and therefore a Roberts Court majority post-*Rapanos* jurisprudence and instrumentalism. Even supposing such a step, its character and its significance for policy is altogether uncertain granted the complicating factors of those forthcoming elections, their impact on executive and legislative branch politics and policy, divided or unitary government, EPA discretion over its agenda, its budget, and policy, as well as possible changes in the composition of the Court.

In a nutshell, where *Rapanos* and its wake are concerned, there are good reasons to hesitate in making predictions about its legal and political meanings, and therefore to distrust preconceived notions and blanket conceptual and normative generalizations about the implications of conservative judicial domination, as frustrating as that is, or might be, from partisan or ideological perspectives.

CONCLUSION

The preceding case study illustrates what the indifference thesis looks for and how it analyzes indeterminacy, activism, the judicial process, and impact of the law on the social welfare of the polity. In view of that, its salient strength is that it illustrates why, and how, it is prudent to distrust preconceived notions and blanket generalizations about (conservative) law and politics once it is established that there are competing reasonable ways to address "conservative domination of the judiciary." Another strength of indifference analysis is that it situates commentary to be relentlessly "matter-of-fact" about law and politics. By that I mean being especially and intentionally attentive to circumstantial social fact and consequentialist considerations which are all too easily eclipsed, obscured, or evaded by analyses which, intentionally or not, depend heavily on preconceived notions and blanket generalizations about law and politics.

Yet, as indicated at the beginning, indifference analysis does not exempt itself from its own pragmatism. To the contrary, it challenges its own presuppositions and generalizations and calls explicit attention to its weaknesses. Two examples: First, if its two strengths have been demonstrated then conceivably Commerce Clause federalism makes too easy a case for indifference analysis and for being uncertain about the implications of conservative domination. This criticism cuts more or less deeply. The deeper cut is that, if federalism is different in kind and not degree from other law and politics, then indifference analysis and its premises are a mistake for other commentary. The less deep cut is that, if federalism is different in degree from other law and politics then the strengths of indifference analysis and its premises will vary from case study to case study. Although I am suspicious of the deeper cut, only subsequent case studies would substantiate how deep the cut is.

Second, perhaps the salient weakness of indifference analysis is its salient strength. Its supposed "realism" apparently provides no criteria for saying whether conservative domination of the judiciary is good, bad, or much ado about nothing, at least in relation to Commerce Clause federalism. This is odd, if not perverse. Whether this criticism cuts deeply or not is a matter of perspective. It does not cut deeply if one mixes the various hypotheses about domination (giving them different weights); the resulting blend would provide criteria for saying something more definitive about conservative domination of the judiciary. Also, competing blends would provide competing criteria, thereby setting the stage for competing sides to debate conservative domination. These debates might not (although they could) coincide with ideological or partisan notions and generalizations, but if they did, a gap between indifference analysis and ideology and partisanship is not necessarily a disappointing result, except from an ideological or partisan perspective.

There exactly is where the criticism cuts deeply. If one takes the hard view that commentary *is* ideology and partisanship, then the cut goes to the heart of indifference analysis. Perhaps one way to blunt the criticism is to say that indifference analysis can be a test of the strengths and weaknesses of ideological and partisan analysis. But saying that does not actually blunt the cut because indifference analysis presupposes that it, rather than ideology or partisanship, should be given primary weight in commentary. So, from the perspective of ideology and partisanship there is no escaping the conclusion that indifference analysis, whatever its inspiration, is odd and perverse.

NOTES

1. I use the term "judiciary" to refer to both the Supreme Court and the lower courts, otherwise specifying the Supreme Court or lower courts accordingly as the context requires.

2. *Are judges political? An empirical analysis of the Federal Judiciary* (Sunstein, Schkade, Ellman, & Sawicki, 2006) provides an empirical analysis of the conservative turn in the Federal judiciary.

3. I would like to thank the anonymous reviewer for a number of specific suggestions that provided opportunities to improve the analytic focus of this essay. I would also like to thank my research assistant, Whitney Knopf, for her diligent work and patience with this essay.

4. The indifference thesis arises from, and develops, arguments for an "agnostic skepticism" in commentary (Strauber, 2002) and a subsequent elaboration and specification of this skepticism related to relationships between ideals as aspirations, on the one hand, and social fact and consequentialist considerations on the other (Strauber, 2003). I refer to the thesis as a bold one because of the pervasiveness in commentary of simultaneous putative resistance to preconceptions about law and politics and implicit or explicit manifestations of advocacy scholarship. An extended discussion of continuities and discontinuities between the agnostic skepticism (and therefore the indifference thesis) and other approaches to commentary (e.g., the New Institutionalism, the New Constitutionalism) can be found in *Neglected Policies* (Strauber, 2002, pp. 27–35).

5. The conclusion addresses some of the relative strengths and weaknesses of indifference analysis.

6. See Strauber (2003, pp. 32, 45–49).

7. Internal citations omitted.

8. Richard Posner uses these words to describe a pragmatic "disposition" for legal decision making, and I have appropriated them to characterize commentary.

9. Of the four hypotheses, the hegemonic and cultural efficacy hypotheses are derived (i.e., extrapolated and interpolated) from "How the Supreme Court matters in American politics: New Institutionalist perspectives" (McCann, 1999). The implementation hypothesis is derived from *Judicial policies: Implementation and impact* (Canon & Johnson, 1998), "Social Constructions, Supreme Court reversals, and American political development: *Lochner, Plessy, Bowers,* but not *Roe*" (Kahn, 2006), and *The hollow hope: Can courts bring about social change?* (Rosenberg, 1991). And the electoral competition hypothesis is derived from *Towards juristocracy: The origins and consequences of the New Constitutionalism* (Hirschl, 2004), *Legislative deferrals: Statutory ambiguity, judicial power, and American democracy* (Lovell, 2003), *Courts and Political Institutions, A comparative view* (Koopmans, 2003), and *Judicial review in new democracies, Constitutional Courts in Asian cases* (Ginsburg, 2003).

10. Internal citations omitted.

11. These claims are derived from Canon and Johnson (1998, pp. 16–26). Also Kahn (2006) and Rosenberg (1991).

12. The following discussion focuses on some of the major implications of the electoral competition hypothesis for understanding the role of the judiciary and power relations in periods of divided government. The similarities and differences between the implications for divided and unified government are beyond the scope of this essay.

13. The South has been something of an exception to this patter (Fiorina, 1992, p. 31).

14. There is variation in the incumbency effect, and for a variety of factors the effect is somewhat greater at the national than State levels (Hershey, 2007, pp. 29–30; Keefe & Ogul, 1997, p. 118).

15. Although not exhaustive, the following provides a good sample of what I have in mind: convictions about how business efficiency and competitiveness are undermined by post-New Deal national regulatory power; concerns about how economic growth have been stalled and inflationary pressures aggravated by high taxes, the growth of bureaucracies, and minimum wage; perceptions that values and attitudes related to individual freedom, personal choice, self-reliance and responsibility have been undermined by nanny-like social welfare policies; complaints that the autonomy of the States and their proper role as co-equal partners in constitutional government have been undermined by Congressional and judicial policies; criticisms of Warren Court decisions as "undemocratic" and the impositions of an imperial judiciary (e.g., desegregation of schools and the rights of criminal defendants).

16. *United States v. Darby* (1941) declared that 10th Amendment was not to be read as constitutional limit on national power but as a "truism" or "declaratory" statement indicating a constitutional system of national and state powers wherein the national government may exercise powers granted to and states exercise their respective powers.

17. This parenthetic information could be, and should be, elaborated along jurisprudential, instrumental lines, and ideological lines which would open up to layers of lines of analysis and many more pages of text.

18. Those criteria were that an activity must involve either a channel of interstate commerce or an instrumentality of interstate commerce, or there must be substantial relationship between a regulation and interstate commerce.

19. This material is generated from Klein (2003, p. 6).

20. Greenhouse (2006, p. A1).
21. See Strauber (2002, pp. 148–152).

REFERENCES

Adamany, D., & Meinhold, S. (2003). Robert Dahl: Democracy, judicial review, and the study of law and courts. In: N. Maveety (Ed.), *The pioneers of judicial behavior* (pp. 361–386). Ann Arbor, MI: The University of Michigan Press.

Adler, R. W., Landman, J. C., & Cameron, D. M. (1993). *The Clean Water Act 20 years later*. Washington, DC.: Island Press.

Andreen, W. L. (2004). Water quality today – Has the Clean Water Act been a success?. *Alabama Law Review, 55,* 537–593.

Barringer, F. (2006). Supreme Court case threatens many wetlands. *The New York Times,* February 20, p. A4.

Baum, L. (2007). *The Supreme Court* (9th ed.). Washington, DC.: Congressional Press Quarterly.

Belknap, M. R. (2005). *The Supreme Court under Earl Warren 1953–1969*. Columbia, SC: University of South Carolina Press.

Bergeson, L. L. (1993). The debate over the definition of wetlands continues. *Environmental Issues, 21*(September), 21.

Brady Handgun Violence Prevention Act. Pub. L. No. 103–159, 107 Stat. 1536 (1993).

Buchwalter, B. (2006). Supreme Court decision a warning on wetlands. *Great Lakes Bulletin New Service,* July 20. From http://mlui.org/landwater (Retrieved February 21, 2007).

Canon, B. C., & Johnson, C. A. (1998). *Judicial policies: Implementation and impact* (2nd ed.). Washington, DC.: CQ Press.

Cardozo, B. N. (1921, 1974). *The nature of the judicial process*. New Haven, CT: Yale University Press.

Clayton, C. W., & Pickerill, J. M. (2004). Guess what happened on the way to the revolution? Precursors to the Supreme Court's federalism revolution. *Publius, 34*(3), 85–114.

Clean Water Act. 33 U.S.C. § 1251 (1977).

Compassionate Use Act. Cal. S. Health and Safety C. §§ 11362.7–11362.9 (1996).

Controlled Substances Act. Title II, Pub. L. No. 91–513, 84 Stat. 1236 (1970).

Dewey, J. (1935). *Liberalism and social action*. New York: G. P. Putnam's Sons.

Fair Labor Standards Act. 29 U.S.C. 8 (1938).

Fiorina, M. (1992). *Divided government*. New York: Macmillan.

Fish, S. (1999). *The trouble with principle*. Cambridge: Harvard University Press.

Flournoy, A. C. (2004). Section 404 at thirty-something: A program in search of a policy. *Alabama Law Review, 55,* 607–649.

Foster, J. C., & Leeson, S. M. (1992, 1998). *Constitutional law: Cases in context: Vol. 1. Federal governmental powers and federalism*. New Jersey: Prentice Hall.

Gerhardt, M. J., Rowe, T. D., Brown, R. L., & Spann, G. A. (2000). *Constitutional theory: Arguments and perspectives* (2nd ed.). New York: LexisNexis.

Gillman, H. (2006). Party politics and constitutional change: The political origins of liberal judicial activism. In: R. Kahn & K. I. Kersch (Eds), *The Supreme Court and American political development*. Lawrence, KS: University Press of Kansas.

Ginsburg, T. (2003). *Judicial review in new democracies, constitutional courts in Asian cases.* New York: Cambridge University Press.

Graber, M. A. (1993). The nonmajoritarian difficulty: Legislative deference to the judiciary. *Studies in American Political Development, 7,* 35–73.

Graber, M. A. (1999). The problematic establishment of judicial review. In: H. Gillman & C. Clayton (Eds), *The Supreme Court in American politics: New institutionalist interpretations* (pp. 28–42). Lawrence, KS: University Press of Kansas.

Graber, M. A. (2006a). Legal, strategic or legal strategy: Deciding to decide during the civil war and reconstruction. In: R. Kahn & K. I. Kersch (Eds), *The Supreme Court and American political development* (pp. 33–66). Lawrence, KS: University Press of Kansas.

Graber, M. A. (2006b). Symposium: A new constitutional order? Panel IV: Towards juristocracy: The origins and consequences of the new constitutionalism: Does it really matter? Conservative courts in a conservative era. *Fordham Law Review, 75*(November), 675–708.

Greenhouse, L. (2006). Justices divided on protections over wetlands. *The New York Times,* June 20, p. A1.

Gun-Free School Zones Act. § 1702, 18 U.S.C. § 922 (1990).

Hensley, T. R., Hale, K., & Snook, C. (2006). *The Rehnquist Court: Justices, rulings, and legacy.* Santa Barbara, CA: ABC-CLIO.

Hershey, M. R. (2007). *Party politics in America.* New York: Pearson Longman.

Hirschl, R. (2004). *Towards juristocracy: The origins and consequences of the new constitutionalism.* Cambridge, MA: Harvard University Press.

Kahn, R. (2006). Social constructions, Supreme Court reversals, and American political development: *Lochner, plessy, bowers,* but not *roe.* In: R. Kahn & K. I. Kersch (Eds), *The Supreme Court and American political development.* Lawrence, KS: University Press of Kansas.

Keefe, W., & Ogul, M. (1997). *The American legislative process: Congress and the states.* Upper Saddle River, NJ: Prentice-Hall.

Klein, C. A. (2003). The environmental Commerce Clause. *Harvard Environmental Law Review, 27,* 1–69.

Koopmans, T. (2003). *Courts and political institutions, a comparative view.* Cambridge: Cambridge University Press.

Lovell, G. (2003). *Legislative deferrals: Statutory ambiguity, judicial power, and American democracy.* Cambridge: Cambridge University Press.

McCann, M. (1999). How the Supreme Court matters in American politics: New institutionalist perspectives. In: H. Gillman & C. Clayton (Eds), *The Supreme Court in American politics: New institutionalist interpretations* (pp. 63–97). Lawrence, KS: University Press of Kansas.

Michelman, F. I. (1989). Conceptions of democracy in American constitutional argument: The case of pornography regulation. *Tennessee Law Review, 56,* 291–319.

Mikalonis, S. K. (2006). Commentary: 'Significant nexus' likely to determine federally regulated wetlands. *Michigan Lawyers Weekly* (November 6).

Nagel, R. F. (2001). *The implosion of American federalism.* Oxford: Oxford University Press.

O'Brien, D. M. (2005). *Constitutional law and politics: Vol. 2. Civil rights and civil liberties* (6th ed.). New York: W.W. Norton.

Parenteau, P. (2004/2005). Anything industry wants: Environmental policy under Bush II. *Vermont Journal of Environmental Law, 6,* 1–405.

Posner, R. A. (2003). *Law, pragmatism, and democracy*. Cambridge, MA: Harvard University Press.

Quade, E. S. (1982). *Analysis for public decisions* (2nd ed.). New York: Elsevier Science.

Rosenberg, G. N. (1991). *The hollow hope: Can courts bring about social change?*. Chicago: University of Chicago Press.

Savage, D. G. (2006). Going with the flow: Wetlands cases raise anew the question of the environment and federal power. *American Bar Association Journal, 92*, 18.

Strauber, I. L. (2002). *Neglected policies: Constitutional law and legal commentary as civic education*. Durham, NC: Duke University Press.

Strauber, I. L. (2003). Framing pragmatic aspirations. *Polity, 35*, 491–512.

Sunstein, C. R., Schkade, D., Ellman, L. M., & Sawicki, A. (2006). *Are judges political? An empirical analysis of the federal judiciary*. Washington, DC: Brookings Institution Press.

Tupi, B. S. (2006, July 28). Muddy waters: Supreme Court *Rapanos* decision fails to clarify reach of federal wetlands power. *Real Estate/Environmental Liability News, 17*.

Tushnet, M. (2003). *The new constitutional order*. Princeton, NJ: Princeton University Press.

Tushnet, M. (2006a). *A court divided: The Rehnquist Court and the future of constitutional law*. New York: W.W. Norton.

Tushnet, M. (2006b). Symposium: A new constitutional order? Panel IV: Towards juristicracy: The origins and consequences of the new constitutionalism: Political power and judicial power: Some observations on their relation. *Fordham Law Review, 75*(November), 755–768.

Tushnet, M. V. (1985). Federalism and the traditions of American political theory. *Georgia Law Review, 19*, 981–997.

Violence Against Women Act. Title IV, §§ 40001 – 40703, Pub. L. 103–322, § 108 Stat. 1796 (1994).

Whittington, K. E. (2005). "Interpose your friendly hand": Political supports for the exercise of judicial review by the United States Supreme Court. *American Political Science Review, 99*(4), 583–596.

Young, E. A. (2005). Just blowing smoke? Politics, doctrine, and the federalist revival after *Gonzales v. Raich*. In: D. J. Hutchinson, D. A. Strauss & G. Stone (Eds), *Supreme Court review* (pp. 1–50). Chicago and London: The University of Chicago Press.

Zuckerman, A. (1991). *Doing political science: An introduction to political analysis*. Boulder, CO, San Francisco, Oxford: Westview Press.

CASES CITED

Garcia v. San Antonio Metropolitan Transit Authority. 469 U.S. 528 (1985).

Gonzales v. Raich. 545 U.S. 1 (2005).

Massachusetts et al. v. Environmental Protection Agency et al. 05–1120 (2007).

National League of Cities v. Usery. 426 U.S. 833 (1976).

New York v. United States. 505 U.S. 144 (1992).

Northern California River Watch v. City of Healdsburg, Civil Action No. C01-04686WHA. (C.A. 9; Aug. 10, 2006).

Printz v. United States. 521 U.S. 898 (1997).

Rapanos et. ux., et al. v. United States. Slip Opinion, 547 U.S. 898 (2006).

Solid Waste Agency of Northern Cook County v. United States Army Corps of Engineers. 531 U.S. 159 (2001).

United States v. Charles Johnson, Genelda Johnson, Francis Vaner Johnson, and Johnson Cranberries. 467 F.3d 56; 2006 U.S. App. (1st Cir. Mass., 2006).

United States v. Chevron Pipe Line Co., Civil Action. No. 5:05-CV-293-C. (N.D. Tex.; June 28, 2006).

United States v. Darby. 312 U.S. 100 (1941).

United States v. Gerke Excavating, Inc., Civil Action. No. 04-3941. (C.A. 7; September 22, 2006).

United States v. Lopez. 514 U.S. 549 (1995)

United States v. Morrison. 529 U.S. 598 (2000).

United States v. Riverside Bayview Homes. 474 U.S. 121 (1985).

POPULAR CONSTITUTIONALISM: THE NEW LIVING CONSTITUTIONALISM

George Thomas

> The new assertion of popular political power and responsibility is not equivalent to the substitution of democratic absolutism for democratic constitutionalism. Constitutionalism necessarily remains; but the constitutions are instructed frankly to the people instead of the people to the constitutions.
>
>   – Herbert Croly, Progressive Democracy

We live in peculiar times. Pleas for judicial restraint have become ubiquitous as both the left and the right accuse the Court for engaging in judicial activism. And yet they do so, at times, in near oblivion of one another. Thus Dean Larry Kramer of the Stanford Law School can write: "Outside the liberal academy and the ever shrinking liberal wing of the Democratic party, ... it may simply be that no one thinks the Rehnquist Court is doing anything all that wrong" (Kramer, 2004, p. 230). But the conservative journal *First Things* – to take but one very clear example – had years earlier organized a symposium on "The End of Democracy? The Judicial Usurpation of Politics" that criticized the Rehnquist Court for doing much wrong (*First Things*, 1996; see also Wolfe, 2004). Many of the essays did so, moreover, in a manner that could find common cause with elements of Dean Kramer's call for popular constitutionalism as he insisted that the Court "is ultimately supposed to yield to our judgments about what the Constitution means and not the reverse" (Kramer, 2004, p. 248).

Special Issue: Constitutional Politics in a Conservative Era
Studies in Law, Politics, and Society, Volume 44, 73–105
Copyright © 2008 by Emerald Group Publishing Limited
All rights of reproduction in any form reserved
ISSN: 1059-4337/doi:10.1016/S1059-4337(08)00803-X

Kramer even issued a democratic call to arms: "The Supreme Court has made its grab for power. The question is: will we let them get away with it?" (p. 249). Kramer's question echoes Robert Bork's insistence in *First Things* that the Court was becoming our "judicial oligarchy." It might also find common cause with a one conservative scholars' more tempered contemplation of "constitutional resistance" to judicial supremacy (Stoner, 2006), or another's lament that more and more the Court was "removing from the arena of public deliberation questions that were once thought to be at the center of our public lives" (Wolfe, 2004, p. 4).

The seeming agreement does not end here. Indeed, what is most remarkable about the new wave of scholarship on popular constitutionalism is that it is often expressed by left of center scholars who have come to embrace positions that, only a decade or two ago, were deemed a threat to the very notion of constitutionalism by many on the left. This suggests that criticism of judicial supremacy was not a passing fancy aimed at the Warren Court, but like original meaning, has taken solid root in ways that cannot be easily characterized as left or right (Thomas, 2008; Balkin, 2006). And yet left critics of the Court and right critics of the Court, not surprisingly, take issue with different opinions, with the former focusing on the Rehnquist Court's opinions such as *United States v. Lopez* and the latter on its opinions in cases such as *Planned Parenthood v. Casey*, even though they now do so using a common vocabulary. This tension is indicative of our current constitutional order.

This chapter explores the discontinuities in the current constitutional order as both conservatives and liberals insist on "taking the Constitution away from the Court." It does so by focusing on the turn to popular constitutionalism by prominent liberal legal scholars, illustrating how elements that were most prominently associated with conservatives have been used to criticize and even hold at bay aspects of a potentially conservative constitutional vision. In fact, popular constitutionalism shares many of the features – as do calls for judicial minimalism – that were expressed in conservative critiques of the Warren Court. Yet left constitutional scholars have turned to these very features to prop up the legacy of the Warren Court against its conservative critics. The turn to popular constitutionalism is a result, I suggest, of popular constitutionalists' position in "political time" – that is, after Ronald Reagan's 1980 election and subsequent conservative electoral victories which sparked a debate about constitutional fundamentals that shapes our current constitutional discourse (Skowronek, 1993; Busch, 2006). Not only has the character of national politics changed, but this has included a change in our constitutional thought and culture, particularly in the kinds of constitutional arguments that are viably put forward.

While popular constitutionalism is part of a broader scholarly turn in constitutional theory which has happily gone beyond the Court in examining the contours of American constitutionalism, popular constitutionalists have drawn on these elements to insist upon the terms of progressive and New Deal constitutionalism as the equivalent of a "new" Constitution or a foundational "settlement." If conservatives challenged the "liberal order" of the Warren Court years and the New Deal "breakthrough" on some issues, liberals have sought to preserve this order against what many of them deemed a conservative or "collaborationist" Court (Tushnet, 2006). But, as the prominent conservative critiques of the Court indicate, the Rehnquist Court has been "liberal" as often at it has been "conservative" (Wolfe, 2004, pp. 1–3; Nagel, 2001).[1] In fact, arguments about the Rehnquist Court, and now the Roberts' Court, are often proxies for arguments about the continued legitimacy of the New Deal breakthrough.

Yet, in defending the New Deal order these scholars have attempted to merge the Great Society and the Warren Court as natural developments of the New Deal, which might be best seen as attempts to prop up a fractured constitutional order, uneasily pushing it in new directions, while holding conservative constitutional understandings at bay. In a curious inversion, I argue that left liberal defenders of the New Deal order have already broken with parts of its legacy, while conservative critics of the Court adhere to elements of the New Deal breakthrough. To some degree, both liberals and conservatives remain plagued by the progressive and New Deal preoccupation with the "problem" of judicial review in a democracy, which has prevented them from offering a coherent foundation to the Constitution.[2]

Given these discontinuities, our constitutional politics cannot be readily characterized as liberal or conservative. It is not simply that the Court itself embraces these discontinuities, which may well be why both the left and the right seek to "take the Constitution away from the courts" at particular moments. While the Court may reflect the current "political regime" (Tushnet, 2005), such a descriptive understanding does not capture the particular shape that constitutional arguments – including Supreme Court opinions – have taken in the wake of the New Deal breakthrough (Keck, 2004, p. 11). Nor does this understanding explain the arguments put forward by popular constitutionalists[3] in relation to the success of conservatives in partially altering the constitutional landscape. The connection between these two is the focus of this chapter.

In tracing out these incongruities, this chapter begins by examining the turn to popular constitutionalism, rooting it in earlier progressive thought. Popular constitutionalism reconnects to the original understanding of living constitutionalism, where the Constitution is understood in light of prevailing democratic sentiment and subordinated to the "will of the people." This recasting of living constitutionalism is then situated as an attempt to preserve "mid-century constitutionalism liberalism" against an at times conservative Rehnquist Court and now possibly more conservative Roberts Court. Yet the popular constitutionalist rediscovery of the progressive critique of judicial power does not provide the illusive foundation for the Warren Court within the contours of the New Deal breakthrough. It is, rather, ultimately riddled by many of the same problems that beset an earlier insistence on judicial restraint, or a historically evolving constitution. Taking popular constitutionalism seriously, it is not clear why a conservative turn is not simply the newest manifestation of constitutional "development."

THE TURN TO POPULAR CONSTITUTIONALISM

Popular constitutionalists seek to recover the popular sovereignty founda-tions of American constitutionalism, bringing the people in as active participants in the constitutional enterprise as they create and refashion the Constitution by "majoritarian and populist mechanisms" (Amar, 1995, p. 89). The result is to recover an understanding, in FDR's words, of constitution as a "layman's document, not a lawyer's contract" (Kramer, 2004, p. 207). This understanding has deep roots in American constitu-tionalism, tracing its lineage back to the founding and, as popular constitutionalists insist, finds powerful expression in the likes of *The Federalist* and Abraham Lincoln (Ackerman, 1991; Tushnet, 1998). In exercising popular sovereignty, the people founded the Constitution, but they did not simply retreat from the trajectory of constitutional develop-ment. Rather, as Bruce Ackerman argues, since the Constitution of 1787 the people have spoken in a manner that has re-founded the Constitution giving us a "multiple origins originalism" (Kersch, 2006a, p. 801; see also Amar, 1998 and 2005). In turning to founding era thought and the notion of constitutional foundations, popular constitutionalists like Ackerman and Amar make common cause with conservatives who turn to original intent, but then they seek to synthesize this understanding with democratic expressions of popular will by emphasizing both formal and informal constitutional change, giving us layered "foundings," and a more complex version of "living constitutionalism." Such constitutional change, however, can only legitimately come from an authentic expression of "We the People."

As Ackerman argues, in *The Federalist*, Publius justifies the extra-legal founding of a new constitution by recourse to an extraordinary act of "We the People" through the ratifying conventions (Ackerman, 1991, p. 171). For Ackerman, Publius inspired and defended a dualist democracy that, at a foundational level, places republicanism prior to constitutionalism. Thus the people, in an act of democratic "higher lawmaking," create and authorize a constitution. This foundational act establishes fundamental law, which the government must operate within until the next act of "higher lawmaking" whereby the people recreate the fundamental law giving us a new constitution (Ackerman, 1991, pp. 6–7, 165–199). Ackerman's Yale Law School colleague, Akhil Amar, similarly emphasizes the republican foundations of American constitutionalism to insist upon popular constitutional change outside the formal confines of Article V. As Amar argues, Article V specifies the formal channels the *government* must act through to initiate constitutional change, while the people, acting as *the people*, can alter the Constitution outside the confines of Article V. In this, Amar is a careful reader of texts, not only focusing on the text of Article V, but on the subsequent amendments to illuminate how the people have "re-founded" the Constitution, which, like Ackerman, yields a multiple origins originalism (Amar, 1995, 1998, 2005). At the same time, Amar's understanding of popular sovereignty is less formulaic than Ackerman's understanding of dualist democracy where the people have only acted as "We the People" on three occasions. Thus Amar's popular sovereignty is more fluid in bringing about constitutional change, but also more carefully rooted in constitutional text.

This less formulaic view of popular constitutionalism is even more apparent in the scholarship of Mark Tushnet and Larry Kramer insofar as they view popular constitutionalism as a more continuous influence on our constitutional understandings. In *The People Themselves*, Kramer masterfully traces the emergence of revolutionary constitutionalism in America and its deep connection with an active and spirited people. Constitutionalism is less about formal written limits as embraced by law, he argues, than a custom of politics that attempts to limit arbitrary government by way of popular sovereignty. Thus, Kramer insists, constitutionalism is too often seen as working *within* a particular constitutional order rather than *working out* that order (Kramer, 2004, p. 8). For Kramer, the heart of American constitutionalism has been the popular working out of our constitutional understandings where the people themselves, rather than the Court, act as the authoritative interpreter of constitutional meaning – at least until the modern area where judicial supremacy has become the norm.

Tushnet speaks in similar terms, seeing popular constitutionalism as a continuous act of constituting the American people rooted in the Declaration of Independence and the Constitution's preamble, where "We the People" speak (Tushnet, 1998, p. 11). These principles represent what Tushnet calls the "thin" constitution and take primacy over "thick" constitutional forms, which are meant to serve the ends of the "thin" constitution. Such an understanding is found most powerfully, Tushnet argues, in Lincoln's insistence in his First Inaugural that "this country with its institutions, belongs to the people who inhabit it" (Tushnet, 1998, p. 181).

Following the work of political scientists, these legal scholars have recovered a robust tradition of American constitutionalism "outside the courts."[4] And they have done so in a manner that gives us a more capacious view of American constitutional development that cannot be understood from an analysis of courts alone. Drawing on the eclipsed views of Judge John Bannister Gibson, these scholars remind us that written constitutionalism does not necessarily call for or depend on courts and lawyers: "The principles of a written constitution are more fixed and certain, and more apparent to the apprehension of the people, than principles which depend on tradition and the vague comprehension of the individuals who compose the nation, and who cannot all be expected to receive the same impressions or entertain the same notions on any given subject" (*Eakin v. Raub*, 62). Like Gibson, popular constitutionalists insist that "We the People," or "the people themselves," are the primary enforces of constitutional meaning through the legislature and elections: "for, after all, there is no effectual guard against legislative usurpation but public opinion, the force of which, in this country is inconceivably great" (*Eakin*, 62). Therefore, "it rests with the people, in whom full and absolute sovereign power resides, to correct abuses in legislation, by instructing their representatives to repeal the obnoxious act." For Gibson, the written constitution was directed to the people and the legislature. And while legislatures were bound by the constitution, legislative representatives themselves were the primary interpreters of a constitution when they were engaged in passing laws. If, however, the legislature went beyond constitutional limits, the people, acting in elections, were the central mechanism to enforce the terms of a written constitution against legislative encroachments. While this did not give the legislature omnipotence – it could act against the Constitution – it did yield legislative supremacy in constitutional interpretation with the people as the central check on legislative power. This might allow, as Gibson said, violations of the written Constitution, but, as he reminded us, there is "no magic power inherent in parchment and ink" (*Eakin*, 62).

Yet popular constitutionalists are less clear about how the people act and about how far they may act within the constitutional order. The people act through critical elections, through institutions and debate about constitutional issues, in the streets, and, so it seems, through the Court itself. For Ackerman and Kramer, much of popular constitutionalism from the New Deal breakthrough on seems to be best captured by the Court – until, that is, the Court returned to enforcing federalism (Ackerman, 1998, pp. 397–406; Kramer, 2004, pp. 218–220). Moreover, while popular constitutionalists offer vivid descriptions of constitutionalism outside the Courts, the normative arguments they put forward are not always clearly grounded in their descriptive scholarship. At times they seem to move a great distance from Gibson, potentially dissolving the notion of a fixed constitutional foundation, positing popular sovereignty as the defining feature of the American constitutionalism. Thus "We the People" can remake the Constitution in an act of popular sovereignty outside of Article V (Ackerman, 1998, pp. 15–17). This not only positions "the people" as the authoritative interpreter of the Constitution, but seemingly goes so far as to suggest that the people, acting as "the people," can trump the written Constitution. While Kramer is not clear on this point, his persistent criticism of the Court always casts it in opposition to "the public's view of things" and not as having misinterpreted the Constitution (p. 253). What appears wrong is not that the Court misinterpreted the Constitution, but that it acts against the people, who, so it seems, are not bound by the written Constitution in any significant way.

Even if we accept popular sovereignty and think of the people as the source of all legitimate constitutional authority, the Constitution itself may limit how the people act within the confines of the Constitution they brought to life (Whittington, 1999). As William Harris puts it, "This people may be the author of the text, but it [is] also a textually bounded creature of its own constituent act" (Harris, 1993, p. 202). To draw this out, Harris offers an illuminating distinction between "The Constitutional People" and the "Sovereign People." The constitutional people, no less than the institutions they call to life, are bound by this constitution. The sovereign people remain "outside" the constitutional order, where they might, in a revolutionary act, alter or abolish this constitutional order (p. 201). Popular constitutionalists reject this distinction – placing transformative or revolutionary acts of the people within the confines of remaking the existent constitutional order (although Ackerman's dualist democracy attempts to formalize the informality of popular sovereignty).

This understanding blurs – if it does not conflate – the people's constitutional right of amendment with its revolutionary right to "dismember or overthrow" the Constitution (Lincoln, 1992, p. 291; see also Finn, 1999). And yet there is an important distinction between the sovereign people as the legitimate authority establishing the Constitution and the people as the authoritative interpreter of the Constitution once established.[5] But in collapsing this distinction, popular constitutionalists, like progressives before them, seemingly place democracy as the primary value within the American regime so that "the people" cannot legitimately be bound by a constitution, but are rather engaged in a perpetual process of constitution-making.[6]

While this sense of constitutionalism recovers important features that have been obscured by a scholarly preoccupation with the Court, it threatens to reduce constitutional meaning to whatever comes out of the throws of democratic politics. This not only turns our attention to interpreting democratic will or "authentic" acts of popular sovereignty, but effectively undoes any sense of constitutional identity. In some of the heady abstraction, popular constitutionalism often reads as akin to Rousseau's version of popular sovereignty, which "is nothing but the exercise of the general will." Here popular constitutionalists owe a heavy debt to progressives who often insisted on "pure democracy" and "the will of the people" as legitimately altering the Constitution.

THE PROGRESSIVE ROOTS OF POPULAR CONSTITUTIONALISM

Kramer sees the progressive promotion of "direct democracy" as an effort to "reconstruct the nation's constitutions, root and branch," presumably including the U.S. Constitution (p. 215). He approvingly quotes the 1912 Progressive Party Platform as capturing the spirit of popular constitution-alism, " 'We hold with Thomas Jefferson and Abraham Lincoln that the people are the masters of their Constitution [and that in] accordance with the needs of each generation the people must use their sovereign power to

establish and maintain' the ends of republican government" (p. 215). Like
the progressives, much of popular constitutionalism gets carried away in
dizzying abstractions about "the people" and their unbound right to rule
that, at least rhetorically, is not tempered by substantive limits, in contrast
to Thomas Jefferson or Abraham Lincoln, who are drawn on by both
progressive and popular constitutionalists (see, in contrast, Jacobsohn,
1986, pp. 111–112).[7] This heady abstraction is in contrast to the often subtle
and informative descriptions of American constitutional practice, where the
people debate foundational issues by way of elections and often through
constitutional forms. And, as these scholars have shown, such debates have
often had an impact on the development of constitutional meaning as we
wrestle with foundational constitutional questions (see, also, Kahn and
Kersch, 2006). This understanding fits much of the valuable description
on display in these works and often fits the explicit claims of such works
(see Tushnet, 1998, p. 14). But it does not accord easily with the more airy
claims of the people's "prophetic voice" where "The People must retake
control of their government" and transform our constitutional commitments in any manner we see fit, or where the Constitution must accord to
popular understandings (Ackerman, 1998, pp. 3, 5–6). At these moments,
popular constitutionalism seems not so much a rejection of judicial
supremacy, but a rejection of constitutional identity and limits that might
temper and confine popular desires. As Teddy Roosevelt put it in the throws
of progressive politics, "the first essential of the Progressive program is the
right of the people to rule" (Milkis & Tichenor, 1994, p. 329). In this, as Ken
Kersch reminds us, progressives often cast themselves as anti-constitutionalist
and anti-rights insofar as such understandings were wed to more traditional
notions of *liberal* constitutionalism (Kersch, 2004; see also Murphy, 2007).

At this more abstract level, the progressive insistence on "pure
democracy," often in direct antagonism to liberal elements of American
constitutionalism, bears a striking resemblance to Rousseau's insistence on
the sovereign will of the people against the earlier progenitors of modern
(liberal) constitutionalism like Montesquieu. Indeed, the progressive
insistence on pure democracy at times reads as an application of Rousseau's
theory of the general will, much as *The Federalist* reads as an application of
Montesquieu's theory of the separation of powers. Even Woodrow Wilson's
often subtle critique of the separation of powers finds expression in *The
Social Contract*, where Rousseau rejected the notion that sovereignty itself
could be divided, taking aim at "separations" in politics altogether: "But
our politicians, being unable to divide sovereignty in its principle, divide it in
its object. They divide it into force and will, into legislative power and

executive power; into rights of taxation, or justice, and of war; into internal administration and foreign relations – sometimes conflating all these branches into a fantastic being, formed of disparate parts; it is as if they created a man from several different bodies, one with eyes, another with arms, another with feet, and nothing else" (Rousseau, 2002, p. 171).

If sovereignty cannot be divided, for Rousseau, neither can it be bound: "If, then, the people simply promises to obey, it dissolves itself by that act and loses its character as a people; the moment there is a master, there is no longer a sovereign, and forthwith the body politic is destroyed" (p. 170). Such an understanding threads its way through popular constitutionalism insofar as the constitutional elements are clearly subordinate to popular will. This understanding found expression in the great progressive thinker Herbert Croly, whom Kersch (2004) aptly dubs the "father of modern constitutional theory" (p. 16), and who may justly lay claim to being the father of popular constitutionalism. Critical of our inherited Constitution, as the epigraph to this chapter illustrates, Croly often cast himself as fundamentally restructuring our constitutionalism rather than doing away with it altogether. But any sense of constitutionalism would need to be subordinated to popular will: "The socially righteous expression of the popular will is to be brought about by frank and complete confidence in its own necessary and ultimate custodian" (p. 211). He went on to reject the traditional notion of a constitution as binding the polity, "Any particular method of securing order, such as that prescribed by the Constitution, must not be exalted from a method or an instrument into a Higher Law" (Croly, 1914, p. 227). Rather, as Croly insisted, we "must make the Constitution alterable at the demand and according to the dictates of a preponderant prevailing public opinion." Indeed, Croly insists that the "power of revision should be possessed by a majority of the electorate," so the Constitution can change with the people's demands (p. 231).

For Croly, as for popular constitutionalists, constitutionalism is essentially about a particular style of popular politics that often conflicts with the more conventional understanding of the Constitution as a substantive limit on the power of the government and the people (Murphy, 2007).[8] Throughout *Progressive Democracy*, for instance, Croly insists that government must be government by men rather than government by law. This understanding of law as fundamentally binding popular sovereignty is, at root, a pernicious limitation upon democratic politics. Accordingly, and capturing much of the ethos of popular constitutionalism, Croly insists that the "only limits placed on this power should be a method of procedure which allowed sufficient time for deliberation and a certain territorial distribution of the prevailing majority" (p. 231). He rejects any notion that popular sovereignty can be theoretically bound by claims of rights rather than procedures. An acute manifestation of this for Croly is the Bill of Rights, although it applies with equal force to other aspects of the Constitution that bind and limit an authentic act of popular sovereignty. As Croly insists, "whether reasonable or not, the insertion of the bill of rights in the Constitution contributed more than any other feature to convert it into a monarchy of the Law superior in right to the monarchy of the people."

It is this monarchy of the people, as expressed in reworking their constitutional order, which popular constitutionalists seek to recover. Constitutional meaning, then, is created in the throws of popular constitutional politics as "We the People" work out our constitutional understandings and obligations. The result is a "living" constitution, but one rooted in popular understandings. Like the mid-twentieth-century living constitution, constitutional meaning is open to historical evolution, but it occurs by the way of popular acts and not by the way of Supreme Court opinions. This recovers, in a sense, the original context of living constitutionalism. That is, the people and the democratic branches ought to be able to forge new constitutional understandings based on historical changes that make the Constitution "theirs." Such a sentiment is obvious in the constitutional vision of leading progressives like Croly and Wilson, the original theorists of living constitutionalism. In his *The New Freedom*, Wilson not only calls for the "emancipation of the generous energies of a people," but speaks of "the parliament of the people," where such understandings would inform an evolving constitution (Wilson, 1913, p. 90).

And yet, while the turn to popular constitutionalism recaptures the connection between democracy and the living constitution, in the hands of current constitutional theorists it is often centered on maintaining judicial opinions as the ultimate expression of popular will. This understanding also found expression in Croly, "The fault with the American system in this respect consists not in the independence of the Federal judiciary, but in the practical immutability of the Constitution. If the instrument which the Supreme Court expounds could be altered whenever a sufficiently large body of public opinion has demanded change for a sufficiently long time, the American democracy would have much more to gain than to fear form the independence of the Federal judiciary" (Croly, 1914, p. 200). This understanding informs the somewhat peculiar relationship between popular constitutionalism and living constitutionalism in contemporary constitutional politics.

CONSERVATIVE POLITICS AND CONTEMPORARY CONSTITUTIONAL THEORY

If popular constitutionalists begin with the people "acting in the street" or by way of elections, they remain wed to the judiciary insofar as it enforces the last great expression of popular will as solidified by the New Deal. This is particularly true of Ackerman and Kramer, but, at moments, of fellow travelers to popular constitutionalism like Cass Sunstein. While the arguments of these scholars vary widely, this scholarship is linked insofar as it (1) melds the New Deal and Warren Court together and (2) insists that the judiciary should operate within the contours of the New Deal/Warren Court order. The result is to preserve the fundamentals of the Warren Court, often by insisting upon judicial restraint, minimalism or rejecting judicial review altogether (Kramer, 2004; Sunstein, 1999; Tushnet, 1998). In turning to these works of constitutional scholarship, I treat them as endogenous aspects of the project of maintaining the legitimacy of the Warren Court and elements of the New Deal against the reconstructive efforts of conservatives. In doing so, I do not mean to suggest that these scholars are being disingenuous about the arguments they put forward. The project of creating and maintaining constitutional authority is necessarily a political one (Kersch, 2004, p. 11; Moore, 2006). Thus I seek to situate these arguments in "political time," suggesting that the arguments made by popular constitutionalists must be understood against the backdrop of prior arguments and action (Skowronek, 1993; Orren & Skowronek, 2004; Whittington, 2007).

Still, it is not a coincidence that many scholars of popular constitu-tionalism sought to "take the Constitution away from the courts" at the very moment that the courts began to articulate elements of Reagan's more conservative constitutional vision. In the wake of the 1995 case of *United States v. Lopez*, where the Court rejected a congressional act as beyond the scope of the commerce power for the first time since the New Deal,[9] Mark Tushnet asked if we were living in a constitutional moment (Tushnet, 1996, 2003). Three years later, he argued at great length that judicial review was unnecessary and potentially harmful in *Taking the Constitution Away from the Courts*. Here Tushnet sought to return to elements of progressivism, rejecting judicial review, which would allow the people to adapt the Constitution to their understanding of themselves: "It would make populist constitutional law the only constitutional law there is" (Tushnet, 1998, p. 154). Taking his bearings from the Constitution's "thin" principles of popular sovereignty, Tushnet argued that "thick" constitutional formalities were not central to our identity and, so it seemed, could possibly be altered to accord with our more democratic aspirations. As he explained popular constitutionalism, "we can start telling a different story about ourselves precisely because we constitute *ourselves*. We can, in short, change who we are." And, in the process, change the Constitution to accord with our understandings of who we are by way of populist constitutional law. Thus even while Tushnet begins by speaking of the inalienable rights of human beings (p. 11), which might provide some grounding to popular constitutionalism, he then insists that "the Declaration's principles, the values that constitute the American people, are always subject to change as the people change," which seems to reject foundations beyond "the people."

That very year, Ackerman's second volume of *We the People* insisted that "We the People" had already spoken. And in speaking, we had rejected Reagan's transformative constitutional ambitions in an affirmation of our New Deal Constitution (Ackerman, 1998, pp. 390–391). Building on the first volume of *We the People*, Ackerman put flesh on his view of dualist democracy, arguing that the New Deal had been an example of popular "higher lawmaking." Franklin Roosevelt's intention to transform the Constitution had been "ratified" by the people in a series of critical elections that legitimately gave us a "new" Constitution. Reagan, on the other hand, had sought to challenge the "continuing validity of New Deal liberalism," but his attempted transformation was not ratified by the people in a process of higher lawmaking. So while "We the People," in acts of Rousseauian popular sovereignty, can transform the Constitution in whatever manner we see fit, and wholly outside of Article V's specific procedures for amendment, as a people we decided not to alter it from its New Deal/Warren Court path. Ackerman's argument, as I note below, abounds in ironies. The people speak as sovereign through the Court, which tends to reinforce judicial supremacy. Indeed, Ackerman seems to take seriously the Court's insistence that our belief in ourselves as a constitutional people "is not readily separable from [our] understanding of the Court invested with the authority to decide [our] constitutional cases and speak before all others for [our] constitutional ideals" within the confines of a particular constitutional regime. And it is fitting, as Ackerman insists that the Court's opinion here, in *Casey*, is precisely what squashed Reagan's conservative constitutional ambitions. In upholding *Roe v. Wade*, the *Casey* opinion halted Reagan's transformative project, making judicial decisions such as *Lopez*, which possibly rejected elements of the New Deal, "unconstitutional."

This is stunning insofar as *Roe* itself is a break with New Deal constitutionalism. It is very difficult to argue that "We the People" rejected a conservative constitutional reconstruction and, therefore, the New Deal Constitution stands because *the Court* upheld a precedent that itself was at odds with the central lines of New Deal constitutional thought. I take this up below, but *Casey* is interesting in its own light. Consider the quote above, which is worth pondering in its full context:

> Like the character of an individual, the legitimacy of the Court must be earned over time. So, indeed, must be the character of a Nation of people who aspire to live according to the rule of law. Their belief in themselves as such a people is not readily separable from their understanding of the Court invested with the authority to decide their constitutional cases and speak before all others for their constitutional ideals. If the Court's legitimacy should be undermined, then, so would the country be in its very ability to see itself through its constitutional ideals. The Court's concern with legitimacy is not for the sake of the Court but for the sake of the Nation to which it is responsible.

One would be hard pressed to come up with a statement more at odds with popular constitutionalism. Even alongside other Rehnquist Court opinions that insist upon judicial supremacy (e.g. *Boerne*), this is an extraordinary statement of the role of the Court within our constitutional system. *Lopez*, of which popular constitutionalists have been so critical, did not even speak the language of judicial supremacy. And yet, popular constitutionalists say very little about *Casey*. It is not discussed, or even found in the index, of Kramer's *The People Themselves*. While Tushnet begins *Taking the Constitution Away From the Courts* by noting the paradox of calling for popular constitutionalism while celebrating *Roe v. Wade*, he, too, says nothing about *Casey* (1998, IX). Nor does Sunstein discuss *Casey*, though he discusses abortion at length, and views Justice O'Connor, who along with Kennedy was the author of *Casey*, as a model of "judicial minimalism" (Sunstein, 1999, p. 9; in contrast, see Keck, 2004, pp. 271–276).[10] *Casey*, the clearest judicial challenge to anything smacking of popular constitutionalism, is featured prominently only in the work of Ackerman. And then, as we have seen, it is cast as holding conservatives at bay to embrace the popular higher lawmaking of the New Deal years. The result is not only a sort of New Deal originalism, but makes the New Deal "the end of history" in constitutional development (Thomas, 2000; Kersch, 2006a, 2006b).

Tushnet played this out, in a far more subtle and grounded manner, in his *The New Constitutional Order*, where he argued that we are not living in a constitutional moment with grand constitutional ambitions. Rather, we are living in a new constitutional order that is characterized by "chastened constitutional ambitions" and symbolized by "the end of big government" (Tushnet, 2003, pp. 8–9). This was not the victory for conservatives that it might seem, though time will tell whether the appointments of Chief Justice

Roberts and Justice Alito will alter this equation. Rather, the conservative reconstructive effort, consolidated by President Clinton, halted the growth of the old order, but did not recast it in an ambitious conservative direction. Thus the grand constitutional ambitions of the Warren Court and the New Deal, merged together, have been largely preserved. For Tushnet, this represents the state of our current regime, which is reflected by a divide polity, where the Court reflects the politics of the "governing coalition" or a divide between "two types of Republicans" (Tushnet, 2003, p. 125, 2005, p. 9). This new order is best reflected, Tushnet suggests, by a jurisprudence of "minimalism" as described, and endorsed, by Cass Sunstein (Tushnet, 2003, p. 130).[11]

The preservation of the New Deal/Great Society order is more vividly evident in Sunstein's argument for "judicial minimalism." Sunstein argues that the Court should move "one case at a time," handing down opinions on the narrowest possible ground. According to Sunstein (1999), the Court ought to be "minimalist" so as to allow for "democratic deliberation" as we the people work out our constitutional aspirations. Sunstein (2004) himself has called for us, as a polity, to complete FDR's unfinished revolution by creating a second bill of rights – including positive constitutional rights. Thus Sunstein is most skeptical of judicial power – indeed what he calls judicial "activism" – when it might prohibit such "popular constitutional self-government." While not a popular constitutionalist himself, Sunstein situates popular constitutionalists like Tushnet and Kramer as "minimalists," whom he contrasts with "fundamentalists," which are largely conservatives like Justices Scalia and Thomas (Sunstein, 2005, p. 49). In thwarting democratic deliberation, conservatives are "radicals in robes" that seek to adhere to "history's dead hand" by bringing back "a constitution-in-exile" (Sunstein, 2005, pp. 53–78).

Sunstein's argument for judicial modesty serves the dual function in a conservative era of preserving the inheritance of the New Deal and Warren Courts, while preventing conservative judicial appointees from writing their constitutional understandings into constitutional law. This is evident in Sunstein's choice of cases. Sunstein prefers "minimalist" constitutional law that forgoes deep theorizing of a "fundamentalist" variety, but the cases accord neatly with left/liberal political desires even when the reasoning of those cases – consider *Casey* – could hardly be described as "minimalist." Not surprisingly, *United States v. Lopez*, in second guessing a congressional determination about interstate commerce is cast as a fundamentalist opinion that even nodes to returning the "constitution-in-exile" (Sunstein, 2005, p. 237). Yet, as Keith Whittington argues, this inverts the political consequences of these cases: "in brief, *Casey* is about stopping political debate and legislative action. *Lopez* and its brethren are about redirecting political activism into different channels. Ultimately, *Casey* is intended to have substantial political and policy consequences. By contrast, *Lopez* has only modest policy consequences" (Whittington, 2004, p. 184). Rather than minimalism per se, it seems, the virtue of minimalism for Sunstein, given our position in "political time," is that it preserves the inherited order. Thus overturning *Roe* would be "fundamentalist," while preserving it would be "minimalist" (Sunstein, 2005, pp. 108–109).[12]

Larry Kramer's *The People Themselves* also has this preservationist turn. Following FDR, Kramer argues that the Constitution is a laymen's instrument of governance, not a lawyer's document. In Kramer's hands, the people have a strong role in constitutional interpretation and, at some moments as I noted above, it seems that the Constitution can be whatever the people want – that there is no fixed meaning inherent in its written nature. Yet, as with other popular constitutionalists, Kramer focuses on popular constitutionalism as it culminates in the New Deal breakthrough, but then seeks to discount current popular efforts to alter these inherited constitutional understandings. Indeed, Kramer merges the New Deal and the Warren Court, even while noting the tension "liberal intellectuals" faced as the heirs of anti-Court progressive popular constitutionalism when confronted with "a liberal activist Court" that gave progressives a reason to hope (p. 222). And while Kramer notes the immense body of scholarship that emerged to "rationalize and explain the post-New Deal structure of judicial review," his real criticism is aimed at the Rehnquist Court justices who rejected the New Deal "settlement" and started enforcing constitutional limits on governmental power (p. 225). In this, Kramer seems to accept judicial supremacy of the Warren Court variety, as it protects rights, but rejects judicial review of "the whole Constitution," which includes governmental limits (p. 225).

In fact, as with Ackerman, the Court seems to be the expressive voice of the people in these instances. As Kramer argues, "While making their presence felt on questions of individual rights, these Courts carefully respected the space carved out for popular constitutionalism at the time of the New Deal and left questions respecting the scope of national powers to the political process" (Kramer, 2004, p. 220). In rejecting this accommodation, striking down laws on the basis of federalism, the Rehnquist Court thwarted popular constitutional understandings. Kramer, though, ducks the hard questions of why the judicial protection of some liberties is consistent with popular constitutionalism, while the judicial limitation of national power, or the protection of other liberties, is not (p. 225). Indeed, Kramer altogether ignores the fact that much of what the pre-New Deal Court did was protect liberties that progressives rejected. Our constitutional politics involved clashes over liberties and rights, which makes it very difficult to say that the Warren Court was simply protecting "civil liberties" (Kersch, 2004, pp. 1–2). Nor does Kramer explain (1) how liberties that were seemingly rejected by the popular constitutionalism of the New Deal in the arena of due process (e.g. "privacy") are deserving of judicial protection within the contours of the "New Deal accommodation" or (2) why Reagan's rejection of elements of the New Deal reconstruction, particularly as articulated by the Rehnquist Court federalism jurisprudence, is not the most recent manifestation of popular constitutionalism.

This last point is particularly pressing for popular constitutionalists. Reagan, for instance, frequently invoked the phrase "We the people," long before it was fashionable for law professors to do so, insisting that "Our Constitution is a document in which 'We the people' tell the government what it is allowed to do" (Reagan, "Farwell Address"). This put the people as placing limitations on the national government, while allowing them to operate widely within the states. Thus the central criticism leveled by conservatives at the Warren Court, and the Burger and Rehnquist Courts as well, was that it was preventing the people, acting in their states and local communities, from making decisions they had a constitutional right to make. Thus many conservatives have been most critical of the Court when it strikes down state laws (but see also Wolfe, 1986, 2004; Rossum, 2002). Such critiques, however, often invoked "judicial activism" without tethering it to any sense of constitutional foundations, as if "restraint" was simply to be preferred. Though the connection between judicial power and constitutional foundations was often unclear, there was an insistence that the Court was *writing* a constitution rather than interpreting one. To some degree, popular constitutionalists agree. Yet they insist that the Warren Court was *writing* a constitution to accord with popular aspirations – but popular *national* aspirations, which often required bringing "outlier" states into the fold. Thus popular constitutionalists, following the progressive vision of national democracy, have been most critical of Court opinions striking down national laws.

This understanding is supported by recent empirical scholarship (Powe, 2000; Gillman, 2006). Or, rather, popularly elected national officials encouraged the "activism" of the Warren Court for political reasons (Whittington, 2007, p. 271). Yet, scholarship along these lines also views the Rehnquist Court's federalism opinions as a natural result of national elections, which reflect the current makeup of the "national governing coalition" (Pickerill & Clayton, 2004a, 2004b; Tushnet, 2005; Balkin & Sanford, 2001). Thus the Court's recent federalism decisions are, much as the Warren Court's opinions before it, the result of popular choices, or at least reflect the essentials of the current political order (Tushnet, 2005). There is a good deal of truth to this understanding. Though this conclusion is too easily arrived at and too often results in tautological reasoning, whereby scholars insist that the Court acted as it did because that is what the "governing coalition" wanted. But the "governing coalition" is often so broad that the opposite result could just as easily comport with elements of it. The result is that whatever the Court does, it is supported by "the governing coalition," which explains far too much (Keck, 2007; see also Whittington, 2007, pp. 41–45).

Empirically speaking, a "living constitution" may manifest itself as a reflection of complex democratic politics, of which the Court is a part, but that might also give it wide autonomy (Whittington, 2007). If conservatives are successful in national politics, we should expect to see a "living constitution" turn in a more conservative direction. (It is plausible to read John Yoo's insistence on an extraordinarily powerful executive in a post 9/11 world in evolutionary terms (see Silverstein, 2006; Yoo, 2005)). But popular constitutionalists like Ackerman, Kramer and Sunstein have vehemently rejected this putatively conservative turn, seeking not only to preserve the essentials of the Warren Court merged with the New Deal as if it were the "end of history," but seeking to expand this trajectory in many areas (Kersch, 2006a, 2006b). In this, Kramer and Ackerman have proffered a sort of "New Deal Originalism" (Thomas, 2000; White, 2000).

In merging the Warren Court with the New Deal, however, popular constitutionalists tend to neglect the arguments at the heart of the New Deal breakthrough. This is most evident in Ackerman's thought, which defends the New Deal as a constitutional transformation by neglecting many of the constitutional arguments put forward by the New Dealers themselves, arguments that defended the New Deal as a restoration of the Founder's Constitution not a transformation of it (Roosevelt, 1932; Frankfurter, 1937; Jackson, 1941; see also Jaffa, 1962; Tulis, 1991; Storing, 1995). Before further examining this point, however, Ackerman's argument also illustrates the dilemmas of "regime" politics whereby Court opinions are seen to reflect democratic political desires. As I noted above, Ackerman explicitly draws a connection between FDR and Reagan, arguing that Reagan attempted to reconstruct constitutional authority in a peculiarly New Deal style: by way of transformative judicial appointments. Ackerman argues that one of the fundamental changes wrought by the New Deal was the "self-conscious use of *transformative judicial appointments* as a central tool for constitutional change" (Ackerman, 1998, p. 26). Yet Ackerman paints Reagan's attempted constitutional transformation as a failure. Unlike Roosevelt, Reagan did not win a solid Republican majority in the Congress in the 1984 election, and in 1986 the Republicans lost the Senate, which very likely resulted in the defeat of Reagan's nomination of Judge Robert Bork to the Supreme Court. Bork's confirmation, for Ackerman, combined with Reagan's earlier elevation of William Rehnquist to the Chief Justiceship and the appointment of Antonin Scalia to the Court, may well have culminated in a series of transformative constitutional opinions – namely the overruling of *Roe v. Wade*. Instead, failing to win wide-spread popular support for his attempted constitutional transformation, Reagan was forced to appoint the more moderate Anthony Kennedy to the Court, who brought Reagan's transformative ambitions to a halt when he joined Justice O'Connor, another Reagan appointee, and Justice Souter, a Bush appointee, in a plurality opinion upholding *Roe* in *Casey*.

But what if Kennedy had voted to overturn *Roe*? Even if presidents and political coalitions might attempt to produce constitutional change – or stasis – through the judiciary, in our constitutional framework, given judicial independence, this is hardly a guarantee.[13] It is also to focus too narrowly on the Court, as if presidents can only bring about constitutional change via the judiciary, rather than altering constitutional thought and culture more broadly (Thomas, 2008). And to say that Kennedy's upholding of *Roe* is a reflection of popular constitutionalism runs the risk of tautology: whatever constitutional decisions are reached, are the ones the people wanted. It is, moreover, possible that upholding *Roe* was a reflection of a moderate conservative "governing coalition," which did not want *Roe* overturned and therefore represents Reagan's success at maintaining this coalition rather than a failure (Tushnet, 2005; Whittington, 2007). And what of where Reagan succeeded? In the Rehnquist Court's federalism opinions, Kennedy (as well as O'Connor) did join Reagan's other appointees. And here they did so on ground that was truly in opposition to the New Deal breakthrough – federalism.[14]

Ackerman's odd argument that the New Deal Constitution stands, and hence Reagan's reconstructive efforts failed, because the Court failed to overturn *Roe*, reduces Reagan's constitutional vision to a single issue. Odder, it is the very issue where his thinking was arguably at one with New Deal understandings. The Court's opinion in *Roe* was utterly at odds with the various stands of New Deal constitutional thought, serving to highlight the Warren Court's, and then Burger Court's, departure from the core elements of the New Deal in regard to due process. At the center of the New Deal was a need to tether judicial will against *Lochner* like reasoning that came to symbolize judicial "activism" for progressives and New Dealers (O'Neill, 2005, pp. 28–36). The fundamental agreement in the area of due process was a rejection of "substantive due process." This is evident not just in the insistence on judicial "self-restraint" in the jurisprudence of Felix Frankfurter, who, interestingly, is most open to such reasoning, but in the textualism of Hugo Black, as well as the "democracy reinforcing" defense of judicial review put forward by Harlan Fiske Stone in *Carolene Products* (footnote 4) – which is often taken to embody the essence of New Deal constitutionalism (Keck, 2004). If there was agreement that "fundamental rights" needed to be protected in these central lines of New Deal constitutional jurisprudence, there was not an easy agreement on what rights were "fundamental" and therefore entitled to judicial protection (Gillman, 1994). There was, though, a solid core that rejected earlier views of "substantive due process," congealing around Holmes' famous *Lochner* dissent, which was embraced by all of these strands of New Deal jurisprudence.[15] Moreover, Holmes' opinion insisted on "judicial restraint," which would then allow for a flexible reading of the Constitution to accord with "the natural outcome of dominant opinion[.]"

Dissenting in *Roe*, then Justice Rehnquist drew attention to this fact: "while the Court's opinion quotes from the dissent of Mr. Justice Holmes in *Lochner*, the result it reaches is more closely attuned to the majority opinion of Mr. Justice Peckham in that case" (*Roe*, 174). Rehnquist's dissent echoed New Deal Justice Hugo Black's famous *Griswold* dissent:

> The Due Process Clause with an "arbitrary and capricious" or "shocking the conscience" formula was liberally used by this Court to strike down economic legislation in the early decades of this century, threatening, many people thought, the tranquility and stability of the Nation. See, e.g. Lochner. That formula, based on subjective considerations of "natural justice," is no less dangerous when used to enforce this Court's views about personal rights than those about economic rights. I had thought that we had laid that formula, as a means for striking down state legislation, to rest once and for all in cases like West Coast Hotel Co. (p. 522)

The return of substantive due process, which the New Deal Court had negotiated around, highlighted the fractured state of New Deal jurisprudence and provoked many legal scholars who had been weaned on the progressive critique of the *Lochner* Court to cry foul (Kalman, 1996, pp. 1–10). Even John Hart Ely, who attempted to defend the Warren Court's jurisprudence as an extension of Stone's footnote 4, objected to *Roe* as out of accord with the New Deal accommodation (Ely, 1973, 1980). For progressives, *Lochner* was synonymous with "judicial lawmaking" and "activism" against popular democracy. Digesting this understanding, liberals and conservatives rooted their understandings of judicial review in the contours of progressive/New Deal constitutionalism.

As I tentatively sketch below, the "problem" of judicial review became an organizing feature of constitutional thought as jurists and scholars attempted to make it compatible with democracy. Here both liberals and conservatives have suffered insofar as they have begun by insisting upon judicial restraint, attempting to work the "problem of judicial review" into American constitutionalism (see Whittington, 1999, p. 168). Progressives and New Dealers argued for a flexible understanding of the Constitution, which often included a flexible understanding of judicial review. But there was a tension in how these fit together. Flexibility, as manifest in the progressive and early New Deal years, allowed for democratic adaptation of the Constitution. In the Warren Court years, the Court itself instigated such adaptation. Conservatives accepted judicial restraint, but rejected a flexible Constitution. The return of originalism, in fact, was a means of limiting judicial discretion in positivistic original intent, thereby preventing a judicially instigated flexible reading of the Constitution against democratic legislation (Brubaker, 2005). But there was a tension in conservative thought between the insistence on judicial restraint and the insistence on a fixed Constitution.

JUDICIAL CONSERVATISM AND THE INCONGRUITIES OF CONSTITUTIONAL DEVELOPMENT

The first wave of originalists, conservative jurists like Bork and scholars like Raoul Berger, took the progressive and New Deal critique of judicial lawmaking as their organizing principle, digesting central tenets and lessons from the New Deal breakthrough (O'Neill, 2005, pp. 112–168; Jacobsohn, 1986, pp. 57–58; Barber, 1993, pp. 121–129). Here the first wave of originalists is squarely with the Constitutional Revolution of 1937 as they insist upon a narrow legal positivism to confine the scope of judicial review and reconcile it with what Bork calls the "Madisonian dilemma" (Bork, 1996, p. 139; see also O'Neill, 2005, p. 112); that is, how are we to legitimize judicial limitations on majority rule in democracy. While a leading legal scholar finds it odd that a conservative like Bork would expresses concern about the countermajoritarian nature of judicial review, this is not particularly perplexing (Friedman, 2002, pp. 253–254). The preoccupation of reconciling judicial review with democracy was a central inheritance of the progressive era. Like all legal scholars after the New Deal breakthrough, Bork was weaned on the progressive critique of the *Lochner* Court and the New Deal telling of history.

Consider that the current Court's most powerful articulator of original-ism, Justice Scalia, defends it in precisely these terms: "Now the main danger in judicial interpretation of the Constitution – or, for that matter, in judicial interpretation of any law – is that the judges will mistake their own predilections for the law. Avoiding this error is the hardest part of being a conscientious judge; perhaps no conscientious judge ever succeeds entirely" (Scalia, 1989, p. 863). Originalism, while not perfect – notice that Scalia calls it "the lesser evil" – is the best method of interpretation because it "does not aggravate the principal weakness of the system [judicial discretion], for it establishes a historical criterion that is conceptually quite separate from the preferences of the judge himself" (Scalia, 1989, p. 864). Constitutional text and historical original intent combine to limit judicial discretion.

This is evident in Scalia's substantive due process dissents where he insisted that only rights that were (1) explicitly enumerated in Constitution text or (2) had been accorded long-standing historical protection in American society would qualify for the Court's most exacting level of review, strict scrutiny. As Scalia has put it, drawing on the progressive understanding of *Lochner*, "In my history-book, the Court was covered with dishonor and deprived of legitimacy by *Dred Scott v. Sandford* (1857), an erroneous (and widely opposed) opinion that it did not abandon, rather than by West Coast Hotel (1937), which produced the famous 'switch in time' from the Court's erroneous (and widely opposed) constitutional opposition to the social measures of the New Deal." This version of originalism may well owe more to Oliver Wendell Holmes than the Founders, but this only reaffirms the notion that it is firmly planted within the New Deal breakthrough. The plea for judicial self-restraint and deference to democratic majorities stems from progressive and New Deal thought. Like the New Deal justices, Scalia thinks that constitutional interpretation must, first and foremost, limit judicial will, but he does so by looking to text (Black) and history and tradition (Frankfurter). If conservatives like Scalia draw on the ghost of *Lochner* to criticize "judicial activism" in *Roe*, *Casey* and *Lawrence*, it is because they have digested the New Deal breakthrough (Bork, 1990, p. 81).

But like progressives and New Dealers before them, conservatives did not always attend carefully to what they meant by "activism," or, for that matter, why "restraint" would be constitutionally founded. Rather than speaking to foundational constitutional principles and allowing the judicial role to flow from them, "restraint" was invoked as defining the judicial role in a democracy. But this neglected when the Court should legitimately enforce constitutional meaning and limits, unless it was always supposed to defer to democratic judgments (Jacobsohn, 1977, p. 171). Indeed, much like the various strands of New Deal jurisprudence, originalists like Bork and Scalia saw the central feature of constitutional interpretation as aimed at limiting judicial discretion. Such an understanding inverted the Constitution, viewing it through the lens of the judiciary, rather than situating the judiciary within the contours of the whole Constitution (Thomas, 2008). This left the Rehnquist Court, just as the New Deal Court before it, open to embarrassing charges of hypocrisy and a double standard when the Court persistently struck down national legislation. In fact, one scholar noted, "Today, it is the liberals who protest against activism when a conservative Supreme Court justice asserts a new doctrine of states' rights or limitation on racial preferences" (Rabkin, 2000). The Rehnquist Court has even been labeled "the most activist Court in history" (Keck, 2004) as conservatives struggle with the possible tension between the rhetoric of judicial restraint and an insistence on judicially enforced constitutional limits. Subsequent originalists have jettisoned the link between originalism and judicial restraint. Originalism has thus been defended as central to the nature of a written Constitution, which requires not "restraint" or "activism" from the judiciary, but constitutional fidelity (Whittington, 1999, p. 168). Judicial activism has, accordingly, been refashioned as a departure from original meaning, rather than the act of striking down democratically enacted legislation (Barnett, 2002).

LEGAL LIBERALISM'S BREAK WITH THE NEW DEAL

If judicial conservatism is echoing the various New Deal strands of constitutional thought on the issue of "civil liberties," defenders of the New Deal "transformation" often obscure these earlier arguments. Efforts to rescue *Griswold* and *Roe* by linking them to the "New Deal constitutional synthesis" tend to neglect the very arguments put forward by progressive and New Dealers in arguing for these changes. The difficulty is that very little that was settled in this constitutional shift justifies either opinion, while there is much at the heart of the New Deal's deconstruction of traditional due process that squarely rejects such thinking. At least these were the sort of arguments made by ardent advocates of the New Deal like Wechsler, Alexander Bickel and Learned Hand, not to mention New Deal justices like Frankfurter, Black and Stone (as well as Holmes, Brandeis and Cardozo preceding them). Having accepted these arguments, how does one then embrace "activism"? This was precisely the legal liberal's dilemma typified by the scholarship of Herbert Wechsler (1959), a one-time law clerk to Stone, and his search for "Neutral Principles" in constitutional adjudication. Wechsler captured the central dilemma rooted in the New Deal breakthrough: "The problem for all of us became: How can we defend a judicial veto in areas where we thought it helpful in American life – civil liberties area, personal freedom, First Amendment, and at the same time condemn it in the areas where we considered it unhelpful?" (Leuchtenburg, 1995, p. 234).[16] Taking this critique seriously, Wechsler (1959) raised serious criticism of the Warren Court's *Brown* decision, prior to anything like *Griswold*, in his Holmes Lecture at the Harvard Law School on "Neutral Principles." As Wechsler (1959) argued, neutral principles were necessary in constitutional adjudication so that judges were not simply using judicial review in areas where they happened to like the political result (see also Kalman, 1996, pp. 44–45).

Ackerman focuses on historical constitutional development, as manifest in popular constitutionalism, to unravel the traditional legal liberal dilemma. For Ackerman, *Lochner* and its ilk were rejected in the Constitutional Revolution of 1937 whereby the people ultimately ratified a new Constitution. This New Deal Constitution, according to Ackerman's synthesis, is broad enough to encompass *Griswold* and *Roe*. So simply put: *Roe* is grounded in the (New Deal) Constitution, *Lochner* is not. This is made evident in Ackerman's curious discussion of *Casey* that I took up above. Yet, Ackerman says very little about how the New Deal reconstruction of liberty and due process justifies *Roe*. Rather, Ackerman argues that *Griswold* (and thus presumably *Roe*) was a synthesis of the Founding's concern with personal liberty in a "post-New Deal world of economic and social regulation." To arrive seamlessly at this conclusion, however, Ackerman ignores the very reasoning put forward in Justice Douglas' *Griswold* opinion, which was preoccupied by the very dilemma Ackerman seeks to dissolve (Ackerman, 1991, pp. 131–162; Ackerman, 1998, pp. 390–403). Indeed, Douglas opinion turned to the "penumbras" of the Constitution to ground the right to privacy in constitutional "text," declining to turn to the due process clause precisely because such arguments had been cast as illegitimate since *West Coast Hotel* in the New Deal telling of history. Notice that Black, too, shares this logic in his dissenting opinion in *Griswold*, which also provides the foundation of Rehnquist's dissent in *Roe*.

Such attempts to root the judicial defense of "civil liberties" – particularly "privacy" – in constitutional change amount to "a sophisticated refinement" of the "progressive model of constitutional development" (Kersch, 2002, p. 86). The result is a "Whiggish" view of constitutional development that replicates the idea of a "living constitution" that has evolved in a progressive direction, culminating in the great Warren Court civil liberties and rights decisions. This narrative does not match the actual conflict over "civil liberties" in the wake of the New Deal that shaped subsequent constitutional thought. While many legal liberals attempted to weave these different modes of thought into a coherent order by turning to historical development, these attempts illustrate that the Warren Court had already instituted constitutional change that fell away from New Deal foundations. Unless, that is, the New Deal is simply taken to have brought forth a "living constitution" grounded in legal realism. This is captured, possibly, by FDR's insistence that he sought to restore the Court "to its rightful and historic place in our system of constitutional government and to have it resume its high task of building anew on the Constitution 'a system of living law' " (McMahon, 2004, p. 71).

CONCLUSION: A CONSERVATIVE ERA?

If we accept the "living constitution" as yielding a "present day sense of the Constitution" by way of legal realism, it is not clear why this understanding of a living constitution could not turn in a conservative direction (Whittington, 2007, p. 266). If constitutional meaning must "vary with the adaptation of law to changing" needs, which progressives and New Dealers argued about even in terms of constitutional rights, then a conservative turn is a plausible outcome of this variation. While the scholarship on "political regimes" is largely descriptive, in many ways it supports just such an understanding. The return of constitutional federalism shows signs that conservatism's challenge to the New Deal breakthrough has been partially successful. (Though, casting an eye at issues like gay marriage, it is not clear that federalism necessarily cuts in a conservative direction.) The very same year that *Casey* was handed down, for instance, the Court reopened a debate on the meaning of the Tenth Amendment that had been settled since the late New Deal years in *New York v. United States*. Three years later in *Lopez*, the Court returned to policing the reach of Congress' commerce power for the first time since 1936. Since that time the Court has shown that it is willing to police the boundaries between the states and the national government: limiting Congress' power under the commerce clause (*Lopez* and *Morrison*) and breathing life into the Tenth Amendment (*New York* and *Printz*).[17] With President Bush's appointments of Chief Justice Roberts and Justice Alito to the Court, the return of judicially enforced federalism is likely to continue.

Popular constitutionalists have rejected these developments as unfounded "judicial activism" out of accord with the popular constitution, which remains moored in New Deal understandings (at least on issues of federalism). Taking their own arguments seriously, it is not at all clear that their normative arguments flow from their descriptive and historical analysis. As I have suggested in this article, many progressive developments themselves, such as a narrow right to privacy in abortion, are difficult to reconcile with New Deal constitutionalism. And, if the Constitution does legitimately change with popular aspirations, it is not clear why those aspirations might not move in a conservative direction. After all, on some issues popular constitutionalists are in the odd position of defending *Court* opinions against *popular* legislation. It is as if a "living constitution must accord with "progressive" aspirations.[18] Philosophically rooted arguments for some form of a living constitution may be far more powerful to this end (Barber, 1993; Fleming, 2006; Dworkin, 1996), but popular constitutional-ists have rejected philosophy in favor of history,[19] grounding our constitutionalism in the New Deal regime to hold conservative constitu-tional politics at bay. This lends some credence to James Ceaser's suggestion that, "If ever the 'living constitution' ceases to function in favor of promoting Progressive-Liberal goals, the doctrine is certain to become a dead letter" (Ceaser, 2006, p. 66).

Popular constitutionalists, however, have not abandoned the notion of a living constitution they have simply moved its locus in a more conservative era. In some sense, in fact, they have restored it to its progressive origins as an instrument of the people and not the courts. But, like progressives before them,[20] if judges embrace "progressive" constitutional aspirations, then they are the people's champions. If they do not, then they have made a "power grab" against "We the People." Fittingly, this found expression in Woodrow Wilson's constitutional understandings. In *Constitutional*

Government, Wilson praised the Court in "whiggish" terms as "the balance-wheel of our whole constitutional system," because the Court had, according to Wilson, seen fit to "adapt" the "Darwinian constitution" to the "opinion of the age" (Wilson, 1908, p. 172). Yet where judges were concerned with "fine-spun constitutional argument" rather than democratic adaptation, they should be led "to a back seat" where they might "pass unnoticed from the stage" (Mason, 1965, p. 75). This captures the essence of popular constitutionalism in a (partially) conservative era. If conservatives have turned to historical original intent and the "dead hand of the past," the foundations of popular constitutionalism remain plagued by the same issue that confronted a historically evolving living constitutionalism: Can a constitution whose identity is solely directed by "the live hand of the present" actually be a constitution?[21]

NOTES

1. I fuse these terms for shorthand, realizing that they do not capture the range of thinking among scholars or justices. Both can be very difficult to situate as liberal or conservative, left or right.

2. This is perhaps most evident in the long-standing insistence, at various times by both left and right, on judicial restraint, as if "restraint" could be meaningful or valuable independently of a larger constitutional identity.

3. I focus on Bruce Ackerman (1991, 1998), Larry Kramer (2004) and Mark Tushnet (1998) as leading popular constitutionalists. I also draw on elements of Akhil Amar (1995) and Cass Sunstein (2005, 2004, 1999) both of who, at times, share much of the logic of popular constitutionalism. And, as I note throughout, Tushnet's (2003, 2005, 2006) descriptive work, while often illustrating how the Court reflects popular politics, is not a normative call for popular constitutionalism. See also Michael Perry (1999).

4. Though with the exception of Sanford Levinson, who happens to be a law professor as well, they do not cite this earlier work (e.g. Murphy, 2007 and Moore, 1996) nearly as much as they could.

5. Though the distinction, as Wayne Moore (1996) illustrates, can be difficult to draw as the people may act through official channels as well as independently.

6. Here *popular* constitutionalism is in distinct contrast to *liberal* constitutionalism. Drawing on the republican tradition, popular constitutionalists reject limits to the people's sovereign voice even within the constitutional order and reject the notion that liberalism bounds and limits democratic popular sovereignty (Kramer, 2004, p. 248). Indeed, Ackerman equates liberalism with "foundationalist" constitutionalism that he explicitly rejects: whatever liberal elements exist within a constitutional regime exist wholly at the leave of the people (Ackerman, 1991, pp. 10–16).

7. Mark Tushnet (1998) is potentially different than Ackerman and Kramer if his view of popular constitutionalism is bound by the "inalienable rights" of the people

(p. 11). Here Tushnet even draws on Gary Jacobsohn's use of Lincoln's description of the Constitution as a "picture of silver" around the "apple of gold," which is the Declaration of Independence. Thus the Constitution is best seen in light of the Declaration's principles. Whereas Tushnet finds this an expression of popular sovereignty, in Jacobsohn's hands, this illuminates the natural rights underpinning the Constitution, which binds popular aspirations. As Jacobsohn describes it, this is opposed to "popular constitutionalism." "Lincoln's constitutional theory requires the political realization of the self-evident fact of human equality, which means that the Constitution aspires to a state of affairs where *arbitrary* infringements upon the rights of people to govern themselves do not exist. It does not require that the specific aspirations that at any given time may be pursued under the authority of self-governance be constitutionally mandated" (Jacobsohn, 1986, p. 112).

8. Tushnet and Sunstein, again, may be somewhat different here if their built in limits are really binding (Tushnet, 1998; Sunstein, 2005). Yet, while Sunstein has often been critical of this judicial understanding in the work of Ronald Dworkin, his own use of judicial minimalism tends in this direction.

9. As an isolated case, Rehnquist's opinion for the Court in *National League of Cities v. Usery* (1976) held out limitations on Congress' power under the Commerce Clause, but did so indirectly by way of state sovereignty.

10. Sunstein could argue that the holding is minimal, but this creates a strange sort of maximalism that O'Connor seems to embrace. The Court decides how it decides, and may does so minimally, but it is always up the Court, which does not offer clear rules, but turns on its peculiar readings. The result is that the Constitution is what Justice O'Connor says it is. Or now what Justice Kennedy says it is.

11. As a matter of principle, if judicial review is rejected as Tushnet would prefer, while this might have the short-term impact of preserving Warren era precedents, its long-term impact could go in nearly any political direction.

12. Sustein is critical of Dworkin style jurisprudence and often has been of Roe, but this manifests itself as now preserving much of that inheritance while rejecting foundational jurisprudence that might push in a more conservative direction.

13. This also focuses too exclusively on the Court. Presidents might more broadly influence constitutional discourse and culture without necessarily translating that into Supreme Court opinions (see Thomas, 2008).

14. Though Kennedy and O'Connor possibly qualified this.

15. While the Court would later try to distinguish between personal and economic rights, we should recall that Justice Peckham's opinion in *Lochner* referred to "liberty of contract" as a personal right.

16. Friedman points to the historical contingency of this dilemma, but that itself hardly makes it less powerful if it was the preoccupation at the heart of New Deal constitutionalism, other than to suggest that we should forge a new understanding of judicial review, leaving the preoccupations of the New Dealer's behind us. But this opens the possibility, surely, for a return to older understandings of the Constitution as well.

17. The sovereign immunity cases also fit here, though they have their own peculiar history. *Seminole Tribe of Florida v. Florida* 517 U.S. 44 (1996); *Florida Prepaid Postsecondary Education Expense Board v. College Savings Bank* 527 U.S. 627 (1999); *College Savings Bank v. Florida Prepaid Postsecondary Education Expense Board* 527 U.S. 666 (1999); *Alden v. Maine* 527 U.S. 706 (1999); *Kimel v.*

Florida Board of Regents 528 U.S. 62 (2000); *Trustees of the University of Alabama v. Garrett* 531 U.S. 356 (2001).

18. As Croly (1914) argued, "Popular political authority must be real and it must make for social righteousness" (p. 210).

19. Sunstein (2005) rejects philosophical substance, or deep theorizing, for the procedural conditions which produce "deliberative democracy."

20. This is also true of modern judicial conservatism (Keck, 2004).

21. On constitutional change and identity, see Jacobsohn (2006, p. 394) and on the substantive limits of constitutionalism, see Murphy (2007, pp. 502–508).

REFERENCES

Ackerman, B. (1991). *We the people: Foundations.* Cambridge, MA: Harvard University Press.

Ackerman, B. (1998). *We the people: Transformations.* Cambridge, MA: Harvard University Press.

Amar, A. R. (1995). Popular sovereignty and constitutional amendment. In: S. Levinson (Ed.), *Responding to imperfection: The theory and practice of constitutional amendment.* Princeton, NJ: Princeton University Press.

Amar, A. R. (1998). *The bill of rights: Creation and reconstruction.* New Haven, CT: Yale University Press.

Amar, A. R. (2005). *America's Constitution: A biography.* New York, NY: Random House.

Balkin, J. M. (2006). *Abortion and Original Meaning.* Yale Law School Public Law Working Paper No. 119. Available at SSRN: http://ssrn.com/abstract = 925558.

Balkin, J. M., & Sanford, L. (2001). Understanding the constitutional revolution. *Virginia Law Review, 87*(6).

Barber, S. A. (1993). *The constitution of judicial power.* Baltimore, MD: Johns Hopkins University Press.

Barnett, R. E. (2002). Is the rehnquist court and activist court? The commerce clause cases. *University of Colorado Law Review, 73,* 1275.

Bork, R. H. (1990). *The tempting of America: The political seduction of the law.* New York, NY: Free Press.

Bork, R. H. (1996). Our judicial oligarchy. *First Things,* (November).

Brubaker, S. C. (2005). The countermajoritarian difficulty: Tradition versus original meaning. In: D. W. Kenneth & R. C. Cecilia (Eds), *The Judiciary and American Democracy: Alexander Bickel, the Countermajoritarian Difficult, and Contemporary Constitutional Theory.* Albany, NY: SUNY Press.

Busch, A. (2006). *Reagan's victory: The presidential election of 1980 and the rise of the right.* Lawrence, KS: University Press of Kansas.

Ceaser, J. W. (2006). *Nature and history in American political development.* Cambridge, MA: Harvard University Press.

Croly, H. (1914). *Progressive democracy.* New Brunswick, NJ: Transaction Publishers.

Dworkin, R. (1996). *Freedom's law: The moral reading of the American constitution.* Cambridge, MA: Harvard University Press.

Ely, J. H. (1973). The Wages of Crying Wolf: A Comment *on Roe v. Wade. Yale Law Journal, 82,* 920.

Ely, J. H. (1980). *Democracy and distrust: A theory of judicial review.* Cambridge, MA: Harvard University Press.

Finn, J. (1999). Transformation or transmogrification? Ackerman, Hobbes (as in Calvin and Hobbes), and the puzzle of changing constitutional identity. *Constitutional Political Economy, 10,* 355–365.

First Things. (1996). The End of Democracy? The Judicial Usurpation of Politics? (November).

Fleming, J. E. (2006). *Securing Constitutional democracy: The case of autonomy.* Chicago, IL: University of Chicago Press.

Frankfurter, F. (1937). *The commerce clause under Marshall, Taney, and Waite.* Chapel Hill, NC: University of North Carolina Press.

Friedman, B. (2002). The birth of an academic obsession: The history of the counter-majoritarian difficult, part five. *Yale Law Journal, 112.*

Gillman, H. (1994). Preferred freedoms: The progressive expansion of state power and the rise of modern civil liberties jurisprudence. *Political Research Quarterly, 47*(3).

Gillman, H. (2006). Party politics and constitutional change: The political origins of liberal judicial activism. In: R. Kahn & K. Kersch (Eds), *The Supreme Court and American Political Development.* Lawrence, KS: University Press of Kansas.

Harris, W., II. (1993). *The interpretable constitution.* Baltimore, MD: Johns Hopkins University Press.

Jackson, R. (1941). *The struggle for judicial supremacy: A study in a crisis in American power politics.* New York, NY: Knopf.

Jacobsohn, G. J. (1977). *Pragmatism, statesmanship, and the Supreme Court.* Ithaca, NY: Cornell University Press.

Jacobsohn, G. J. (1986). *The Supreme Court and the decline of constitutional aspiration.* Lanham, MD: Rowman and Littlefield.

Jacobsohn, G. J. (2006). Constitutional identity. *Review of Politics, 68*(3).

Jaffa, H. V. (1962). The case for a stronger national government. In: R. A. Goldwin (Ed.), *A Nation of States: Essay on the American Federal System.* Chicago, IL: Rand McNally.

Kahn, R., & Kersch, K. I. (Eds). (2006). *The Supreme Court and American political development.* Lawrence, KS: University Press of Kansas.

Kalman, L. (1996). *The strange career of legal liberalism.* New Haven, CT: Yale University Press.

Keck, T. M. (2004). *The most activist court in history: The road to modern judicial conservatism.* Chicago, IL: University of Chicago Press.

Keck, T. M. (2007). Party politics or judicial independence? The regime politics literature hits the law schools. *Law & Social Inquiry, 32*(2).

Kersch, K. I. (2002). The reconstruction of constitutional privacy rights and the new American state. *Studies in American Political Development.*

Kersch, K. I. (2004). *Constructing civil liberties: Discontinuities in the development of American constitutional law.* New York, NY: Cambridge University Press.

Kersch, K. I. (2006a). Justice Breyer's mandarin liberty. *University of Chicago Law Review, 73,* 759.

Kersch, K. I (2006b). The New Deal Triumph as the End of History? The Judicial Negotiation of Labor Rights. In: R. Kahn & K. I. Kersch (Eds), *The Supreme Court and American Political Development* (pp. 169–226). Lawrence, KS: University Press of Kansas.

Kramer, L. (2004). *The people themselves: Popular constitutionalism and judicial review.* New York, NY: Oxford University Press.

Leuchtenburg, W. E. (1995). *The Supreme Court Reborn*. New York, NY: Oxford University Press.

Lincoln, A. (1992). First inaugural address. In: *Selected Speeches and Writings*. New York, NY: Vintage Books.

Mason, A. T. (1965). *William Howard Taft: Chief justice*. New York, NY: Simon and Schuster.

McMahon, K. J. (2004). *Reconsidering Roosevelt on race: How the presidency paved the road to Brown*. Chicago, IL: University of Chicago Press.

Milkis, S., & Tichenor, D. (1994). Direct democracy and social justice: The progressive party campaign of 1912. *Studies in American Political Development, 8*, 282–340.

Moore, W. (1996). *Constitutional rights and powers of the people*. Princeton, NJ: Princeton University Press.

Moore, W. (2006). (Re)Construction of constitutional authority and meaning: The fourteenth amendment and slaughter-house cases. In: Kahn & Kersch (Eds), *The Supreme Court and American Political Development*. Lawrence, KS: University Press of Kansas.

Murphy, W. (2007). *Constitutional democracy: The creation and maintenance of a just political order*. Baltimore, MD: Johns Hopkins University Press.

Nagel, R. F. (2001). *The implosion of American federalism*. New York, NY: Oxford University Press.

O'Neill, J. (2005). *Originalism in American law and politics: A constitutional history*. Baltimore, MD: Johns Hopkins University Press.

Orren, K., & Skowronek, S. (2004). *The search for American political development*. New York, NY: Cambridge University Press.

Perry, M. J. (1999). *We the people: The fourteenth amendment and the Supreme Court*. New York, NY: Oxford University Press.

Pickerill, J. M., & Clayton, C. (2004a). The Rehnquist court and the political dynamics of federalism. *Perspectives on Politics, 2*(2).

Pickerill, J. M., & Clayton, C. (2004b). Guess what happened on the way to revolution? Precursors to the Supreme Court's federalism revolution. *Publius, 34*, 3.

Powe, L. A., Jr. (2000). *The Warren court in American politics*. Cambridge, MA: Harvard University Press.

Rabkin, J. (2000). Original dissent: Keith Whittington makes the case for constitutional law. *The Weekly Standard* (March 6), 34–36.

Roosevelt, F. D. (1932). The Commonwealth Club Address. In: *The Public Papers and Addresses of Franklin D. Roosevelt*, Volume One: *The Genesis of the New Deal* (compiled by Samuel I. Rosenman, 1938. New York: Random House).

Rossum, R. (2002). *Federalism, the Supreme Court, and the seventeenth amendment: The irony of constitutional democracy*. Lanham, MD: Lexington Books.

Rousseau, J-J. (2002). *The social contract and the first and second discourses*. New Haven, CT: Yale University Press.

Scalia, A. (1989). Originalism: The lesser evil. *University of Cincinnati Law Review, 57*, 849.

Silverstein, G. 2006. *Review of John Yoo, The Powers of War and Peace*, Constitutional Commentary.

Skowronek, S. (1993). *The politics presidents make: Leadership from John Adams to George Bush*. Cambridge, MA: Harvard University Press.

Stoner, J. R., Jr. (2006). Constitutional resistance. *Claremont Review of Books, 6*(3).

Storing, H. J. (1995). The problem of big government. In: J. Bessette (Ed.), *Toward a More Perfect Union*. Washington, D.C.: AEI Press.

Sunstein, C. (1999). *One case at a time: Judicial minimalism on the Supreme Court.* Cambridge: Harvard University Press.

Sunstein, C. (2004). *The second bill of rights: FDR's unfinished revolution and why we need it more than ever.* New York: Basic Books.

Sunstein, C. (2005). *Radicals in robes: Why extreme right-wing courts are wrong for America.* New York, NY: Basic Books.

Thomas, G. (2000). New deal 'Originalism'. *Polity, 33*(1).

Thomas, G. (2008). *The Madisonian constitution.* Baltimore, MD: The Johns Hopkins University Press.

Tulis, J. K. (1991). The constitutional presidency in American political development. In: L. F. Martin & A. Shank (Eds), *The Constitution and the American Presidency.* Albany, NY: SUNY Press.

Tushnet, M. (1996). Living in a constitutional moment? *Lopez* and constitutional theory. *Case Western Reserve Law Review, 46,* 845.

Tushnet, M. (1998). *Taking the constitution away from the courts.* Princeton, NJ: Princeton University Press.

Tushnet, M. (2003). *The new constitutional order.* Princeton, NJ: Princeton University Press.

Tushnet, M. (2005). *A court divided: The rehnquist court and the future of constitutional law.* New York, NY: W. W. Norton.

Tushnet, M. (2006). The Supreme Court and the national political order: Collaboration and confrontation. In: R. Kahn & K. I. Kersch (Eds), *The Supreme Court and American Political Development.* Lawrence, KS: University Press of Kansas.

Wechsler, H. (1959). Toward neutral principles of constitutional law. *Harvard Law Review, 73.*

White, G. E. (2000). *The constitution and the new deal.* Cambridge, MA: Harvard University Press.

Whittington, K. E. (1999). *Constitutional interpretation: Textual meaning, original intent, and judicial review.* Lawrence, KS: University of Kansas Press.

Whittington, K. E. (2004). The *casey*-five versus the federalism five: Supreme legislator or prudent umpire? In: C. Wolfe (Ed.), *That Eminent Tribunal: Judicial Supremacy and the Constitution.* Princeton, NJ: Princeton University Press.

Whittington, K. E. (2007). *The political foundations of judicial supremacy: The presidency, the Supreme Court, and constitutional leadership in U.S. history.* Princeton, NJ: Princeton University Press.

Wilson, W. (1908). *Constitutional government in the United States.* New York, NY: Columbia University Press.

Wilson, W. (1913). *A New Freedom.* New York, NY: Doubleday, Page and Company.

Wolfe, C. (1986). *The rise of modern judicial review: From constitutional interpretation to judge-made law.* New York, NY: Basic Books.

Wolfe, C. (2004). *That eminent tribunal.* Princeton, NJ: Princeton University Press.

Yoo, J. (2005). *The powers of war and peace: The constitution and foreign affairs after 9/11.* Chicago, IL: University of Chicago Press.

CASES CITED

Alden v. Maine, 527 U.S. 706 (1999).

College Savings Bank v. Florida Prepaid Postsecondary Education Expense Board, 527 U.S. 666 (1999).

Florida Prepaid Postsecondary Education Expense Board v. College Savings Bank, 527 U.S. 627 (1999).

Griswold v. Connecticut, 381 U.S. 479 (1965).

Kimel v. Florida Board of Regents, 528 U.S. 62 (2000).

Lochner v. New York 198 U.S. 45 (1905).

New York v. United States, 505 U.S. 144 (1992).

Planned Parenthood v. Casey, 505 U.S. 833 (1992).

Printz v. United States, 521 U.S. 898 (1997).

Roe v. Wade, 410 U.S. 113 (1973).

Seminole Tribe of Florida v. Florida, 517 U.S. 44 (1996).

Trustees of the University of Alabama v. Garrett, 531 U.S. 356 (2001).

United States v. Lopez 514 U.S. 549 (1995).

United States v. Morrison, 529 U.S. 598 (2000).

POLITICAL REGIMES AND THE FUTURE OF THE FIRST AMENDMENT

Thomas F. Burke

Fifty years ago the political scientist Robert Dahl concluded that courts are usually in sync with "the policy views dominant among the lawmaking majorities" and thus offer little help to aggrieved minorities (Dahl, 1957, p. 285). In recent years, Dahl's classic formulation has received renewed attention. This chapter uses the example of the Rehnquist Court's First Amendment decisions to analyze "regime politics" theory. On religion cases the Rehnquist Court was generally in sync with the socially conservative strain in the Republican Party, but in other First Amendment areas the pattern is far more complex, raising questions about the relationship between conservative judges and the political movements that brought them to office.

To the extent the Constitution really is, as Supreme Court Chief Justice Charles Evan Hughes famously said, what the judges say it is, then of course the future of the First Amendment depends on who will be interpreting it.[1] Predicting the judiciary of the future, though, depends on such small matters as the outcome of the 2008, 2010 and 2012 elections, and the health, well-being and attitude toward retirement of the current corps of Supreme Court justices – all matters on which prophets and soothsayers have as much

Special Issue: Constitutional Politics in a Conservative Era
Studies in Law, Politics, and Society, Volume 44, 107–139
Copyright © 2008 by Emerald Group Publishing Limited
ISSN: 1059-4337/doi:10.1016/S1059-4337(08)00804-1

expertise as legal scholars. With the federal courts now slightly tipped toward Republican appointees, and with two new Supreme Court appointees whose First Amendment views are far from crystal clear, attempting to foretell what courts will be saying in the 21st century about obscenity, or school prayer, or copyright law, is a fool's errand.

This chapter, then, aims at something markedly less ambitious: an examination of changes in how conservative judges approach the First Amendment, and a brief consideration if what this portends for the future. It may be impossible to chart the future of the Roberts Court, much less the entire federal and state judiciaries, with any accuracy, but quite possible to say some interesting things about how conservatives will talk and argue about the First Amendment in the early 21st century.

To do this, though, I examine two Supreme Courts that did their work mostly in the 20th century:

The First Amendment Religion Court. This Court moved First Amendment law in ways that cultural conservatives mostly admired. It chipped away at Warren Court Establishment and Free Exercise precedents, facilitating voucher programs that aid religious schools, and forcing government institutions to provide equal access to religious groups. The Court moved doctrine gradually, and in some areas – most famously school prayer – frustrated the Christian right, but overall, this court as one critic put it has "turned the constitutional law of religion nearly upside down" (Greenawalt, 2004).

The First Amendment Speech and Press Court. This Court often pushed First Amendment law away from the expressed desires of the Christian right. Rather than knocking down Warren and Burger Court precedents, it expanded them. It struck down laws banning flag burning and internet pornography, leaving intact or expanding protections for sexual speech. Some of its decisions, on campaign finance and commercial speech, were more palatable to conservatives, but overall the Court's decisions mostly reversed rather than advanced the expressed desires of cultural conservatives within the Republican Party.

These two courts are, of course, the Rehnquist Court. I have dramatized their differences, but one of them clearly was a more reliable supporter of the policies of the Republican Party, and especially cultural conservatives within the Republican Party, than the other.

The differences are evident not just in the decisions themselves, but also in the justices' explanation of their votes, their published opinions. In the religion cases, the opinions show a Rehnquist Court eager to revisit fundamental assumptions, upend precedents and reconsider the original meaning of the phrases in the Constitution. Indeed the Rehnquist Court's religion opinions sometimes seem like clashes between rival historians, albeit historians with a cause. The obstacles created by a welter of Warren and Burger Court precedents are sometimes swept away, and with them rules that limited religious organizations and religious expression, to the delight of the Christian Right.

The Rehnquist Court's opinions in non-religious First Amendment cases have a markedly different tone. *This* Rehnquist Court usually avoids fundamental questions and fails to explore the "original meaning" of the First Amendment. Instead it works within the conceptual framework of earlier cases, and usually focuses on questions of application and policy. The Court's liberals and conservatives differ, but much more narrowly, on the parameters of precedents and how best to apply them to the facts at hand. Further, there are several instances in which conservatives such as Scalia "switch" and line up with the moderate-to-liberal wing of the Court. The resulting record is a puzzle. This Rehnquist Court, unlike the religion court, seems almost detached from the agenda of Republicans, floating in its own space defined by nearly a century of First Amendment precedents. Flag burners and Internet pornographers are not, one might think, core constituencies of the Republican Party. Why would Reagan and Bush appointees be lining up behind them?

Posing the question in this way is useful, but simpleminded in at least two respects. First, judges are, of course, more than mere agents of their sponsors. Even in the rare case in which they are perfectly aligned in their policy views with their appointers, judges act within an institution and profession that shapes what they think is possible and what counts as good judicial decision making. The task currently at the center of political science scholarship on courts is to understand how these institutional and professional influences on the judiciary interact with appointment patterns and external influences (Keck, 2007a). That turns out be the same challenge presented to anyone interested in charting the future of the First Amendment. The Rehnquist Court's decisions in this realm provide a fascinating case with which to examine how the many influences on federal judges intertwine.

But my question is simpleminded in another, potentially more troublesome way: It is reductive in its portrayal of the appointing regime. Like any political movement, conservatism has internal tensions, competing strands and priorities that change over time. Cultural conservatives, especially Christian conservatives who make up a sizeable bloc within the Republican Party, have been skeptical both of the Warren and Burger Court's rulings on religion and on free expression more generally. Yet there has also always been a libertarian strand even within the Christian Right, and in recent years that strand has flourished (Brown, 2002). The pattern of the Rehnquist Court on First Amendment issues, while undoubtedly irritating to many in the Republican Party, may reflect not merely the libertarian leanings of the justices but a broader shift within American conservatism.

THE INFLUENCE OF POLITICAL REGIMES

At some point most Americans are told, perhaps by civics teachers, that courts serve to protect minorities against tyrannical majorities. Americans are also told – occasionally by presidents and Supreme Court justices – that judicial review represents a threat to democracy because again, courts often side with minorities against majorities – the "countermajoritarian difficulty" (Bickel, 1962; Graber, 1993). In a seminal article, Robert Dahl took on both views. Because of the way justices are selected for the bench, Dahl argued, they are very unlikely to stand up against the governing majority to protect the rights of the minority. That is because, aside from exceptional periods of transition, "the Supreme Court is inevitably a part of the dominant national alliance" (Dahl, 1957, p. 293). Or as another prominent political scientist, Martin Shapiro, put it, "To the extent that courts make law, judges will be incorporated into the governing coalition ..." (Shapiro, 1981, p. 33). Those who staff the Court tend to share the worldviews of their appointers on most major political questions, and so are the least likely to take issue with the governing majority.

From this perspective, federal judges can be seen not so much as protectors of minorities, but of the regimes that appoint them. Court appointments are attempts by presidents and their allies in Congress to entrench the judiciary with allies. This can be a powerful strategy, because unlike all other appointees, federal judges serve life terms, and thus can influence public policy long after the appointing regime has fallen from power. In the late 19th century, the Republican Party was able to entrench its economic nationalist views on the federal judiciary, setting the stage for Progressive Era conflicts between legislatures and the Court on economic regulations (Gillman, 2002). The post-1937 Court is often referred to as the Roosevelt Court because it collaborated so well with New Deal Democrats, deferring on most matters to the national government, but using its power to wipe out "pockets of resistance" and expand the scope of the New Deal (Tushnet, 2006, p. 119). The Kennedy and Johnson administrations created the latter-day Warren Court, liberalizing constitutional politics in a host of areas (Gillman, 2006). The politics of judicial appointments, including appointments to lower federal courts, became far more intense in the late 20th century as presidents increasingly sought to remake the nation by transforming the federal judiciary (Scherer, 2005). As a 199-page guide to judicial appointments created by the Office of Legal Policy in the Reagan Administration put it, "there are few factors that are more critical to determining the course of the Nation ... than the values and philosophies of the men and women who populate the third co-equal branch of the national government – the federal judiciary" (Gillman, 2006, p. 159). No wonder presidents and their allies attempt to "plant" the judiciary with helpful friends, and no wonder political scientists in what has been called "regime politics" school have been drawn to studying the planting strategy.

As regime politics scholars have demonstrated, there are many ways in which the entrenchment project can go wrong. In fact, a list of all the difficulties of the entrenchment strategy suggests just how problematic it is.

First, there is a bit of exaggeration built into such terms as the "dominant national alliance" or the "governing coalition," because such entities, even when electorally successful, are usually internally divided. Moreover, in recent years there has been no dominant national coalition, and appointing presidents have had to deal with senates that are closely divided, or controlled by the opposing party. After the showdown between President Reagan and a Democratic-controlled Senate over Robert Bork, presidents tended to adopt a conflict avoidance strategy, nominating judges who were not so easily associated with the wings of their parties (Clayton, 1999). Whether Roberts and Alito, President George W. Bush's nominees, will mesh with the President's expressed ideal, Justice Scalia, or fall somewhat closer to the more moderate voting patterns of O'Connor and Kennedy, remains to be seen. Further, when a president's party is fractious and far from dominant in the Senate, the risk of an outright "mistake" seems to grow. David Souter, a George H.W. Bush appointee who usually votes against cultural conservatives in First Amendment cases, appears to be such a mistake (Keck, 2003, p. 186).

Second, even if presidents could pick a first-choice nominee who had the support of a unified dominant party, they would not necessarily get a nominee who votes the way they wish on every issue. It is much easier for presidents to find faithful appointees to the Forestry Service than it is for them to find loyal nominees to the Court, simply because the scope of the Court's decision making is so much wider (Gillman, 2006, p. 141). Moreover, presidents cannot know what constitutional issues will emerge in the years after their appointments, much less predict how their nominees will vote on such issues. The freedom of lifetime appointment means that judges can surprise their sponsors. President Nixon was partly successful in his expressed goal of nominating justices who would temper the liberalizing criminal justice decisions of the Warren Court, but one doubts that he anticipated Harry Blackmun's views on *Roe v. Wade*, which became Blackmun's most celebrated (and reviled) contribution to constitutional law. And of course Harry Truman was famously unhappy when his own appointees voted against him in the "Steel Seizure" case (*Youngstown Sheet & Tube v. Sawyer* 343 U.S. 579, 1952).

Third, the concerns of presidents and their governing coalitions do not translate directly into judicial action. Judges act within a "web of 'internal' institutional constraints, perspectives and responsibilities," and so are not of a mind to issue policy proclamations, even if they had the power to do so.[2] Legal actors internalize a way of thinking about and arguing cases that helps them to be effective in their jobs. Judges, for example, have to find ways to explain their choices that the audience for legal decisions finds appropriate (Carter & Burke, 2007). Given that this audience is diverse, and that its expectations leave judges plenty of choices as to how to present themselves, it is not easy to sketch out how these institutional constraints influence judges in the abstract. The constraints are certainly not reducible to a mechanical formula. They are most visible when one encounters their outer edges. Judges, for example, will often say that a result they initially thought correct "would not write" and so they have to rethink their premises. Some policies are harder than others to voice in legal terms. Social security privatization and ending affirmative action are both goals of the Republican Party, but one is more easily translated into the language of constitutional law than the other. Justices on the Warren Court found a right to state-provided criminal counsel in the Constitution, but not a basic "right to welfare" as many liberal legalists had urged. The latter task would have involved, at a minimum, a much more heroic judicial effort to find the right in the Constitution (Rosenberg, 1993).

Among the institutional constraints on judges, potentially, is precedent. Scholars in the behavioral school have debunked the notion that precedent on the Supreme Court operates as a mechanical determinant of rulings, pushing judges of all ideological stripes to the same position (Brenner & Spaeth, 2003). But as Kritzer and Richards have demonstrated, precedent can have more subtle effects, leading judges to pay attention to some factors in a case rather than others, thus "framing" the case in ways that can influence the decision making of judges across the ideological spectrum (Richards & Kritzer, 2002; Kritzer & Richards, 2002). Beyond the narrow rules precedents sometimes create, which as generations of Realists have shown, are highly manipulable; precedent generates certain patterned ways of thinking, broad frameworks and categories, that over time become not merely accepted, but ingrained. Judges dissatisfied with those frameworks can take them on directly, but this is hard work, because they have become taken-for-granted within the legal community and even in the larger culture. Normally judges, even on the Supreme Court, tend to work within these frameworks and categories rather than upending them (Kersch, 2006).

Perhaps because the attitudinal model looms so large within their subfield, political scientists who study courts tend to think of precedent as a constraint on voting, a possible explanation for how "law" might affect people with attitudes. But as Martin Shapiro noted a generation ago, it may be more appropriate to think as precedents as aids to judges. Appellate judges are generalists who must deal with an elaborate array of increasingly complex, often technical fact situations as well as a diverse array of laws. Moreover, judges are embedded in a system that is only modestly hierarchical and far-flung, which makes it difficult for those dealing with the same problem to communicate. Precedent facilitates communication up, down and across courts, and provides judges a path through the chaotic swirl of facts in cases (Shapiro, 2002).

But of course, appointing politicians sometimes choose nominees precisely because they believe judges will overturn particularly noxious precedents. To what extent are the ambitions of appointers crushed by the judges they appoint? The regime politics literature has documented examples of what look like successful collaborations between appointers and the appointed, and some examples in which things seemed to turn out less nicely for the appointing regime. The next step is to think through the patterns of success and failure in the entrenchment strategy (Keck, 2007a). Why do some goals of the appointing regime take root on the Court while others wither? That is one of the questions this chapter explores, by comparing some "successful" and "unsuccessful" areas within the First Amendment jurisprudence of the Rehnquist Court. But I also want to use the example of the First Amendment to show how difficult it can be to measure "success." Conservative views of the First Amendment are diverse and may even be changing, which makes charting the future of First Amendment discourse a particularly difficult task.

THE REHNQUIST COURT AND THE RELIGION CLAUSES

The Rehnquist Court religion cases have, from the perspective of the religious conservatives, been a mixed bag. For Eric Claeys they were a "wasted opportunity" because while the Court made substantial changes in the interpretation of the Free Exercise Clause, it was not nearly as successful with the Establishment Clause, particularly in the school prayer cases (Claeys, 2006, p. 363). But another observer, Jay Wexler, sees a more radical shift, concluding that the Court has "virtually rewritten the entire law regarding the First Amendment's Religion Clauses" (Wexler, 2006, p. 263).

Wexler's comment captures something that is easily missed by those who study the religion clause cases in isolation: Just about everything in this area is up for grabs, with little agreement among the justices even on fundamental principles. The Rehnquist Court shook up an already unstable body of doctrine. Abner Greene has created a useful typology of the Rehnquist Court's religion jurisprudence (Greene, 2006). One group concerns policies that create special benefits (the concern of the Establishment Clause), the other concerns policies that create special burdens (the Exercise Clause). The major change the Rehnquist Court made in both areas was to replace complex rules – The *Lemon* and *Sherbert* Tests – with a seemingly simpler rule of formal neutrality: If the benefit and burden is part of a more general category of benefits or burdens that apply to non-religious entities, it is constitutional. Of course, as Greene himself admits, this is an oversimplified account of a large body of cases, but it is a good starting point. In *most* instances, the move to a formal neutrality standard has shifted First Amendment doctrine in ways that accord with the policy views of Republicans, especially Christian conservatives.

Government Aid to Religious Institutions

In *Lemon v. Kurtzman*, 403 U.S. 602 (1971), the Supreme Court ruled that reimbursing private schools for teachers' salaries and instructional materials resulted in excessive entanglement of church and state. *Lemon*, of course, is best known for the *Lemon* test for Establishment Clause violations:

> First, the statute must have a secular legislative purpose; second its principal or primary effect must be one that neither advances nor inhibits religion ... finally, the statute must not foster an excessive entanglement with religion. (403 U.S. 612–613)

This seemed a tough standard for government programs that provide aid to parochial schools. The Burger Court used the *Lemon* test in *Meek v. Pittinger* 421 U.S. 349 (1975) to strike down a program that lent instructional materials to parochial schools and in *Wollman v. Walter* 433 U.S. 229 (1977) to rule against public transportation for parochial school trips. But in *Mueller v. Allen* 463 U.S. 388 (1983), the Burger Court offered a bit of hope for those supporting aid to parochial schools, concluding that a tax deduction for some educational expenses was constitutional, even though this deduction overwhelmingly was used for expenses at sectarian schools. And in *Witters v. Washington Dept. of Services for the Blind* 474 U.S. 48 (1986), the Court upheld a state program providing vocational assistance to a student studying for the ministry, reasoning that any public money that went to a religious institution "does so only as a result of the genuinely independent and private choices of aid recipients" (474 U.S. at 487).

The crux of the argument in these cases was that aid was constitutional if offered in a formally neutral way, leaving recipients to choose whether to use it for religious or secular schooling. Conservatives on the Court argued that this neutrality standard reflected the original meaning of the First Amendment much more faithfully than the *Lemon* test. Over a series of Establishment cases in the Rehnquist Court, the neutrality standard became more prominent in the Court's opinions while the *Lemon* test receded. In *Zobrest v. Catalina Foothills School District* 509 U.S. 1 (1993), the Court by a 5-4 vote approved government-funded sign-language interpreters in parochial schools, reasoning that the tutors were equally available to children in sectarian and non-sectarian programs. In *Agostini v. Felton* 521 U.S. 203 (1997), the Court upheld the use of federally funded Title One tutors in parochial schools as within the First Amendment, explicitly overruling its contrary holding in *Aguilar v. Felton* 473 U.S. 402 (1984). In her opinion for the Court, O'Connor used the *Lemon* test, but argued that that *Zobrest* and other subsequent cases modified the way the Court interprets both the effects and entanglement prongs. The mere presence of a public employee in a parochial school can no longer be assumed to advance religion, she argued; only evidence that the employee was involved in advancing religion, or that the program "defines its recipients by reference to religion" would make the program unconstitutional (521 U.S. at 234).

Another step toward the neutrality standard came in *Mitchell v. Helms* 530 U.S. 793 (2000), in which the Court by a 5-4 vote approved a federal program providing equipment and educational materials to both public and parochial schools. The majority was split into two camps. Thomas, writing for a plurality, used what he called the *Agostini* test rather than the

Lemon test: Government aid to religious institutions will be approved where it "does not result in governmental indoctrination; define its recipients by reference to religion; or create an excessive entanglement" (530 U.S. at 808, quoting *Agostini* 521 U.S. at 234). Further, in weighing each of the first two prongs, Thomas wrote, the Court should consider whether aid is given in neutrally, "only as a result of the genuinely independent and private choices of individuals" (530 U.S. at 810, quoting *Agostini* at 226). O'Connor, in her concurrence, took issue with Thomas's "near absolute position with respect to neutrality" (838), and insisted on applying the modified version of the *Lemon* test she had announced in *Agostini*, but voted with the majority.

In *Zelman v. Simmons-Harris* 536 U.S. 639 (2002), Chief Justice Rehnquist drew on *Mueller, Witters, Zobrest, Agostini* and *Mitchell* to conclude that a voucher program in which 96% of government aid flowed to religious schools was not a violation of the Establishment Clause. Summarizing this line of cases Rehnquist wrote:

> While our jurisprudence with respect to the constitutionality of direct aid programs has "changed significantly" over the past two decades ... our jurisprudence with respect to true private choice programs has remained consistent and unbroken. (649)

Zelman represented the triumph of the formal neutrality standard. Where in earlier cases the Court had worried about "divertibility," the possibility that the aid in question could be used to support religious instruction, under the neutrality standard this became irrelevant, as long as the aid was shown to flow through individuals who can (at least theoretically) choose between secular and religious institutions.[3] Similarly the actual effect of the program, in this case a large governmental subsidy to religious organizations, is discounted in *Zelman* because of its path through the choices of individuals. By largely substituting a neutrality rule for the *Lemon* test, the Rehnquist Court transformed the Establishment Clause, opening up government funding of religious institutions.

Access to Government Forums

A second line of cases that pleased religious conservatives was the public access cases, in which religious groups used First Amendment lawsuits to fight what they perceived as an unfair bias toward secular organizations in public life. Here again the Rehnquist Court drew on a Burger Court precedent, *Widmar v. Vincent* 454 U.S. 263 (1981), which found that a public university that made its facilities available to registered student groups could not bar groups using the facilities for religious discussion and worship. As in the government aid cases, the Court progressively expanded the contexts in which religious organizations could be accommodated. Further, it supplanted the *Lemon* test with the more permissive formal neutrality standard in evaluating whether granting the claimed access rights to religious groups would violate the Establishment Clause.

The first step was *Board of Education v. Mergens* 496 U.S. 226 (1990), in which the Court upheld the constitutionality of the Equal Access Act, which prohibits public schools that open up their facilities to student groups from discriminating on the basis of the "religious, political philosophical or other content of the speech." Applying the *Lemon* test, the Court found that the Access Act did not have the effect or purpose of advancing religion and did not create an excessive entanglement; it merely ensured government neutrality once a public forum is created. In *Lamb's Chapel v. Center Moriches Union Free School District* 508 U.S. 384 (1993), the Court unanimously ruled that a school district that opened its facilities to outside groups for "social, civic or recreational uses" violated the First Amendment's freedom of speech when it barred a religious group from showing on school grounds a film series with a Christian perspective on child-rearing. White, writing for the Court, concluded that under the *Lemon* test, allowing such a religious perspective on school grounds was not a violation of the Establishment Clause. This stimulated a typically caustic concurrence from Scalia, who compared the *Lemon* test to "some ghoul in a late-night horror movie that repeatedly sits up in its grave and shuffles abroad, after being repeatedly killed and buried" (508 U.S. at 398).

With *Rosenberger v. Rector* 515 U.S. 819 (1995), the Court expanded the principle of the equal access cases to include access to government funding. The Court, this time divided 5-4, ruled that the student government of the University of Virginia violated the First Amendment when it denied funding for a religious publication by a student group. Kennedy, writing for the majority, concludes that a University rule against funding "religious activities" constitutes unconstitutional viewpoint discrimination. In weighing the University's Establishment Clause argument, Kennedy eschewed *Lemon* and instead employed the neutrality rule, finding government funding of religious publications unproblematic as long as the state does not discriminate between religious and non-religious groups. O'Connor's concurrence typically downplayed the precedential value of the case, claiming that "the nature of the dispute does not admit of categorical answers, nor should any be inferred from the Court's decision today" (515 U.S. at 849).

In *Good News Club v. Milford Central School* 533 U.S. 98 (2001) the Court expanded the access cases in another direction, holding that a school that opened its doors to after-hours student clubs could not prohibit the use of school facilities for meetings that included prayer and discussion of scripture. These meetings, the school contended, amounted to religious worship. The school argued that it had the right to determine the range of activities conducted on school grounds – sports but not political meetings, for example – and that allowing religious worship violated the Establishment Clause. But the Court, on a 6-3 majority, characterized the school's actions as unconstitutional "viewpoint discrimination." Writing for the majority, Justice Thomas noted that the school had allowed groups, like the Boy Scouts, whose activities include speech about moral and character development. The Good News Club, he argued, simply provided a more religious perspective on character development, and excluding the Club while including other groups was a violation of the First Amendment. Finally, Thomas argued that including the Club would not coerce children into religion, nor would it fail the neutrality test, thus access – even for activity that includes "worship" – did not violate the Establishment Clause. With *Good News* and *Rosenberger*, the Court used the First Amendment to pry open the doors of government forums, and paved the way for much greater cooperation between government and religious institutions than the Warren Court precedents had countenanced.

School Prayer

The flip side to aid and access decisions were the Rehnquist Court's two major school prayer rulings. Cultural conservatives in the Republican Party were infuriated by the Court's holdings in *Lee v. Weisman* 505 U.S. 577 (1992) and *Sante Fe Independent School District v. Doe* 530 U.S. 290 (2000), which not only upheld Warren Court precedents but expanded them.

Weisman concerned a prayer given at a middle-school graduation by a Rabbi. The school district pointed to the non-sectarian language of the prayer and the nature of the setting, a graduation ceremony that did not, unlike previous school prayer cases, take place within a classroom, and at which attendance was voluntary. The Court, on a 5-4 vote, ruled that the school had nonetheless violated the Establishment Clause. Kennedy's opinion steered clear of *Lemon*. Instead he based his ruling on the principle that the "government may not coerce anyone to support or participate in religion or its exercise ..." (505 U.S. at 587). A concurrence by Justice Blackmun, joined by O'Connor and Stevens, made clear that Kennedy's "coercion test" was tolerated but not enthusiastically endorsed by his fellow justices in the majority. The concurrence used the *Lemon* test to analyze the case, and suggested that coercion is a sufficient, though not necessary, indication of an Establishment Clause violation (505 U.S. at 604). Scalia, in his dissent, was predictably scornful of the psychological aspects of Kennedy's coercion test, noting that while he had been critical of the nuances in the Court's religious display jurisprudence, "interior decorating is rock-hard science compared to psychology as practiced by amateurs" (636).

Sante Fe involved a nondenominational prayer led by a student before a high school football game in Texas. In what was perhaps a misguided attempt to ward off judicial scrutiny, the school had conducted a secret ballot election of the senior class to determine what form of prayer, if any, would be given and who would lead it. The school argued that its elections system was a public forum, and that as in *Rosenberger*, the University of Virginia student publications case, it was simply granting equal access to the religious and irreligious. Stevens wrote for a 6-3 majority that included O'Connor, who had flipped sides after voting with the minority in *Weisman*. He dismissed the analogy to *Rosenberger*, noting that in Sante Fe's voting system, the minority would get no access at all to the purported forum. Stevens then employed an O'Connor innovation, the "endorsement test," judging the school's actions by "whether an objective observer, acquainted with the text, legislative history and implementation of the statute, would perceive it as a state endorsement of prayer in public schools" (530 U.S. at 12 quoting *Wallace v. Jaffee* 472 U.S. at 73). Stevens concluded that the school policy failed both the endorsement test and Kennedy's coercion test.

The school prayer decisions expanded Warren and Burger precedents beyond the classroom and outside curricular instruction. That said, the majority opinions in the case suggest discomfort with the *Lemon* test. Whether as alternatives, or as glosses on *Lemon*, Kennedy's "coercion test," and O'Connor's "endorsement test," have not, however, won over their colleagues, further muddling law in this area. The result in these cases sharply contrasts with the aid and access decisions, suggesting that the Rehnquist Court, even in its religious clause decisions, did not march in lockstep with the religious right.

Free Exercise

Another area, the Free Exercise cases regarding "generally applicable" laws, can also be scored as a defeat for cultural conservatives, though the scoring here is not nearly as clear-cut as in the prayer cases. In *Sherbert v. Verner* 374

U.S. 398 (1963), the Warren Court had established the rule that a generally applicable law affecting religious practice, in this case an unemployment law that cut off benefits to a Seventh-Day Adventist who refused as part of his religion to work on Saturday, had to be justified by a "compelling state interest," a high standard. *Sherbert*, was, however, from the beginning a shaky precedent, and the Court often found ways to uphold general laws that affected religious practice (*Goldman v. Weinberger* 475 U.S. 503, 1986; *Bowen v. Roy* 476 U.S. 693, 1986; *Lyng v. Northwest Indian Cemetery Protective Association* 485 U.S. 439, 1988). Nonetheless, the Rehnquist Court attracted great attention when, in *Employment Division v. Smith* 494 U.S. 872 (1990), Scalia's majority opinion declared that generally applicable laws that affect religious exercise would be presumed constitutional.

Smith succeeded in uniting a diverse array of religious groups, along with congressional Democrats and Republicans: they could all agree the Court had badly erred. Soon after *Smith*, Congress by a lopsided vote enacted the "Religious Freedom Restoration Act," which created a statutory right that mirrored the *Sherbert* doctrine: neutral laws that affect religious exercise had to be justified by a compelling interest. But the Rehnquist Court returned the volley: In *Boerne v. Flores* 521 U.S. 507 (1997), it struck down RFRA, at least as it applied to states. Finally, in *Church of Lukumi Babalu Aye, Inc. v. City of Hialeah* 508 U.S. 520 (1993), the Court clarified that it would be very tough on cases in which public officials aimed specifically to curb the religious exercise of some group, as the city of Hialeah had done in enacting animal sacrifice laws targeting practitioners of Santeria.

Smith, *Boerne* and *Lukumi Babulu Aye* are hard to analyze from a regime politics perspective. Many religious conservatives joined the broad coalition that attempted to use the Religious Freedom Restoration Act to "overturn" *Smith*. That said, it seems unlikely that the rule in *Smith* had much effect on the religious practices of Christians, who can campaign effectively in legislatures for exemptions from general laws that affect their religious practices. *Smith* and *Lukumi* are much more relevant to members of minority religions, because their religious practices are much more likely to come into conflict with general laws.

THE REHNQUIST COURT AND THE NON-RELIGION FIRST AMENDMENT CASES

An exhaustive review of the Rehnquist Court speech and press decisions – one study counts 143 non-religion First Amendment cases (Epstein & Segal,

2006) – would be exhausting indeed. Given the task of this chapter, though, it is best to compare areas in which the Court was either most out of line with its Republican appointers and those in which it was most active in support of traditional Republican constituencies.[4] Thus I focus on the Court's flag-burning, sexual speech and commercial speech cases. Here, unlike in most of the religion cases, conservatives on the Court mostly extended the frameworks of previous more liberal courts, in ways that sometimes displeased cultural conservatives.

Flag-Burning

In *Texas v. Johnson* (491 U.S. 397, 1989), the Court reversed a conviction under a state law prohibiting desecration of "sacred objects." Writing for the majority, Justice Brennan found flag-burning to be a type of symbolic speech protected by the First Amendment and applied the *O'Brien* test for mixed conduct/speech cases (*United States v. O'Brien.* 301 U.S. 367, 1968). Finding no governmental interest unrelated to the speech in the case, Brennan applied "exacting scrutiny" and found no interest sufficiently compelling to justify punishing Johnson's speech.

Brennan's opinion was joined by the traditional liberals Marshall and Blackmun, but also by Reagan appointees Scalia and Kennedy. Kennedy wrote an extraordinary concurrence expressing his pain in siding with a flag-burner:

> The hard fact is that sometimes we must make decisions we do not like. We make them because they are right, right in the sense that the law and the Constitution, as we see them, compel the result. (*Texas v. Johnson*, 491 U.S. at 420–421)

Four dissenters were not compelled. Writing for justices White and O'Connor, Chief Justice Rehnquist framed the case not as an example of symbolic speech, but rather as "low-value" speech, as described in the classic 1942 case *Chaplinsky v. New Hampshire* (315 U.S. 568, 1942). Quoting *Chaplinsky*, Rehnquist argued that flag-burning is "'no essential part of the exposition of ideas and [is] of such slight social value as a step to truth that any benefit that may be derived from [it] is clearly outweighed' by the public interest in avoiding a probable beach of the peace" (491 U.S. at 431). Justice Stevens wrote a brief concurrence arguing that the flag was a special symbol and thus immune from normal First Amendment analysis.

Congress, reacting to the public uproar over *Texas v. Johnson*, enacted the "Flag Protection Act of 1989." Thus flag-burning returned to the Court in

United States v. Eichman, 496 U.S. 310 (1990). Although the Protection Act had been crafted to pass the *O'Brien* test as a restriction on conduct rather than speech, the same majority as in *Texas v. Johnson* rejected the law, on similar grounds.

In these cases two Reagan appointees – Kennedy and Scalia – helped to form the majority, and one of the Court's moderates, Stevens, voted with the minority. In siding with the majority, Kennedy and Scalia accepted and extended several frameworks for thinking about free speech developed in the Warren and Burger Courts. It is useful to list all the ways in which Kennedy and Scalia (and to some extent even the dissenters) accepted these frameworks, some of which were controversial with cultural conservatives when first proposed, but have subsequently become part of the architecture of free speech law.

First Kennedy and Scalia went along with using the *O'Brien* test in this case, which frames this case as an example of symbolic speech, or speech mixed with action. This concedes a central claim, that an action – burning the flag – is a kind of expression, a "medium for the communication of ideas" as another flag case, *Spence v. Washington* (18 U.S. 405, 1974), put it, and thus though literally not speech, falls under the First Amendment. This concession is so unremarkable today that it barely receives mention, but at one time it would have been fiercely argued. Instead the sides in the flag-burning cases concentrated on the follow-up issue, as articulated in *O'Brien* – whether the state had an interest unrelated to the suppression of ideas. The dissenters struggled to articulate an interest that could be considered unrelated to expression, one that was "content-neutral."

Rehnquist's dissent in *Texas v. Johnson* points to another, largely taken-for-granted backdrop to the flag-burning cases: The erosion of the *Chaplinsky* "two-tier" approach to speech, in which some forms of speech – libel, obscenity, "fighting words" – are said to fall entirely outside the First Amendment. While *Chaplinsky* has never been explicitly overruled, the core idea in the passage Rehnquist quoted – that some forms of speech deserve no constitutional protection – has largely been abandoned. As Robert Post has argued, one of Justice William Brennan's major contributions to constitutional law was to focus on its effects rather than its abstract categories. In First Amendment law, this led to a newfound concern that laws punishing "bad speech" like libel could in operation deter all kinds of good speech (Post, 1993). Libel, for example, is still a disfavored category, but doctrines such as vagueness, overbreadth and the "actual malice" test for defamatory material about public figures are used to insure that libel laws do not create a "chilling effect" on journalists. Similarly, obscenity can still be regulated, but only within a framework, the *Miller* test, designed to ensure that non-obscene sexual speech is not chilled.

Despite Rehnquist's quotation from *Chaplinsky*, none of the justices on the Rehnquist Court has called for rolling back the many Warren and Burger Court precedents that have undermined the "in–out" approach to the First Amendment. That is not because conservatives have failed to attack these decisions. It is certainly plausible to argue, as Robert Bork has, that the First Amendment was understood by the Framers to protect only "political" speech – speech relevant to decision-making in a democracy. Under Bork's conception of "political" speech, libel, obscenity, flag-burning and even commercial speech would not fall within the ambit of the First Amendment (Bork, 1971). Bork's call for a narrowed, original under-standing of the First Amendment has, however, gone unheeded, even among the purportedly originalist conservatives on the Court. Indeed there is remarkably little analysis of the original meaning of the First Amendment in the Rehnquist Court's Speech and Press Clause jurisprudence.

Thus in siding with the majority, Kennedy and Scalia were not simply agreeing with a result, but acquiescing to a set of frameworks developed by liberals in the Warren and Burger courts over the past 30 years. Of course, even while bowing to all the precedents in the case, Kennedy and Scalia still could have accepted Stevens' invitation to make a special exception for the flag, a "ticket for this show only" precedent. In that sense, accepting the frameworks I have described did not mechanically obligate Kennedy and Scalia to overturn flag-burning laws, as the votes of the dissenters demonstrate. It did, however, frame their choices. If the two were to vote to approve flag-burning laws, they would have to acknowledge, as Stevens did, that they were making a special exception by making some very fine (and to many in the legal community unconvincing) distinctions. By choosing the easier path, Kennedy and Scalia extended the First Amendment precedents in this area, and in turn made it just a little bit harder for future judges to reframe the issue of flag-burning.

Sexual Speech on the Internet

The Rehnquist Court was confronted by a new medium, the Internet, and had to wrestle with how the First Amendment applied to it. Understandably the justices were drawn to analogies to older media as a way of making sense of the Internet. But which ones? Telephones, like the Internet, are used by individuals in ways that make it hard for the companies carrying the signal to monitor. Television, like the Internet, comes into the home in a way that makes it arguably hard to shield children from unwanted messages. But then again, the Internet also could be analogized to the print media, the most protected from regulation under the First Amendment. The Court chose the print analogy, and in a series of cases provided the same broad protections for expression on the Internet that had previously been given to print media.

The Internet had implications for many aspects of First Amendment law, but the area the Rehnquist Court confronted most often was sexual speech. Put bluntly, the Internet offers everyone, minors included, unprecedented access to sexual imagery and sexual speech. The Rehnquist Court's first major encounter with Internet sexuality came in *Reno v. ACLU*, 521 U.S. 844 (1997). By a vote of 7-2, the Court struck down the Communications Decency Act, which prohibited transmission of obscene or "indecent" materials to minors, either through intentional communication with children or by displaying them "in a manner available" to those under 18.

Prohibiting obscene materials on the Internet posed no particular issue; under the reigning obscenity precedent, *Miller v. California* 413 U.S. 15 (1973), the Court had approved of obscenity regulations for the print media. But "indecent" material was another matter. In *FCC v. Pacifica* 438 U.S. 726 (1978), the Court had upheld regulations for the broadcast media that regulated the times when indecent speech could be aired. In *Renton v. Playtimes Theatres* 475 U.S. 41 (1986), the Court had approved zoning rules that limited the locations of businesses selling sexually explicit materials. The Decency Act's defenders urged the Court to consider the Act a kind of zoning rule on the Internet, restricting children's access to sexual material but leaving it generally available to adults.

Writing for the majority, Justice Stevens concluded that the Decency Act could not be compared to zoning or broadcast indecency laws. He rejected the analogy to regulations on broadcasting, concluding that the Internet was not as intrusive as television – viewers, he claimed, were not likely to arrive at a sexually explicit website by accident. Further, the Internet did not have the long history of regulation that had affected broadcasting, a pattern of government involvement justified by the relative "scarcity" of spectrum on which to broadcast. Stevens also rejected the zoning analogy, in part because he concluded that there was no effective way for content providers on the Internet to zone. Keeping only children away from sexually explicit material, he concluded, was technologically impossible. Only Chief Justice Rehnquist and Justice O'Connor dissented, and on narrow grounds: They would have ruled the law as constitutional as applied to intentional communication between an adult and a child.

After the Decency Act was struck down, Congress passed a new, more carefully crafted statute, the Child Online Protection Act (COPA). To define what it criminalized, the Act drew on the test created in *Miller v. California* for obscenity, slightly altering its language to refer specifically to minors. One of the prongs in the statute, paralleling *Miller*, asked if "the average person, applying contemporary community standards, would find, taking the material as a whole *and with respect to minors*, is designed to appeal to *or is designed to pander to* the prurient interest ..." [Italicized phrases are amendments to the *Miller* prong.] In *Ashcroft v. ACLU* 535 U.S. 564 (2001), the Court encountered a fascinating question raised by the collision of the Internet with the *Miller* test: If obscenity is judged by "community standards," what is the community that decides whether Internet pornography is obscene? Under the COPA, the job of deciding whether Internet pornography is obscene would fall to local juries, who tend to interpret the law in light of local standards, raising the possibility that juries in the most puritan communities would have the greatest influence over Internet content. On this narrow question – whether local juries should decide what count as "community standards" for Internet pornography – the Court on an 8-1 vote upheld the COPA. The majority was badly divided, but Justice Thomas's lead opinion was unsympathetic to the arguably distinct problems posed to purveyors of sexual material on the Internet, who do not have the option of sending mild versions of their stuff to Mississippi and raunchy versions to Manhattan. If that was their problem, he suggested, they should try another medium. In any case, the Court was not going to create a new regulatory scheme for the Internet; the *Miller* test would do.

The Rehnquist Court encountered yet another Internet regulation, the Child Pornography Protection Act, in *Ashcroft v. Free Speech Coalition* 535 U.S. 234 (2002). This law criminalized the possession and distribution of Internet pornography involving children, but went beyond this to include material that merely appeared to be children – computer-generated images, or adult actors who looked childlike. The government argued that this "virtual child pornography" stoked viewer's interest in the real kind, and made it harder to detect when actual children were involved. Writing for a 6-3 majority, Kennedy noted that under *New York v. Ferber* 458 U.S. 7474 (1982), child pornography did not have to meet the *Miller* test for obscenity to be criminalized. But Kennedy distinguished *Ferber* as involving actual children, and ruled that the CPPA was overbroad and unconstitutional. Rehnquist, O'Connor and Scalia dissented, arguing that parts of the law could be constitutionally applied, and concluded that the majority's overbreadth analysis itself swept too broadly.

Finally, in *U.S. v. American Library Association* 539 U.S. 194 (2003), the Court upheld a provision in a grant program for libraries requiring them to install filtering software on Internet terminals. Rehnquist, in his majority opinion, noted that no one considers it a First Amendment violation when libraries choose which books to circulate, even if patrons might choose other books. Installing filtering software on computers, he noted, is even less restrictive to patrons because the software can always be turned off if the patron requests.

The library case aside, in the Internet cases, the Rehnquist Court mostly took Warren and Burger Court precedents such as *Miller* and applied them to a new medium. In so doing, the Court reinforced speech-protective precedents, and made it difficult for Congress to slow down the proliferation of sexual imagery on the Internet. The Rehnquist Court, including some of its most conservative members, found itself siding with pornographers, even child pornographers, against large majorities in Congress.

Commercial Speech

From a regime politics perspective, commercial speech offers an odd case. Freeing up the speech of businesses that advertise seems like a Republican project, but it was the liberals on the Burger Court who were the biggest champions of commercial speech, and William Rehnquist the biggest foe. Moreover, the businesses that came before the Rehnquist Court to plead their case against government regulation sold alcohol, cigarettes, games of chance and personal injury litigation – not products close to the heart of cultural conservatives.

In an early case on commercial speech, the Court had declared that the First Amendment created no obstacle at all to regulation of advertising (*Valentine v. Chrestenson* 316 U.S. 52, 1942). But in the Burger Court commercial speech, like libel and other "low-value" expression, found some shelter under the First Amendment. The Burger Court summarized its standards for gauging the constitutionality of commercial speech regulation in *Central Hudson Gas v. Public Service Commission* 447 U.S. 557 (1980):

> At the outset, we must determine whether the expression is protected by the First Amendment. For commercial speech to come within that provision, it at least must concern lawful activity and not be misleading. Next, we ask whether the asserted governmental interest is substantial. If both inquiries yield positive answers, we must determine whether the regulation directly advances the governmental interest asserted, and whether it is not more extensive than is necessary to serve that interest. (566)

The *Hudson* test was criticized by several members of the Rehnquist Court, but unlike the *Lemon* and *Sherbert* tests lived to see the beginnings of the Roberts Court undiminished.

Hudson survived partly because the Court found it easy to strike down objectionable laws under its aegis. In *Rubin v. Coors Brewing* 514 U.S. 476 (1996), the Court used the *Hudson* test to unanimously strike down a federal law banning labels on beer from describing their alcohol content. Two years later, in another liquor case, *44 Liquormart v. Rhode Island* 517 U.S. 484 (1996), all nine justices voted to strike down a state law banning the advertising of liquor prices, though they divided on the rationale. Stevens, together with Kennedy and Ginsburg, concluded that regulations against truthful commercial messages "for reasons unrelated to the preservation of a fair bargaining process" should receive strict scrutiny rather than the more deferential *Hudson* test. Most of the other justices found the law unconstitutional under *Hudson*. Thomas argued that where "the government's asserted interest is to keep legal users of a product or service ignorant" *Hudson* should not be used; the law should be considered per se unconstitutional (518). But while Thomas's concurrence was quite critical of *Hudson*, he did not argue for wholly overruling it; he simply wanted to carve out a large exception to it. *In Greater New Orleans Broadcasting Association v. U.S.* 527 U.S. 173 (1999), the Court was unanimous in striking down a federal law prohibiting advertising for private casino gambling. Stevens, in his opinion, concluded that there was no need to revisit the validity of the *Hudson* test because the statute clearly fails it. Thomas concurred to reiterate his contention that governmental attempts to manipulate consumer choice in the marketplace by keeping consumers ignorant are "per se illegitimate" (197). Finally, in *Lorillard Tobacco Co. v. Reilly* 533 U.S. 525 (2001), the Court struck down two state restrictions on tobacco advertising, though it did leave intact regulations requiring that tobacco products be displayed behind counters. Once again, the Court was badly divided on the rationale, with Kennedy, Scalia and Thomas all expressing concerns about *Hudson*. Souter, Stevens, Ginsburg and Breyer, meanwhile, dissented from parts of the result. *Lorillard* then, is a "flipped" decision where the Court's conservatives were most sympathetic to a free expression argument.

Just as confusing was the lineup in a rare case in which the Rehnquist Court rejected a First Amendment commercial speech challenge (*Florida Bar v. Went for It* 515 U.S. 618, 1995). The case tested the constitutionality of a rule prohibiting lawyers from mailing solicitations to victims within 30 days of an accident. This decision found Breyer in a five-person majority alongside O'Connor, Rehnquist, Scalia and Thomas, while Kennedy wrote for the dissenters. Both sides used *Hudson* to frame the issues.

It is hard to summarize the scrambled voting patterns in the commercial speech cases; indeed in cases like *Lorillard* it is hard enough to even describe the votes. The clearest pattern that emerges is of a Court that retains the *Hudson* test, grumbles about it occasionally, and seems to use it more and more aggressively to scrutinize speech restrictions, *Went for It* to the contrary.

EXPLAINING THE DIVERGENCE(S)

Conservative Republicans who had a hand in appointing the majority of the Rehnquist Court might, on balance, have been satisfied with its rulings on religion – except for its ruling on school prayer. On the other side, the Court's decisions on sexual speech and flag-burning could not have satisfied them – though its commercial speech rulings might have had some use for business constituencies. (More if the Court had brought commercial speech to parity with other kinds of protected expression, a move that would have required overruling *Hudson*.) What explains this very mixed pattern of support and opposition to the preferences of the appointing regime?

Sorting through the common explanations is difficult, because many of them do not generate a hard and fast mechanical prediction about how the Court will act in a particular case. Whether this is an indication of the richness and subtlety of the explanations, or a flaw rendering them nearly useless, depends in large part on one's view of the enterprise of social science, a matter clearly outside the scope of this chapter. That said, despite the "nuance," or, as some may view it, the "squishiness," of these explanations, the example of the Rehnquist Court First Amendment cases does help us think through some of them.

The Deviant Cases Help the Regime

One common claim in the regime politics literature is that judicial decisions that seem to go against the appointing regime are actually helpful to it. The Rehnquist Court's decision in *Planned Parenthood v. Casey*, for example, is said to have kept a troublesome issue for Republicans off the legislative agenda (Clayton, 1999; Rosen, 2006). On this account, the First

Amendment cases that superficially look like departures from Republican goals are in fact in the long-run interest of the Party. The flag-burning, school prayer, Internet pornography and obscenity cases can be explained because they give legislators, including Republicans, the ability to vote for the statute, then castigate the judges who make the ruling (and then, once the statute is struck down, get credit for voting for yet another statute on the same topic, as Congress has in both the flag-burning and Internet pornography cases). This is especially true if Republican legislators consider the statutes unconstitutional, but need to vote for them to curry favor with voters.

One does not have to be a hard-core positivist to notice that once even apparent reversals count as victories, presidents can never be shown to "lose" – any outcome can be explained as supporting the appointing coalition (Keck, 2007b). Moreover, the counterfactuals are harder to measure than is commonly supposed. Would it really hurt the Republican Party to make flag-burning, Internet pornography and school prayer into prominent legislative controversies? It is probably best to think of the "apparent reversal" analysis as an interesting description of how judicial outcomes can be used by governing regimes, rather than an *explanation* of those outcomes. It seems just a bit too subtle to believe that presidents, seeing an opportunity to gain from a backlash, appoint justices who they know will rule against them in high-profile cases.

The Deviant Cases Line up with Public Opinion

There is a large literature on the significant influence of public opinion on rulings of the Supreme Court (Mischler & Sheehan, 1996). Indeed, Rosen claims in a recent book that the judiciary has become "The Most Democratic Branch" because its decisions align much more closely with public opinion than those of the other branches (Rosen, 2006).

Public opinion, however, is not terribly helpful for explaining the Rehnquist Court's decision making in First Amendment cases. That is because most of the things the Court has done, including many of those most disappointing to the appointing regime, are also very unpopular with the public. Forty years of negative court decisions have not reduced the allure of school prayer for the public. Laws against flag-burning and sexual portrayals on the Internet are very popular; it seems unlikely that any politician, seeking public approval, would campaign against them.

Kennedy and O'Connor

Thomas Keck points out that Kennedy and O'Connor are the reason the Supreme Court has become "the most activist court of all," because they strike down both liberal and conservative policies, and thus provide the deciding votes in either circumstance (Keck, 2004). To what extent do the votes and opinions of Kennedy and O'Connor also explain the diverging pattern of First Amendment Rehnquist Court decisions?

In the religion cases Kennedy and O'Connor are crucial. They have often provided the fourth and fifth votes in the access and aid cases, and they were the swing voters in the school prayer cases. Because of their position they determined the Court's religious clause jurisprudence, supporting a move away from the strict interpretation of the *Lemon* test – grudgingly in O'Connor's case. They have, however, been much less successful as policy entrepreneurs. Kennedy's coercion test and O'Connor's endorsement test have not gained the support of a majority of their colleagues.[5]

In the non-religion cases the pattern is much less clear. Often the votes of Kennedy and O'Connor cancel each other out. O'Connor tends to vote with the government; Kennedy is usually found with the Court's liberals. Moreover, in these cases Thomas (sexual speech) and Scalia (flag-burning) make a difference by contributing votes to the libertarian side. Further, in the commercial speech cases all of the conservative justice have at one time or another voted with the plaintiffs.

Putting all this together, at least in the areas reviewed in this chapter, Kennedy's vote helps to explain the divergence, but so do some of the votes of Thomas and Scalia. Strangely enough, O'Connor, so often at the center of anything involving the Rehnquist Court, does nothing to solve this mystery because she lined up with the government in both the Internet sex and flag-burning cases.

The Outcomes Demonstrate the Weight of Precedent

If precedent matters the way Kritzer and Richards suggest, its does so by focusing judges on certain aspects of cases, framing what matters and what does not among the many case facts. If precedent matters the way Kersch suggests, it matters because it creates frameworks that resonate even beyond the judiciary, in popular culture.

Just as Kritzer and Richards found in their more systematic study, there is evidence throughout the cases reviewed here that judges reason "in the shadow of precedent," even where they ultimately break away from it. In the access and aid cases, for example, the Court moved gradually away from the *Lemon* test, diminishing by small increments the obstacles to government involvement with religion. In the absence of *Lemon* and other precedents it is hard to believe this group of justices would have taken the same slow path. *Smith* may seem a sharper break, though Scalia's claim that the Court had already backed away from the implications of *Sherbert* in previous cases rings true. And of course, in the expression cases that do not deal with religion the justices largely stick with the precedents, even when they admit some disgruntlement with them. That may be, as Kersch suggests, because the intellectual scaffolding of expression law, and concepts such as symbolic speech, are now built into the popular culture, so that any attempt to transform this realm would pit the justices not just against their colleagues, but the broader society (Kersch, 2006). It was Justice Rehnquist, after all, who explained why he voted to uphold the core of the *Miranda* decision by citing its entrenchment within "our national culture" (*Dickerson v. United States* 530 U.S. 428 at 443, 2000).

But all that said, the "weight of precedent" ultimately did not stop the Rehnquist Court from making fundamental changes in First Amendment law. Why were *Lemon* and *Sherbert* largely discarded while *O'Brien*, *Miller Hudson* and all the supporting free expression precedents were followed, even reinforced?

An institutional explanation starts with the mundane observation that justices are judges, and thus care about how well crafted the law is. Conservative judges, at least, found *Lemon* and *Sherbert* to be poorly crafted. The justices rejected them because they provided fuzzy ways to think through what should matter in Religion Clause jurisprudence – and uncertain guides to lower court judges. That is certainly Scalia's opinion. The flip side of this analysis is the claim that conservative judges have accepted "liberal" expression precedents because they work well enough in practice. This is the account of Suzanna Sherry, who argues that expression law has become more pragmatic and less ideological, a shift she approves (Sherry, 2004).

But in law, utility, like beauty, lies in the eyes of the beholder. A justice who concludes that the expression precedents "work well" or at least, well enough, must evaluate them partly on how well they reflect the justice's understanding of the First Amendment. It is hard to believe, in turn, that this understanding has nothing to do with the justice's political beliefs. The liberals on the Rehnquist Court evinced no great dissatisfaction with *Lemon*, after all. Meanwhile the Court's conservatives did not seem particularly enamored with the *Hudson* test, but failed to argue for overruling it, probably because they could work within it to get the result they deemed correct. While judicial craft almost certainly affects the way the Court evaluates precedents, its influence is hard to measure – especially where judges seem to evaluate craft of a precedent in line with their political beliefs.

The Outcomes Reflect the Libertarian Strand within Conservatism

One way to think about the divergent outcomes in these religion and expression cases is to see them as arising out of different brands of conservatism. In the expression cases, the libertarianism of Kennedy, and to a lesser extent Scalia and Thomas, is matched against the more statist conservatism of William Rehnquist and O'Connor. In the religion cases, by contrast, the differences in these brands of conservatism are muted, and all five vote together.

Lining the justices up this way, however, is a bit puzzling. For example, in Mark Tushnet's generally persuasive account, the battle on the Court is between Country-Club Republicanism, personified by O'Connor and Kennedy, and Modern Republicanism, the club of Rehnquist, Scalia and Thomas (Tushnet, 2005). The expression votes, though, sometimes match Kennedy, Scalia and Thomas against O'Connor and Rehnquist. First Amendment expert Eugene Volokh explains that "The justices' First Amendment ideologies just do not obviously match their ideologies on other matters" (Volokh, 2004, p. 40), but this seems a bit too convenient – and unlikely given the reams of behavioral studies that suggest justices' votes tend to factor together pretty well on at most two dimensions, suggesting that there is no special "expression" ideology.[6]

That said, a libertarian strain within conservatism does help account for the overall pattern of the cases, nearly all of which can be seen as expanding individual rights. The aid cases expand the ability of individuals to choose to participate in religious organizations, especially schools. The access cases grant religious organizations the ability to use government forums. The expression cases expand individuals' rights to burn the flag, contribute sexually explicit materials to the Internet, and advertise products. Only *Smith*, the Free Exercise case, looks like an example of diminished individual rights – and only if one believes that the Court before *Smith* was in fact dedicated to strictly scrutinizing laws that affected religious practice.

As Mark Graber has argued, conservative judges are likely to be libertarian, or at least more libertarian than voters (Graber, 2006a, 2006b; Keck, 2004). This is because judges, like other officeholders, are much more likely than voters to come from the educational and financial elite, which tends to be more libertarian than the masses. But judges are also affected by the institution in which they serve (Keck, 2007a). They interpret a Constitution that has many more negative than positive rights, and they lead a judiciary which has proven more effective in stopping governments from doing things than it is in getting governments to do more things. It is not so surprising, given all this, that the Rehnquist Court's First Amendment jurisprudence tended toward more libertarianism than some cultural conservatives in the Republican Party might have wished.

The Outcomes Reflect the Efforts of Conservative Legal Groups

Because I have been surveying the Court's First Amendment decisions from the "top down," I have neglected a crucial actor: the conservative legal groups that have been bringing religious liberty claims to the federal judiciary. Indeed, from the perspective of sociolegal studies, this is the place to start in analyzing legal change – rights "on the books," this body of scholarship suggests, cannot be effectively mobilized without a legal support structure (Epp, 1998). And indeed, religious liberty groups have been among the most effective litigators in the federal courts in recent years. As Steven Brown shows in his cogent study, conservative Christian legal groups have learned to employ the techniques of their predecessors on the left, most famously the NAACP. Brown describes a wide-ranging legal infrastructure, with thousands of attorney volunteers, several groups with professional staff and millions of dollars in funding, topped by star Supreme Court litigators such as Jay Sekulow, labeled the "Thurgood Marshall" of the movement by one Christian right leader (Brown, 2002, p. 37). Of 44 religion cases argued at the Supreme Court between 1980 and 2000, Christian right groups appeared as amici in 29, and as sponsors or funders in 9, among them *Rosenberger* and *Lambs Chapel*, two of the most significant First Amendment victories for conservatives (Brown, Figure 1, p. 84).

Can the efforts of these Christian groups explain the divergence between the religion and non-religion cases? Conservative legal groups have clearly focused more on religious liberty than other First Amendment issues. One of the major organizations, the Alliance Defense Fund, describes itself as "a national Alliance funding the legal defense and advocacy of religious freedom, the sanctity of human life, and family values" (Brown, 2002, p. 41). Brown points out that, as the order of this list suggests, cases involving religious liberty get the largest proportion of the ADF's funding (42). Another group, the Rutherford Institute, has an even greater focus on religious liberty. The Institute's founder, John Whitehead, advocates that Christian organizations take a libertarian approach to law: "If you don't want others ramming their views down your throat, you can't ram your views down their's" (Brown, p. 35). It is unsurprising that conservative lawyers, like conservative judges, tend to be more libertarian than the conservative movement as a whole. Like the judges, lawyers are elites who have been socialized into a culture of negative rights – a tendency Tocqueville noted and applauded many years ago (Tocqueville, 2000, p. 258).

Yet while the lawyers and organizations in Brown's study clearly have a libertarian cast, Brown's study also notes they have been responsive to cues provided by the federal judiciary. He points out, for example, that Christian groups came to their public forum free speech arguments only after years of "beating our heads against the wall," as one litigator put it, by making pure Establishment Clause and Free Exercise claims that were rejected (58). As is common in such circumstances, it is hard to know exactly how much judges are following the litigators' lead in First Amendment cases and to what extent the influence flows in the other direction. Nonetheless, the rise of a liberty-oriented conservative legal movement is an important part of the story of the Rehnquist Court's First Amendment jurisprudence.

THE CONSERVATIVE FIRST AMENDMENT

This chapter has offered a few carefully selected scenes from the Rehnquist Court's handling of First Amendment cases. To reflect the full sweep of First Amendment law, one would have to include many more such scenes: the Court's cases on campaign finance, or hate speech, or religious displays, or time, place and manner regulation. Nonetheless, even this narrowed review demonstrates that the conservatives who came to power on the Rehnquist Court have reshaped the First Amendment in some areas and merely extended older, liberal precedents in others. The Rehnquist Court's record in First Amendment cases suggests some intriguing patterns that are likely to extend well into the 21st century.

First, there is a radical divergence between the religion cases and the non-religious cases. In the religion cases, the Court's conservatives have been pushing hard against the categories created by precedent. They often use extensive quotations and examples from the founding period to challenge fundamental premises about meaning of the Constitution. Reading these cases, one sometimes feels stuck in a rather old-fashioned history seminar, where the deeds and words of great men from the past are argued over (Strang, 2006).

The opinions in the non-religion cases, by contrast, seem much more technical and policy-oriented, even technocratic. There is relatively little discussion of fundamental premises, and almost no invocation of history. On a Court that has a couple of self-proclaimed "originalists" that in itself is notable. In the First Amendment cases that do not directly involve religion, originalism takes a backseat to stare decisis. The Court's conservatives are willing to apply the frameworks they have inherited, often with "liberal" results. Much of the discussion in the opinions, then, is about how agreed-upon principles are applied. Typically, liberals and conservatives disagree, but their disagreements are muted.

Both patterns – fundamental disputes in the religion cases, narrower technical disputes in the non-religious expression cases – are likely to continue on the Roberts Court. It is hard to see how differences over the meaning of the religion clauses can be worked out anytime soon. The Rehnquist Court has uprooted the *Lemon* and *Sherbert* tests, and in so doing has pushed Establishment and Free Exercise law in new directions whose parameters are not yet clear. Although the "neutrality" test seems to have become accepted in the aid and access cases, Kennedy's "coercion" test and O'Connor's "endorsement" test have not been accepted in the school prayer and religious display cases, leaving a vacuum. The law journals are filled with proposals to go even further in rethinking traditional approaches to the religion clauses, and there are indications that some justices, especially Thomas, are receptive to these more far-reaching suggestions.

O'Connor's departure removes a significant obstacle to further innova-tion in the religion cases. On the Rehnquist Court O'Connor acted as an anchor for the conservative majority, usually providing a fifth vote, but always slowing the direction her colleagues were moving. It was O'Connor who kept the ghost of *Lemon* from fading from view, to the considerable annoyance of Scalia. Roberts or Alito could take on the O'Connor role of frustrating more rapid change. But even if they do, they will still have to wrestle with unsettled doctrine in the school prayer and religious display cases.

It is hard to imagine expression law transformed by the Roberts Court the way the religion clauses were reshaped by the Rehnquist Court. Conservative groups learned to use public forum arguments effectively, but outside of this realm they have not had any effect on free expression law. The typical free expression case is presented with many layers of judicial scaffolding. In the flag-burning case, for example, there was *Spence, O'Brien* and many symbolic speech, fighting words and public expression precedents. The justices often tinker with the top layer, but rarely dig down to the bottom. It is a thankless task, and one almost guaranteed to have little payoff.

Where conservatives do shift First Amendment law, they are likely to frame their changes as expanding rights rather than retracting them. As several scholars have suggested, there is a libertarian tilt to legal conservatism that partly reflects tensions within the Republican Party, but also the professional and institutional positioning of both conservative public interest law groups and conservative judges. Moreover, as many have observed, the nature of First Amendment disputing has shifted over time. Where before, the typical First Amendment plaintiff was an outsider, or a group marginalized by the community, more and more today the expression cases pit organizations, often corporations, against government regulations. It is unsurprising that in such areas as campaign finance and commercial speech conservatives have become associated with the pro-plaintiff side. *Lorillard*'s "flipped" result, in which conservatives cast their votes in favor of a First Amendment plaintiff, and liberals dissent, is likely to become more common. To the extent that First Amendment cases still involve the classic pattern – a freedom-loving individual pitted against a repressive institution – conservatives have in some cases recast themselves as the insurgents. In the religious access cases, for example, religious groups portrayed themselves as an oppressed minority, discriminated against by government institutions controlled by secularists. Similarly in abortion protest cases, it is pro-life conservatives who claim their rights to free expression are being trampled. Arguments over campus "hate speech" regulation also have this quality, as conservatives argue that they are the victims of overzealous university regulators.

Do all these developments presage a more fundamental shift in the political culture, in which cultural conservatives give up their longstanding ambition to use the state's authority to curb expression deemed harmful? There is no sign of this in Congress, where laws regulating controversial forms of expression regularly gather overwhelming support among Republicans. Of course such laws also get many Democratic votes, as they reflect public demands for action on such troublesome forms of expression such as sexual speech, flag-burning and broadcast indecency (Keck, 2007a). The record in Congress, though, suggests a continuing disjunction between judicial and legislative conservatives. Indeed, there is no reason to believe that simply because conservatives have taken up the cudgels of freedom of expression in some realms that cultural conservatives as a group will give up on the tools of state intervention in others. That said, the Rehnquist Court's rulings may have a modest influence on the agenda of conservatives, bolstering the libertarian strain within the movement, and discouraging those who seek to curb speech they consider corrosive to moral values. With its path-breaking rulings in the religion cases, and path-following rulings in other realms of First Amendment law, the Rehnquist Court has set a pattern that is likely to endure well into the 21st century.

NOTES

1. Powell (2006, p. 381), quoting Charles Evans Hughes, *Addresses of Charles Evans Hughes* 185 (1916). In fact as Powell notes, Hughes did not literally believe that the Supreme Court controlled the meaning of the Constitution, and lived to regret the way the quotation was used. On the many ways in which the Constitution is fought over outside the judiciary, see Whittington (2001).

2. See Gillman (2006, p. 141). Malcolm Feeley and Edward Rubin offer a particularly nuanced account of how internal constraints on judicial policymaking operate (Feeley & Rubin, 1998).

3. In *Locke v. Davey* 540 U.S.712 (2004), the Rehnquist Court upheld the constitutionality of a Washington state scholarship program that excluded students studying for the ministry. Chief Justice Rehnquist, writing for a 7-2 majority, concluded that while the Establishment Clause did not foreclose state subsidies to such students, the Free Exercise Clause did not require the subsidies either. *Locke v. Davey*, then, suggests the limits of the government aid cases – with the important exception of the "public forum" cases, the Court has not interpreted the religion clauses to require equal support to religious and non-religious activities.

4. My selection criteria lead me to focus in this chapter on surprising cases, those in which simple generalizations about conservatives do not hold true. Thus the cases I analyze may be unrepresentative of the larger group of Rehnquist Court First Amendment decisions. Epstein and Segal, using a well-known database, code 40 of 143 Rehnquist non-religious First Amendment cases as "value conflict" cases, in which the First Amendment is weighed again another "constitutional or political" value. In pure cases, those coded as without "value conflict," the traditional liberal-conservative split appears, but in the "value conflict" cases the relationship between ideology and vote fades, or depending on the measure of ideology, actually reverses (Epstein & Segal, 2006, p. 104). Of course this result depends on the authors code the decisions; one could argue that all First Amendment cases involve constitutional or political value conflicts.

5. Wexler (2006) claims that the endorsement test has become quite influential in the lower federal courts.

6. See note 3 above on this point.

REFERENCES

Bork, R. H. (1971). Neutral principles and some First Amendment problems. *Indiana Law Journal, 47*, 1–35.

Bickel, A. M. (1962). *The least dangerous branch: The Supreme Court at the bar of politics.* New York: Bobbs-Merrill.

Brenner, S., & Spaeth, H. J. (2003). *Stare indecisis: The alteration on the precedent on the Supreme Court, 1946–1992.* New York: Cambridge University Press.

Brown, S. P. (2002). *Trumping religion: The new Christian right, the Free Speech Clause, and the courts.* Tuscaloosa, AL: University of Alabama Press.

Carter, L., & Burke, T. (2007). *Reason in law* (7th ed.). New York: Pearson.

Claeys, E. R. (2006). Justice Scalia and the religion clauses: A comment on professor Epps. *Washington University Journal of Law and Policy, 21*, 349–377.

Clayton, C. (1999). Law, politics and the Rehnquist Court: Structural influences on Supreme Court decision making. In: C. Clayton & H. Gillman (Eds), *The Supreme Court in American politics: New instituitionalist approaches* (pp. 151–177). Lawrence: University of Kansas Press.

Dahl, R. A. (1957). Decision-making in a democracy: The Supreme Court as a national policy maker. *Journal of Public Law, 6*, 279–295.

Epp, C. R. (1998). *The Rights Revolution: Lawyers, activist and Supreme Courts in comparative perspective.* Chicago: University of Chicago Press.

Epstein, L., & Segal, J. A. (2006). The Rehnquist Court and the First Amendment: Trumping the First Amendment? *Washington University Journal of Law, 21*, 81–120.

Feeley, M. M., & Rubin, E. L. (1998). *Judicial policy making and the modern state.* New York: Cambridge University Press.

Gillman, H. (2002). How political parties can use the courts to advance their agendas: Federal courts in the United States, 1875–1891. *American Political Science Review, 96*(3), 511–524.

Gillman, H. (2006). Party politics and constitutional change. In: R. Kahn & K. I. Kersch (Eds), *The Supreme Court and American political development* (pp. 138–168). Lawrence: University Press of Kansas.

Graber, M. A. (1993). The nonmajoritarian difficulty: Legislative deference to the judiciary. *Studies in American Political Development, 7*, 35–72.

Graber, M. A. (2006a). Legal, strategic or legal strategy: Deciding to decide during the civil war and reconstruction. In: R. Kahn & K. I. Kersch (Eds), *The Supreme Court and American political development* (pp. 33–66). Lawrence: University Press of Kansas.

Graber, M. A. (2006b). The origins and consequences of the new constitutionalism. Does it really matter? *Fordham Law Review, 75*, 675–708.

Greenawalt, K. (2004). Religion and the Rehnquist Court. *Northwestern University Law Review, 99*, 145–174.

Greene, A. (2006). The apparent consistency of Religion Clause doctrine. *Washington University Journal of Law and Policy, 21*, 225–261.

Keck, T. M. (2003). David H. Souter: Liberal constitutionalism and the Brennan seat. In: E. M. Maltz (Ed.), *Rehnquist justice: Understanding the court dynamic* (pp. 185–211). Lawrence: University Press of Kansas.

Keck, T. M. (2004). *The most activist Supreme Court in history: The road to modern judicial conservatism.* Chicago: University of Chicago Press.

Keck, T. M. (2007a). Party, policy or duty: Why does the Supreme Court invalidate federal statutes? *American Political Science Review, 101*, 321–338.

Keck, T. M. (2007b). Party politics or judicial independence: The regime politics literature hits the law schools. *Law and Social Inquiry, 32*, 511–544.

Kersch, K. I. (2006). How conduct became speech and speech became conduct. *University of Pennsylvania Journal of Constitutional Law, 8*, 255–297.

Kritzer, H. M., & Richards, M. J. (2002). Jurisprudential regimes and Supreme Court decisionmaking: The Lemon regime and the Establishment Clause cases. *Law and Society Review, 37*, 827–840.

Mischler, W., & Sheehan, R. S. (1996). Public opinion, the attitudinal model and Supreme Court decision-making. *Journal of Politics, 58*, 169–200.

Post, R. C. (1993). William J. Brennan and the Warren Court. In: M. Tushnet (Ed.), *The Warren Court in historical and political perspective*. Charlotte: University of Virginia Press.

Powell, H. J. (2006). Constitutional virtues. *Green Bag, 9*, 379–389.

Richards, M. J., & Kritzer, H. M. (2002). Jurisprudential regimes in Supreme Court decision making. *The American Political Science Review, 96*, 305–320.

Rosen, J. (2006). *The most democratic branch: How the courts serve America*. New York: Oxford University Press.

Rosenberg, G. N. (1993). *The hollow hope: Can courts bring about social change?* Chicago: University of Chicago Press.

Scherer, N. (2005). *Scoring points: Politicians, activists and the lower federal court appointment process*. Palo Alto: Stanford University Press.

Shapiro, M. (1981). *Courts: A comparative and political analysis*. Chicago: University of Chicago Press.

Shapiro, M. (2002). Towards a theory of stare decisis. In: M. Shapiro & A. S. Sweet (Eds), *On law, politics and judicialization* (pp. 112–135). New York: Oxford University Press.

Sherry, S. (2004). Symposium: The Rehnquist Court: Hard cases make good judges. *Northwestern University Law Review, 99*, 3–31.

Strang, L. J. (2006). Symposium: The (Re)turn to history in Religion Clause law and scholarship: Introduction. *Notre Dame Law Review*, 1697–1716.

Tocqueville, A. (2000). *Democracy in America*. H. C. Mansfield & D. Winthrop (Trs.), Chicago: University of Chicago Press.

Tushnet, M. V. (2005). *A court divided: The Rehnquist Court and the future of constitutional law*. New York: W.W. Norton & Company.

Tushnet, M. V. (2006). The Supreme Court and the national political order. In: R. Kahn & K. I. Kersch (Eds), *The Supreme Court and American political development* (pp. 117–135). Lawrence: University Press of Kansas.

Volokh, E. (2004). Symposium: The Rehnquist Court: Pragmatism vs. ideology in free speech cases. *Northwestern University Law Review, 99*, 33–46.

Wexler, J. D. (2006). The endorsement court. *Washington University Journal of Law and Policy, 21*, 263–306.

Whittington, K. (2001). *Constitutional construction: Divided powers and constitutional meaning*. Cambridge: Harvard University Press.

CONFIRMATION OBFUSCATION: SUPREME COURT CONFIRMATION POLITICS IN A CONSERVATIVE ERA

David A. Yalof

ABSTRACT

The premise that the U.S. Supreme Court never veers too far off from the dominant national political coalition (Dahl, 1957) has become widely accepted among social scientists today. To fulfill that promise, however, the confirmation process for justices must serve as a plebiscite through which the public can ratify or reject future justices based on their views. Unfortunately, modern confirmation hearings have become an exercise in obfuscation, providing little meaningful dialogue on important issues. Because conservative Republican presidents have made the lion's share of appointments in recent times, social conservatives have most often benefited from a process that has severed the link between Supreme Court nominees and the polity they must serve.

1. INTRODUCTION

Dissenting in the landmark abortion case of *Planned Parenthood v. Casey*, a frustrated Justice Scalia remarked that if the High Court had indeed become

Special Issue: Constitutional Politics in a Conservative Era
Studies in Law, Politics, and Society, Volume 44, 141–171
ISSN: 1059-4337/doi:10.1016/S1059-4337(08)00805-3

141

the equivalent of a "super legislature" in the modern era, "at least we can have a sort of plebiscite each time a new nominee to that body is put forth." (*Planned Parenthood v. Casey*, 505 U.S. 833, 1001 (1992) (Scalia, J., dissenting)). Recognizing the conflict between lifetime appointments and fundamental notions of democratic accountability, Scalia's solution inherently accepts the possibility of a veritable free-for-all of interest groups, the media and other political actors attempting to make their voices heard in the modern-day Supreme Court confirmation process. Still, do not expect Justice Scalia to back away from the implications of his suggestion: After all, to him the "American people love democracy and the American people are not fools ... Value judgments [] should be voted on, not dictated."

If the Supreme Court appointment process was laden with real public accountability, it would help to affirm the premise underlying a long line of social science scholarship which posits that political constraints on the Supreme Court prevent that body from continuously thwarting the dominant national coalition in the long run (see Dahl, 1957; Funston, 1975). Although Dahl's thesis has been occasionally criticized (e.g. Casper, 1976), the premise that the Supreme Court shifts its ideological positions based on changes in its personnel to reflect the dominant "national lawmaking majority" has been given a new voice in recent years by scholars relying on developmental approaches to analyze how the Supreme Court positions itself in the American political system. Mark Tushnet has persuasively argued that a Supreme Court that is "collaborative" – featuring deference to or confrontation with legislatures, depending on the political requirements of the governing national coalition – can most effectively enforce national norms against sectional resistance in the national political system (Tushnet, 2006, p. 118). For Tushnet, the Roosevelt Court epitomized this form of collaboration with the New Deal order; the Warren Court too collaborated with the Great Society's civil rights agenda. Howard Gillman takes this notion a step further, arguing that partisan regimes consider judges as akin to appointed policymakers; changes in the Supreme Court's understandings of the Constitution can thus be explained only with reference to the policy agendas of national governing coalitions (Gillman, 2006, p. 138). Thus the Court's aggressive constitutional decision-making of the 1960s can only be understood by situating the Court in the larger context of Democratic party politics, which dominated the American political scene during that decade (Gillman, 2006, p. 154). Of course Supreme Court appointments provide a crucial means by which governing coalitions can pursue these goals.

Yet to maintain that connection between the Supreme Court and the national governing coalition, at least two fundamental conditions must be in place. First, the president of the United States must wield his power to nominate Supreme Court Justices with an eye towards influencing Supreme Court decision-making outcomes; if the High Court offers the chief executive a venue for personal patronage and little more, a key link in the chain that leads to public accountability is undermined. Second, given that the president does not always epitomize the national lawmaking majority at any given moment in time, the appointment process must offer other parts of that majority (including Senators and the greater public) an opportunity to participate in a real dialogue concerning where the nominee sits on the political–judicial spectrum. In sum, the process must offer a public education about the nominee, encouraging the "plebiscite" that Scalia was referring to in his Casey dissent.

Senate confirmation hearings are by far the most public aspect of the appointment process. Yet rather than serving an educative function for the masses and their representatives on the constitutional landscape and the place an individual nominee fits within that landscape, these hearings tend to feature well-rehearsed Supreme Court nominees offering proverbial seminars in the art of dodging, ducking and otherwise avoiding Senators' inquiries. Rather than educating Senators or the polity as a whole as to where they stand on key issues of Constitutional law, most nominees assume a stance similar to that of defendants at a criminal trial: The less said the better. Prospective justices expertly avoid pointed inquiries by resorting to general recitations about the importance of "the judicial process" and other vague ambiguities. Accordingly, modern-day Senate confirmation hearings have devolved into a form of gamesmanship on both sides, with little real engagement on issues of substance. In truth, this process falls so far short of a genuine plebiscite that it serves to undermine any possible connection between justices and the national governing coalition.

Because Republican presidents willing to cater to ideological conservatives have made the lion's share of Supreme Court nominations since 1969, this practice of confirmation by obfuscation has significant ramifications for the Court's ideological composition – far more often than not, it has benefited conservatives. Together, the three most recent Republican presidents (Ronald Reagan, George H.W. Bush and George W. Bush) have managed to transform the composition of the federal judiciary into one dominated by conservatives. Ronald Reagan's 1980 campaign for the presidency offered a call to arms for those frustrated with the Warren Court and its liberal legacy; since then social conservatives have increasingly looked to the judiciary for important victories on social issues. The successful confirmations of conservatives John Roberts and Samuel Alito in 2005 and 2006 prove that highly qualified nominees can in fact be approved for the Court, no matter how conservative they may be, so long as their confirmations hearings provide no real opportunity for the public to determine the extent to which they might go against the opinions of the larger ruling majority.

Duly frustrated by this state of affairs, some commentators have advocated abandoning all hopes of a true public education by moving confirmation hearings behind closed doors (e.g. Wittes, 2006). Yet the need for public validation of Supreme Court nomination counsels us against such an approach. In fact, nominees must be prepared to undergo even more intense forms of public scrutiny, if only so that ties between the Court and the polity as a whole may be strengthened.

2. THE CONFIRMATION PROCESS IN HISTORICAL PERSPECTIVE: KEEPING NOMINEES AT A DISTANCE

Prior to the modern era, Senate confirmation hearings failed to provide much suspense either for Supreme Court nominees or for the Senators charged with evaluating them. Certainly the nominee's absence contributed to keeping the process dry and uneventful. Given that Supreme Court nominees only began appearing on a regular basis at their own hearings starting in 1954, it would have been difficult (if not impossible) for Senators to learn much about a nominee's ideological positions within the framework of the hearings themselves. And given that the hearings were not even televised for the first time until 1981, the public would have little real opportunity to evaluate these carefully guarded Supreme Court nominees for themselves.

How then did individual Senators effectively perform their "advice and consent" role in prior eras? Unlike in recent times, Supreme Court nominees did not benefit from a generally recognized presumption in favor of the president's nominee and political ideology. The simple fact that a president won a national election did not necessarily translate into an acceptance on the part of opposition Senators that he now enjoys a mandate to place likeminded individuals on the Supreme Court. Scholars George Watson and John Stookey identify numerous potential Senate roles in this more open-ended appointments landscape, including: (1) the open-minded "evaluator," who uses the confirmation process to help make up his or her mind about the nominee; (2) the "validator," who uses the confirmation process to confirm or validate his or her preliminary decision on the nominee; (3) the "partisan," who seeks to use the process to press a partisan view as far as he can; and (4) the "educator" or "advertiser," who wishes to use the confirmation process as an opportunity to inform and perhaps influence the nominee, fellow committee members, fellow Senators, or perhaps the public (Watson & Stookey, 1988, pp. 190–194).

Up until the middle of the 20th century, Supreme Court appointments usually played themselves out beyond the public's continuous glare. As a consequence, confirmation hearings (to the extent any were held) did not offer much opportunity for Senators to act as "educators" or "advertisers" to any significant degree. Moreover, the limited nature of committee work meant that the "evaluator" and the "validator" would have to seek and get his information elsewhere. By contrast, Senators could always perform their role as "partisans," and many did exactly that. In fact, partisan politics helps to explain why approximately a quarter of all Supreme Court nominees were rejected up until 1900.

To be sure, the Senate often rejected earlier nominees on strictly ideological grounds (Danelski, 1987), because of a perceived lack of ability or proper qualifications, or because of some problem in the nominee's background. John Rutledge's opposition to the Jay Treaty with Great Britain sealed his defeat as President George Washington's nominee for chief justice in 1795, despite Jay's successful service as an associate Justice from 1789 to 1791.

Washington's experience with Rutledge was a rare occurrence, however, for a chief executive who enjoyed relatively strong political standing. By contrast, Senators acting as "partisans" made considerable headway undermining nominations made by weaker presidents who enjoyed limited support in Congress. The "accidental president," John Tyler, saw eight of his Supreme Court nominees defeated, tabled or withdrawn in the early 1840s, while only one was confirmed. Another unelected president, Millard Fillmore, ran into serious problems as well, with three of his nominees turned back after just one successful Supreme Court appointment. One of Ulysses Grant's nominees was outright rejected, while two others were withdrawn. Thus many of these rejections during the 19th century can be explained by considerations of political power, which made life difficult for weak presidents – especially those who were "unelected, those who face[d] a Senate controlled by the opposition, and those in the terminal year in office" (Maltese, 1995, p. 5).

As for the confirmation process itself, it offered quite a limited forum for Senators who actually wished to evaluate the merits of individual nominees. Records of the early Senate Judiciary Committee, originally established in 1816, are mostly unavailable or incomplete. Although the committee during its first half-century of existence met to offer its recommendation on nominees to the full Senate, actual formal hearings on Supreme Court nominations – including listening to live testimony from witnesses – probably did not begin until 1873, with Ulysses Grant's unsuccessful nomination of George Williams to be chief justice (Maltese, 1995, p. 88). Williams' case led to closed-door hearings only because so many already felt he was not qualified for having allegedly used public money for private purposes (the purchase of a carriage) when he was attorney general (Maltese, 1995, p. 142). The most critical evaluations of Williams' suitability for the Court had thus already been rendered before hearings even occurred (President Grant ultimately withdrew Williams' nomination before a final Senate vote on the merits).

Meanwhile, the Senate Judiciary Committee did not hold its first public hearings on a Supreme Court nomination until the controversial progressive advocate, Louis Brandeis, was nominated in 1916. Already a well-known public figure, those hearings produced few important insights (Brandeis himself was never asked to appear). The committee then went back into seclusion for another 14 years, declining to hold full-fledged public hearings again until Hoover's unsuccessful nomination of John Parker in 1930, when a subcommittee of the full Judiciary Committee listened to and discussed witness testimony for nearly three hours (albeit without the nominee himself appearing). That practice continued until the late 1940s, although in these other cases the hearings lasted less than an hour. Meanwhile, the full Senate Judiciary Committee did not even take up the task of holding hearings until 1949; even then, such hearings rarely lasted more than two days at the most. Senators hoping to use such hearings to "evaluate" or "validate" their confirmation decisions could not have benefited much from what amounted to perfunctory hearings on prospective members of the High Court.

Still, the greatest obstacle to Senators genuinely evaluating nominees through the confirmation process was the complete absence of the nominee himself from the proceedings. The first breakthrough on this front did not occur until 1925 when President Calvin Coolidge's nominee for associate Justice, Attorney General Harlan Fiske Stone, agreed to appear before a Senate subcommittee to answer questions about the Justice Department's pursuit of an indictment against Senator Burton Wheeler (D.-Mon.) relating to Wheeler's conduct of his private law practice (Senator Wheeler was eventually acquitted on all charges). Stone masterfully handled the committee's questions about the Wheeler indictment during several hours of public testimony. Still, none of the Senators took the opportunity to interrogate Stone about positions he might take as a Supreme Court Justice (he was in fact confirmed only a short time later). Thus Stone's appearance failed to launch an era in which Senators could more directly evaluate nominees. In 1937, prior to taking his seat on the High Court, the newly confirmed Associate Justice Hugo Black of Alabama defended himself publicly against accusations that he had been a member of the Ku Klux Klan earlier in his career. Of course in that case Black's national radio address about his past occurred only *after* he had already been successfully confirmed for the High Court.

3. A NEW ROLE FOR SENATORS? INVITING THE PUBLIC INTO THE CONFIRMATION PROCESS

Some scholars date the era of more substantive Supreme Court confirmation hearings to 1954 – beginning that year with John Marshall Harlan's appointment to the High Court, every Supreme Court nominee has at least been forced to testify before the Senate Judiciary Committee. According to Stephen Carter, the event that led to this more direct inquiry was *Brown v. Board of Education* (1954) – after that decision, Southern Senators insisted on questioning all post-*Brown* nominees about their views on the civil rights revolution (Carter, 1994, p. 193). In fact, the chairman of the Senate Judiciary committee that year, Senator Harley Kilgore (D.-W.Va.), wanted all such inquiries to occur in public and under oath.

Eisenhower's Supreme Court nominees were among the first to face Senators assuming new roles in the confirmation process, whether as "evaluators" and "validators," or more likely as "educators" and "advertisers" attempting to use the process as a means of criticizing the Supreme Court's desegregation decisions. Some Senators on the Judiciary Committee were determined to create a public demonstration of hostility to *Brown* in the hope that they might (1) intimidate judges from imposing court desegregation orders in the South; and/or (2) discourage President Dwight D. Eisenhower and Attorney General Herbert Brownell from mobilizing the resources of the federal government (military and otherwise) to defend the decision in the South. The Southern Manifesto (signed by 19 Senators and 77 House members, all hailing from one of the 11 former Confederate

States), which promised to use all "lawful means" to bring about a reversal of *Brown,* was just one element of this strategy; forcing Supreme Court nominees to undergo greater public scrutiny of their views was another. In this way, the era of more regular dialogue between nominees and Senators was born.

Yet while a significant breakthrough, this era of give-and-take was still quite limited, frustrating these new Senate roles at the outset. Before Thurgood Marshall's historic nomination in 1967, the total amount of hearing time conducted on each Supreme Court nominee usually amounted to less than a day, with most nominees testifying for a few hours at the most. Indeed, up until 1967, only two sets of confirmation hearings had managed to extend into a third day of gathering testimony. Thus the true modern era of Supreme Court confirmation hearings – in which the Senate Judiciary Committee would willingly engage nominees in more protracted struggles over controversial legal issues – began in the late 1960s with the nomination of Marshall (his hearing went five days) and the attempted promotion of Fortas to Chief Justice. The interrogation of Fortas in particular by Senator Strom Thurmond (R.-S.C.), acting in the role of public "educator" effectively became a referendum on the Warren Court as a whole, with Fortas compelled to defend the body of work by the Warren Court, including some opinions handed down even before his arrival on the Court as an Associate Justice in 1965. The Fortas appointment created national headlines, symbolizing not only public frustrations with the Warren Court, but frustrations with his appointing president, Lyndon B. Johnson, who by the summer of 1968 had seen his entire presidency embroiled in the Vietnam War quagmire. In this tense political environment, Fortas became the first Supreme nominee to be defeated (technically withdrawn) after 38 years of otherwise successful High Court appointments.

As far as national media attention goes, the Fortas hearings drew more than their share against the backdrop of a heated presidential election contest. So too did the public take note when the Senate rejected two of Richard Nixon's first three nominations to the High Court in 1969–1970. After so many years of a conflict-free process, the media suddenly fixated on the conduct of hearings that resulted in the rejection or withdrawal of four Supreme Court nominees during the period spanning from 1968 through January of 1970. Yet all these Capitol Hill battles occurred before the age of gavel-to-gavel coverage on C-Span, and of 24-hour news networks such as CNN, MSNBC and Fox News. Regular televised coverage of Congressional proceedings did not begin in any form until 1979; until that point only occasionally did Congressional hearings break through to a television audience. Although little of Senator Joseph McCarthy's (R.-Wi.) Communist witch hunt of the late 1940s was seen on live television, a confrontation between McCarthy and the Army led to the nationally televised "Army-McCarthy hearings" of 1954. (Though McCarthy had longed for the television spotlight, those latter hearings actually revealed the true nature of his tactics to the public and led to his eventual censure by the Senate in December 1954.) Chaired by Senator John McClellan (D-Ark.) and staffed by a young Robert F. Kennedy, the Senate's permanent subcommittee on investigations in 1955 focused its attention on criminal influence over the powerful Teamsters Union, calling Teamsters' leaders Dave Beck and Jimmy Hoffa to testify. Those hearings were also televised, effectively introducing Senate committee members Barry Goldwater and John F. Kennedy to the nation. Television cameras also covered the Watergate hearings live, gavel-to-gavel, in their entirety.

By comparison, the first set of televised confirmation hearings for a Supreme Court nominee did not occur until 1981, when Sandra Day O'Connor testified before the Senate Judiciary Committee. Because the new Senate Republican majority did not want to embarrass a Republican President so early in his first term, most of the objections to O'Connor were raised and resolved behind the scenes, before the formal announcement of her nomination. Senator Jesse Helms (R.-N.C.) was one of a handful of more conservative Senators worried that O'Connor was not nearly conservative enough on social issues such as abortion: Helms felt that in attempting to make history (and fulfill a presidential campaign promise) to name the first woman justice, President Reagan had compromised on his administration's socially conservative agenda for the High Court. Yet all the Republican Senators fell quickly into line after her nomination was announced, as evidenced by the overwhelming 99-0 vote the Republican-controlled Senate produced in her favor.

Despite the seeming inevitability of O'Connor's confirmation, some hallmarks of the confirmation wars to come within the next decade were already in evidence. By 1968 the traditional distinction between so-called Senate "whales" (who ran the chamber) and "minnows" (who silently followed) had largely disappeared (Bell, 2002, p. 46). Senators themselves were becoming less beholden to their respective parties, as the upper chamber slowly transformed during the 20th century from a collegial body of specialists in different areas of public policy into a body of independent thinkers who would be more willing to challenge nominations made by their own party's presidents (Gerhardt, 2000, pp. 168–169). The middle part of the 20th century also witnessed a sudden surge in intense interest group activity, with Senators increasingly compelled to interact with those groups, and respond to their agendas by more aggressively challenging nominees.

It would take a little time before interest groups and Senators caught on to the potential that televised confirmation hearings held for engaging nominees in a true public dialogue on the state of constitutional politics. But President Reagan's determination to appoint ideological conservatives to the bench effectively forced such reconsideration of the process and its possibilities. Social conservatives would eventually respond with tactics of their own to avoid the fate of fighting the "good battle" over and over without winning any of the more essential political wars.

4. "PACKING THE COURTS": SOCIAL CONSERVATIVES ADOPT A NEW POLITICAL STRATEGY

Just as Sandra Day O'Connor was taking her oath of office to become the first female Justice in Supreme Court history on September 25, 1981, conservative activists were reveling in a level of success at the national level that no one would have thought possible less than two decades earlier. Republican victories must have even surprised O'Connor herself, an Arizonan who had supported Republican presidential candidate Barry Goldwater's failed campaign for the presidency in 1964. That year Goldwater suffered a landslide defeat of epic proportions, winning just 52 electoral votes and 38.4% of the popular vote. Surviving that low point in presidential politics, and the Watergate scandals it endured less than 10 years later, the national Republican party marched back to prominence in 1980 led by a former California Governor, Ronald Reagan, espousing his desire to cut the bureaucracy, lower taxes and overturn liberal Supreme Court opinions such as *Miranda v. Arizona, Engel v. Vitale,* and of course, *Roe v. Wade.*

When one considers how low the Republican Party stood in January of 1965, the party's eventual political resuscitation was that much more impressive. Beginning in 1968, the Republicans would win 7 of the next 10 presidential elections. Richard Nixon and Ronald Reagan each managed to top the 60% mark in coasting to reelection victories in 1972 and 1984, respectively. President George H.W. Bush and his son, President George W. Bush, each topped the 50% mark in the popular vote at least once as well. By contrast, the only Democratic presidential candidate to top the 50%

mark since 1964 was Jimmy Carter in 1976. To be sure, many modern presidential elections (1968, 1976, 2000 and 2004) have been narrow, hard-fought victories. But the Republicans have more often than not ended up the victor in such presidential election battles, outflanking the Democrats in the Electoral College – and when necessary (as was the case in 2000) – in the courts as well.

Given the Republicans' overall success in presidential elections since 1968, the party's failure to win back both houses of the Congress until 1994 was a significant development. Unified control of the branches was the norm earlier in the century when the White House changed party hands in 1912, 1932 and then again in 1952. Despite his landslide election victory in 1972, Richard Nixon never once worked with a Republican House or Senate during his five-plus years as president. The same fate was visited on George H.W. Bush, whose entire tenure as president was subject to the harsh realities of divided party government. Ronald Reagan worked with a Republican Senate for six of his eight years as president, but the Democratic House, led initially by the cantankerous House Speaker from Massachusetts, Thomas P. "Tip" O'Neil, controlled the fate of Reagan's legislative packages throughout his eight years in office. When the Republicans finally did capture both houses of Congress in 1994, they faced off against a popular Democratic President (Bill Clinton) who coasted to reelection on their watch in 1996. Statistically speaking, the close of President George W. Bush's second term in office marks the end of a period in which Republican presidents have controlled the White House for 28 of the previous 40 years. And yet over this exact same period the Republicans controlled the Senate for just a bit more than 16 of 40 years, and the House of Representatives for a mere 12 of those 40 years.

The conservative movement has reacted accordingly to the harsh reality that a national legislature hostile to its agenda has been in place for much of the modern political era. How have conservatives navigated this contentious environment? Two central strategies have prevailed at the national level. First, despite traditional hesitations about excessive government power per se, conservatives have willingly embraced an especially broad interpretation of executive power over this same period, in part as a way of sidelining an uncooperative Congress whenever necessary. Almost two decades before the tragic events of September 11th spurred a Republican administration to embrace broad executive discretion in order to prosecute its expanded war on terrorism, young conservative lawyers (including future chief justice John Roberts) were articulating a broad theory of executive power within the Reagan administration itself. That theory was used to justify Ronald

Reagan's aggressive executive branch initiatives, including his decisions to fire air-traffic controllers, expand the war on drugs, invade Grenada and most controversially of all, to support insurgent movements against communist-controlled regimes in Latin America and elsewhere.

A second strategy has been no less important a pillar in the conservatives' agenda. In theory, frequent control of the White House by Republicans has offered conservatives an opportunity to transform the constitutional landscape by placing a large number of conservative jurists on the federal bench. Thanks to a sizeable increase in federal judgeships created by Congress during the Carter presidency, the federal judiciary was populated by 50% more Democrats than Republicans when Ronald Reagan initially took office in 1981. Even without more judgeships created, Reagan and his Republican successors were in a position to reverse this trend and help build a sizeable conservative majority in the federal judiciary. The Burger Court's attempted "counterrevolution" largely failed: In the 1970s, the High Court refused to overturn precedents such as *Miranda v. Arizona* and *Engel v. Vitale* (Blasi, 1983). In some cases, the Burger Court even advanced the liberals' social agenda for the court, such as when it expanded privacy rights in *Roe v. Wade* or read the Establishment Clause even more broadly in *Lemon v. Kurtzman.* By the end of the century, the Supreme Court found itself precariously balanced between two competing visions of the Constitution, with many cutting edge issues hanging in the balance.

To be effective at "packing the courts," social conservatives required both a president dedicated to using ideology as an important criterion in filling vacancies on the federal bench, and a Senate willing to defer to the president's nominations chosen on ideological grounds, so long as other criteria (competence/qualifications, interest in diversity, etc.) were not completely ignored. In the case of lower court appointments, both these criteria were met, and Republican presidents have effectively remade the judiciary along more conservative lines. Up until the late 1980s and early 1990s, the packing of lower courts with conservatives occurred largely outside the public spotlight, as few lower court appointments lent themselves to being framed as part of a larger cultural or political conflict. The Nixon administration raised the ideological stakes of lower court appointments with its "law and order" rhetoric, but facing a Democratic Senate, it never really threatened to buck traditional considerations of Senatorial courtesy along the way. By contrast, the Reagan administration pushed the envelope by recruiting young conservative intellectuals from the faculty of law schools and from private practice for vacancies on the circuits. Richard Posner, J. Harvie Wilkinson, Kenneth Starr, Alex Kozinski, and

Edith Jones were all part of this youth movement (Schwartz, 1988, p. 60). The administration also focused on the prestigious D.C. Circuit as a venue where no Senatorial considerations existed to scuttle even the most controversial nominations. Both Professors Robert Bork and Antonin Scalia found a home on the D.C. Circuit during the early-to-mid 1980s.

Deploying "conservative revolutionaries" in the Justice Department and the White House, the Reagan administration invested more resources into the search of ideologically desirable jurists than any other administration in American history. Presidents George H.W. Bush and George W. Bush each borrowed from the Reagan administration's playbook on this score. Aided by a Republican-controlled Senate for more than half of his presidency, George W. Bush pushed this process a step further, refusing to consult with Democratic Senators on vacancies in their home states, and urging Senate Republicans to circumvent the so-called Blue Slip system, which had traditionally afforded Senators from *either party* the power to impose a veto on undesirable judicial nominations in their home states (Denning, 2002; Burbank, 2002). As a consequence, some of that administration's more controversial nominations met with levels of resistance unprecedented in the context of lower court appointments.

Despite all the machinations from January 2003 through April of 2005 concerning threatened recess appointments (President Bush used them twice), filibusters and the so-called nuclear option (the term for a Senate rule change that would have eliminated the filibusters of judicial nominees, potentially causing Senate Democrats to shut down the Senate in response), the lower court appointments mill continued to hum throughout the George W. Bush presidency with a general presumption in favor of confirmation. After his first six years in office, President Bush could claim responsibility for the appointment of forty-six judges to the U.S. Courts of Appeals and 203 judges to the federal district courts, figures that amount to nearly three in ten judges staffing the federal judicial system. These numbers compare favorably to those of other recent two-term presidents such as Ronald Reagan and Bill Clinton, each of whom successfully appointed an average of forty-five lower court judges per year.

Moreover, George W. Bush's lower court appointees were on the whole dramatically more conservative than the judges they replaced, successfully transforming the constitutional landscape in a more conservative direction. According to one study of judicial outcomes, Bush's judicial appointees (at least through the summer of 2004) had amassed a record of conservatism that was matched during the past half-century only by President Reagan's appointees (Carp, Manning, & Stidham, 2004). Even more significant, as a result of negotiations entered between 14 moderate Senators representing both sides of the partisan aisle, some of the most controversial conservative lower court nominees were among those ultimately confirmed, including Priscilla Owen and Janice Rogers Brown.

Of course conservative inroads in the lower courts require validation at the Supreme Court level, not just to immunize lower court successes from future challenges, but also because isolated High Court defeats tend to receive disproportionate weight and attention, and thus may dishearten crucial constituencies in the process. When the Supreme Court reversed 17 years of precedent to invalidate sodomy laws in 13 states in *Lawrence v. Texas* (2003), many conservative activists decried it as the "*Roe v. Wade* of the homosexual issue," fearing that the case might eventually snowball into a general sanctioning of gay marriage (Robertson, 2003). Others called it an outright "capitulation to the gay and lesbian agenda" (Lewis, 2003). Although the modern-day Supreme Court decides (on average) less than 50 constitutional cases per year, social conservatives often judge their successes and failures largely on the basis of a Supreme Court-driven report card.

For better or worse, this obsession on the part of so many interested observers with the High Court in particular also aligns with the democratic ideal described in Section 1. Whereas lawyers and litigants must be equally attuned to the law that emanates from lower courts, the national governing coalition and the citizenry it represents pays disproportionate attention to U.S. Supreme Court decisions. At least some of the public recognition afforded to the Supreme Court as an institution stems from the appointment process that produced the nine sitting justices in the first place. The controversial confirmation hearings Clarence Thomas underwent may explain why he enjoys more name recognition than any of his colleagues.[1] Supreme Court Justices do not simply materialize on the court – they must survive the scrutiny of a confirmation process which ensures that every justice meet at least minimum qualifications. The prospective justice must also be deemed acceptable on ideological grounds, as dictated by the degree to which the president's popularity and support in the Senate affords him leverage and power in the appointment process.

When President Nixon captured the presidency in 1968, Conservatives hoped that his and future Republican presidents' High Court nominees would receive the same level of deference Democratic nominees had mostly enjoyed throughout the 20th century. Until President Johnson's bid to promote Abe Fortas to chief Justice failed in 1968, no Democratic president had failed in his bid to fill a Supreme Court vacancy since

Grover Cleveland, whose 1894 nomination of Wheeler H. Peckham was rejected by the Senate. This High rate of confirmation all nominees enjoyed during this era (only Parker was defeated between 1894 and 1968) suggests that "despite the statements of Senators to the contrary, there [was] a Senate presumption in favor of confirmation" throughout this earlier period (Sulfridge, 1980, pp. 562–563). Yet the circumstances facing Republican presidents after 1968 proved dramatically different than in earlier eras when this presumption reigned. In Nixon's case, the ignominious defeat of Fortas was still fresh in the minds of many Democratic Senators; once the Fortas affair unfolded, they would be unlikely to offer any presumption of deference towards a Republican president's nominees.

More significant, however, was the growing trend towards divided party government at the close of the 20th century. Republican Presidents Richard Nixon, Gerald Ford and George H.W. Bush faced a Democrat-controlled Senate for the entirety of their respective presidencies; Ronald Reagan and George W. Bush faced an opposition Senate for a substantial portion of their own presidencies as well. In fact, only a third of the 18 nominations made by those five Republican presidents (O'Connor, Scalia, Rehnquist as chief justice, Roberts, Miers and Alito) actually went before a Senate held by the president's own party. By contrast, all 24 Supreme Court nominations made by Democratic Presidents during the 20th Century were greeted by a Democratically controlled Senate (and only two of those nominations failed: Fortas, and the nominee for Fortas's seat, Homer Thornberry).

Clearly the Supreme Court confirmation process of the modern era has been shaped by a form of partisan conflict that was not present during the first part of the 20th century. This in turn has invited an influx of interest groups and more intense media attention in the process. Throw in the introduction of live televised hearings, and the media circus that has surrounded almost all recent confirmation hearings was perhaps inevitable. A larger question, however, still remained: How would nominees navigate this over-politicized confirmation process to increase their prospects for confirmation?

5. SENATE HEARINGS AS "SHOW BUSINESS": THE MODERN-DAY CONFIRMATION CHARADE

What developed during the 1980s and 1990s was an elaborate confirmation process marked by a delicate nominee dance intended to temper the opposition without sending up red flags of concern among their more natural sources of support. The only exception to this routine occurred with Robert Bork's confirmation hearings in 1987, when the nominee showed unusual amounts of candor in going down to defeat.

Sandra Day O'Connor's confirmation hearings in 1981 were the first to be televised. The importance of this development cannot be overstated: As a medium, television tends to "drown out" traditional channels of political communication that the political parties have relied on in the past to maintain their support (Shogan, 1996, p. 96). When a nomination is controversial, supporters and opponents will vie for control of the issues and images that characterize that nomination; still, televised confirmation hearings offer the public an unmatched opportunity to evaluate the claims and counterclaims that have been made about the nomination by others (Watson & Stookey, 1995, p. 134). Thus television has effectively made Senate confirmation hearings the primary focus of attention. Accordingly, Senators have become more reluctant to declare their position one way or the other before the hearings concluded, lest they appear to have prejudged the nominee only to be embarrassed by new discoveries at the hearings themselves.

O'Connor's nomination also featured interest groups establishing themselves as permanent features of the process, regardless of whether the nomination is controversial or even in doubt. In the past, only two nominations (Clement Haynsworth's in 1969 and William Rehnquist's in 1971) had featured testimony from more than 10 organizations; those two nominations proved controversial enough in turn to result in 45 and 26 votes, respectively, lodged by Senators against those two candidates. By contrast, a record number of organizations (15) testified at the O'Connor hearings despite the lack of any real drama from the outset over whether she would ultimately be confirmed.

Facing Senators more determined to use televised confirmation hearings to "educate" the public about issues, as well as to evaluate the nominee herself, O'Connor was also among the first nominees to stymie them by refusing to respond even in general terms to Senators' questions about issues that might come before the court. She thus offered a preview of the so-called impartiality defense that would eventually prove so difficult for the opposition to puncture. O'Connor's experience as a nominee thus paved the way for candidates to successfully navigate this more "open" era of confirmations. The real battle over a nominee's ideology would be fought not in the confirmation hearings themselves, but in private meetings between the President's advisors and party constituencies. Once O'Connor's strategy succeeded, no level of obfuscation might be deemed unacceptable for a nominee to the Supreme Court.

O'Connor was no doubt apprised by insiders of the last-minute hesitations about her candidacy that had been expressed among White House officials concerned with her views on abortion. In her original interviews with White House aides and President Reagan himself, O'Connor had emphasized her belief that abortion was a legitimate subject for legislative action, and confirmed that as an Arizona state senator she had even sponsored a pro-life bill. However, just prior to President Reagan's July 7, 1981, announcement of her nomination, Attorney General William French Smith dispatched aide Kenneth Starr to telephone O'Connor once last time to investigate her abortion record a bit further. O'Connor told Starr by phone that her record was for the most part silent on abortion: as a judge she had never ruled on the abortion issue, and she had never been an outspoken advocate on behalf of either pro-life or abortion rights organizations (Yalof, 1999, pp. 140–141). Those statements offered Smith enough reassurance so that he could safely recommend that O'Connor's nomination go forward. Based on what Starr learned, the President could defend his selection to Senator Helms and other conservatives skeptical of O'Connor, without fear of a smoking gun arising later in the process.

Testifying before the Senate Judiciary Committee, O'Connor proclaimed to Senators that "[A] statement by me as to how I might resolve a particular issue or what I might do in a future Court action might make it necessary for me to disqualify myself on the matter" (Comiskey, 2004, p. 40). By invoking these concerns of impartiality, O'Connor successfully ducked questions Senators asked her about abortion, affirmative action and the exclusionary rule. All in all, she more than earned her description as "one of the least forthcoming of modern nominees" (Comiskey, 2004, p. 39). Still, she was approved unanimously by all 99 Senators present at her confirmation vote. As a nominee O'Connor found comfortable refuge for her candidacy: skeptical Republican Senators did not want to embarrass President Reagan so early in his presidency with Republican infighting made public. Meanwhile, Senate Democrats considering opposing her candidacy took seriously the warning of party leaders that with Ronald Reagan as president, a moderate like O'Connor was probably the best nominee they could hope for.

O'Connor's unanimous Senate confirmation victory laid the groundwork for future nominees to similarly resort to polite and courteous refusals in response to any questions that might cause even the slightest trouble from opposition or supporters alike. Among all the "artful dodges" documented by scholar Michael Comiskey, none has proven more effective than the "impartiality dodge" because the norm of judicial impartiality is so well-entrenched and powerful that Senators are reluctant to defeat it (Comiskey, 1993, p. 497). At the same time, subsequent nominees did not have the benefit of going before the Senate during Ronald Reagan's honeymoon period as president; some might also be considered more ideological extremist at the outset. Finally, the Senate would not remain Republican forever. Would O'Connor's "impartiality defense" work when the conditions surrounding a nomination were not nearly so favorable?

President Reagan's next opportunity to fill the bench did not come until five years later, when Chief Justice Warren Burger alerted White House officials of his intention to retire at the close of the court's term in 1986. President Reagan's selection of Associate Justice William Rehnquist for the vacant chief justiceship and Judge Antonin Scalia for Rehnquist's associate justice seat offered up two more hard-line conservatives for the Senate's consideration, albeit before a Senate still controlled by the Republicans. And yet the fierce ideological debate over the future of the Court that many on both sides of the aisle were anticipating never actually emerged. Democratic Senators opposed to Rehnquist focused on criticisms unrelated to his service on the court, reviving two principle allegations against him: (1) that as a Republican party poll-watcher in Arizona in the 1960s, he had attempted to discourage minorities from voting; and (2) that as a law clerk to Justice Robert Jackson, he had authored a memo arguing against federal desegregation under the 14th Amendment in *Brown v. Board of Education*. To these allegations, Senator Edward Kennedy added the charge that Rehnquist owned property with a restrictive covenant forbidding sale to Jews.

The first two allegations had been raised in late 1971 when Rehnquist was a nominee for associate justice; his confirmation at that time by a 66-28 vote confirmed that while the charges perhaps had some merit, they were not substantial enough to scuttle his appointment. Fifteen years later these same charges had the same effect: Rehnquist was confirmed by a similar vote of 65-33.

This time, however, the allegations accomplished two other ends. Unlike in 1971, television cameras at his hearings ensured that Rehnquist would be called to account publicly for his many written opinions as a Supreme Court justice, as well as for the thousand-plus votes he cast in his 14-plus years on the Court. Yet by raising these other allegations, Democratic Senators essentially drained away the time Rehnquist might have been otherwise forced to use ducking Senators' questions about these more substantive matters. Given that opposition to Rehnquist emerged mostly from liberal Democrats, the real beef with Rehnquist was certainly ideological; still, media coverage of his confirmation hearings tended to focus on these allegations from before his time on the Court.

A second byproduct of the focus on Rehnquist's earlier foibles was that it sucked up all of the oxygen in the room for contesting Scalia as well. Little time was left for a more intense analysis of the nominee for associate justice. Just 50 years old, Scalia would be in a position to cast his conservative vote much farther into the future than would Rehnquist, 12 years his senior. To be sure, Scalia already benefited from a record on the D.C. Circuit dominated more by complex administrative law precedents than by cases invoking hot-button issues such as concerning abortion, school prayer or affirmative action. All of these factors combined to make Scalia's confirmation a fait accompli, with or without a Republican-controlled Senate.

Yet Scalia went a step further, taking a page from O'Connor's strategy of issue avoidance and obfuscation. Holding firmly to the view that discussion of any live controversy risks "prejudicing future litigants," Scalia employed an especially broad definition of "live controversy" to shield himself from almost all of the Senators' substantive inquiries. At one point he went so far as to fend off questions about as fundamental a decision as *Marbury v. Madison*, the 183-year old precedent that had served as a basis for judicial review for the better part of two centuries:

> As I say, *Marbury v. Madison* is one of the pillars of the Constitution. To the extent that you think a nominee would be so foolish, or so extreme as to kick over one of the pillars of the Constitution, I suppose you should not confirm him. But I do not think I should answer questions regarding any specific Supreme Court opinion, even one as fundamental as *Marbury v. Madison*. (Hearings on the Nomination of Scalia, 1986, p. 33)

If Scalia eventually came to recognize the virtues of a confirmation plebiscite, there was little evidence of that position at work during his own confirmation hearings in 1986.

Robert Bork's nomination in 1987 before Senate Judiciary Committee that was now under Democratic control proved to be a watershed for Supreme Court appointments in terms of interest group involvement and media attention (Maltese, 1995, p. 7). It also offered a rare glimpse into a Supreme Court nominee's future views on the great legal issues of the day. During a record-breaking five days of nominee testimony which began on a

Tuesday afternoon and extended into a rare Saturday Judiciary Committee session, Bork waxed eloquent on his controversial views of free speech (he had authored an article indicating the First Amendment extends to political speech only), privacy (he opposed *Roe v. Wade*) and various other issues. Bork began his testimony with a statement that seemed innocent at first, but which proved to be provocative:

> My philosophy of judging ... is neither liberal nor conservative. It is simply a philosophy of judging which gives the Constitution a full and fair interpretation but, where the Constitution is silent, leaves the policy struggles to the states, and to the American people. (Hearings on the Nomination of Bork, 1987, pt. 1, p. 105)

Yet for Bork, liberty did not just mean freedom from tyranny – it also meant the right of the majority to set society's course. This notion was controversial enough. But on this point, the former Yale Law Professor was prepared to take his old legal seminar at Yale University to the U.S. Senate – and he hoped – to the public as a whole.

Certainly a drawn-out constitutional discussion offered the closest approximation to a plebiscite that's been achieved in the recent history of Supreme Court confirmation proceedings. By engaging frankly at times on the most controversial issues, Bork allowed his own hearings to invite an expression of the people's will on the Constitution and the Bill of Rights. Naturally, the vibrancy of democracy in this instance did not always align with the interests of ideological conservatives, including those within the Reagan Administration's own Justice Department who viewed Bork as the key piece in a strategy to revolutionize the state of constitutional law. Interest groups had painted Bork as a frightening individual prepared to turn back the clock on numerous social issues; to be confirmed, Bork's would have to reassure the public. His strident and lengthy statements during his first few days of testimony proved reassuring only to the arch conservatives who needed no reassuring. Realizing his troubles were mounting, Bork began to step back in his final two days of testimony, leading to accusations from Senator Patrick Leahy and others that he was engaging in a form of "confirmation conversion."

Perhaps the single most important theme that ran through all of Bork's statements at the hearings – and which proved most significant in his eventual undoing – concerned the issue of when and how to overturn precedent. On the afternoon of the fourth day of testimony, Senator Edward Kennedy played a tape of a speech Bork gave in 1985 indicating that he didn't think "that in the field of Constitutional law precedent is all that important." Bork did little to explain the comment other than to term it an "off-the-cuff" reply after a dinner speech. When Bork subsequently demurred on whether *Griswold* should be overturned on the ground that "it would be inappropriate to comment," the damage was already done.

Robert Bork had called the prospect of serving on the Supreme Court an "intellectual feast" and had engaged Senators in Constitutional debates far beyond any other modern Supreme Court nominee. Yet just a few weeks later his nomination was rejected by the full Senate on a 58-42 count, as opposition Senators had more than enough of Bork's own testimony to make their case against him. A highly credentialed nominee has been stopped not because of any troubling political issue in his background, but because the prospect of his future rulings were deemed outside of the judicial mainstream.

Bork's performance went a long way towards addressing the disconnect that had developed between the confirmation process and the public. Not only did Bork spend five days on television; his face was also on the "cover of every major American publication," giving him "just the right mixture of notoriety and fame" (Bronner, 1989, p. 229). For the first time in a long time, politicians had an idea of exactly what type of nominee could be defeated on strictly ideological grounds. Bork's restrictive views went beyond those deemed acceptable by the "national governing majority," and thus could not be ignored by Senators ultimately responsible to the public will. Social conservatives who had supported Ronald Reagan's ascension to office were not prepared to defer their own ideological objectives – they viewed the result as one explained more by poor confirmation strategies and by a candidate who had been effectively demonized.

In response to the Bork fiasco, Presidents Reagan (and later) George H.W. Bush did what conservatives hoped they would not: they ultimately rewarded the national governing majority with nominees of less certain conservative credentials. The next two nominees who actually went before the Senate Judiciary Committee helped their own cause by specifically distancing themselves from Bork's most provocative statements. Judge Anthony Kennedy and David Souter each confirmed that the Constitution's references to liberty included protection of the value of privacy. Both spoke of the capacity of the Constitution to grow with the times. Kennedy, whose own testimony came less than two months after Bork's, was even willing to specifically distance himself from Bork's views on free speech, offering a broader view of free speech to include non-political subjects. But neither was willing to go into any specifics. Kennedy was confirmed 97-0; Souter was similarly confirmed with only modest dissent by a 90-9 score.

Neither Kennedy nor Souter had any writings or other controversial materials in their background that offered the possibility of harsh questioning; if anything, Souter's background offered more red flags for conservatives than liberals. Clarence Thomas, by comparison, was a well-known figure in Washington D.C. based on his service as head of the EEOC during the Reagan Administration. When President George W. Bush named the former EEOC head to a D.C. Circuit vacancy in 1989, most Senators correctly assumed that he was being groomed for a future seat on the Supreme Court, possibly as a successor to Thurgood Marshall, the first African-American named to the Court. With a background spent more in politics than on the bench or a law school faculty, liberal Senators hoped for the opportunity to engage a Supreme Court nominee on the issues once again – their first opportunity since Bork.

The Thomas nomination is remembered primarily for the high drama of seeing a witness and his accuser face off under oath. Accused of sexual harassment after the first phase of his confirmation hearings had concluded, Thomas and his accuser, former EEOC employee (and now law professor) Anita Hill, captivated the nation in a second set of hearings focusing on Hill's accusations about Thomas. Debates over sex and the workplace could be heard in subsequent days around water coolers in offices around the country. The Supreme Court confirmation process thus produced a plebiscite after all – though not one focused on major constitutional issues. The comedy-variety show *Saturday Night Live* had a field day parodying the all-white male Judiciary Committee awkwardly questioning Thomas and his female accuser.

Somewhat lost, however, was the first phase of hearings, when Thomas had been so unwilling to engage Senators on substantive issues. Thomas literally ran away from his record at those initial hearings, disavowing prior statements on property rights, natural law and affirmative action. Thomas also distinguished positions he took as a policy advocate working for the Reagan administration from positions he might take as a justice, a distinction that would make him a blank slate. In his most memorable exchange with a Senator prior to Anita Hill's charges coming to light, Thomas denied to Senator Patrick Leahy ever expressing an opinion on *Roe v. Wade*, and he further implied that he had not thought much about that case (Hearings on the Nomination of Thomas, 1991, pt 1, pp. 222–223). Many Senators who voted against Thomas questioned Thomas' honesty at those first hearings; even some who eventually voted for Thomas, like Sen. Arlen Specter (R.-Pa.) told the nominee he thought his testimony was irreconcilable with his previous statements.

Yet a vast majority of Republican Senators and a handful of Democratic Senators were still willing to support Thomas's nomination because – given the limitations of the Senate Judiciary committee's format – there was no clear-cut way to challenge these perceived discrepancies. Some of these limitations were driven home during the second set of hearings, when Anita Hill came before the Senate to allege sexual harassment. Senator Hank Brown (R.-Col.), while probing Hill for possible political motives, asked her whether she disagreed with Thomas on abortion (Hearings on the Nomination of Thomas, 1991, Pt. 4, p. 133). Allowing Hill to answer that question would have impeached Thomas's earlier testimony that he never expressed an opinion to anyone about abortion. Senate Committee Chairman Joseph Biden cut off Brown's line of questioning immediately, reminding his colleague that the discussion was veering away from the issue of sexual harassment. Not even Senate Democrats on the Judiciary Committee were willing to transform the committee proceedings into a trial on perjury.

After the first set of hearings, Thomas appeared to have a slight majority for confirmation, and the sexual harassment charges that followed ultimately changed few votes: he was eventually confirmed by a 52-48 vote. Even more significant than the vote was the precedent it set: If a nominee chose the path of obfuscation by disavowing all previous statements, but then hid behind the impartiality defense to avoid offering any new positions, the path to confirmation would remain open. More important, if a Supreme Court nominee could navigate the somewhat treacherous path to get to the confirmation hearings themselves (all but two nominees since 1969 have successfully done so) it would be hard (although not impossible) to defeat them.

The hyper politicized confirmation process of the late 1980s and early 1990s began with presidents willing to stake their administration's capital on ideological nominees, even if it meant confronting an opposition Senate equally prepared to engage the nominee on substantive terms. Neither of those two forces were present in the case of President Bill Clinton's two Supreme Court nominees, Ruth Bader Ginsburg and Steven Breyer. Both were considered moderate liberals by Senator Orrin Hatch (R.-Utah) and other Senators who essentially "pre-screened" their nominations for the Clinton White House. Given this level of bipartisan consultation, each of their confirmations was quickly deemed a "fait accompli," as neither suffered as many as 10 negative Senate votes against them.

As president, Bill Clinton was more focused on health care and his domestic agenda; accordingly, his two nominations offered a calm amid the storm. Both Breyer and Ginsburg confessed support for protecting a right to privacy under the Fourteenth Amendment, as Kennedy, Souter and Thomas had done before them. Yet it was Ginsburg who coined the phrase at her own hearing to sum up the impartiality strategy: "No hints, no forecasts, no previews." In practice, no constitutional debate would be forthcoming so long as the issues in question remained potentially live matters. It was a standard that allowed nominees to keep the national governing majority at arm's length in the process.

6. A PUBLIC LEFT BEHIND: THE CONFIRMATION PROCESS AT THE START OF THE 21st CENTURY

Public confirmation proceedings for significant presidential appointees are a recent phenomenon. The standing rules of the Senate were not even modified to require public confirmation proceedings until 1975. Meanwhile, C-Span cameras can now be found at every set of congressional hearings that hold even the slightest potential for public interest. The proliferation of Internet publications (including blogs) and 24-hour cable television news channels has led to wall-to-wall coverage of every aspect of the legislative process, inviting interested citizens into a world formally reserved only for those who could visit the capital personally.

Reacting to the demands of this new, highly transparent television age, Senators have been forced to take appointment politics far more seriously; accordingly, they have significantly increased their opposition to all high-level political nominations. Unlike past presidents who enjoyed nearly absolute deference to appoint executive branch officials of their choosing, presidents since Lyndon Johnson have witnessed at least one in 10 of their Cabinet-level appointments seriously opposed by the Senate (Gerhardt, 2000, p. 168). Naturally, confirmation hearings for executive appointments have become the primary site for confrontational politics. George H. W. Bush's nomination of Senator John Tower in 1989 to serve as Secretary of Defense was effectively doomed when information about the nominee's personal foibles not found in his FBI file nevertheless came to light at his confirmation hearings (Tower's nomination was rejected by a 53-47 vote). Clinton's first nominee for Attorney General, Zoe Baird, saw her nomination run aground when she could not handle Senators' questions about her failure to pay taxes for domestic help.

Even successfully confirmed executive branch appointments must undergo intense Senate interrogation in the modern television age, lest Senators appear to be giving the President a free ride. A refusal to respond to Senators' questions in this context may scuttle otherwise secure nominations. Thus when President George W. Bush nominated the controversial former Senator John Ashcroft to be his first Attorney General in 2001, Ashcroft was compelled to stake positions on *Roe v. Wade* and other issues. Despite his personal views, Ashcroft confessed that the case was the "settled law of the land" and "as attorney general I don't think it could be my agenda" to overturn it. Ashcroft was confirmed by a 58-42 vote; would his nomination have survived if he had refused to answer the Senators' questions? More recently, Senators probed Secretary of Defense-designate Robert Gates at his 2006 hearings concerning whether he thought the U.S. military was winning the war in Iraq; Gates responded "no, sir," but then allowed that he didn't think the military was losing the war either. At least Gates was willing to contribute something to the public dialogue. Ducking hard questions is rarely a winning strategy in executive branch appointment politics.

Unfortunately, the process of confirming Supreme Court nominees, while equally accessible to the public, rarely offers significant insights into the views or judging philosophy of future Justices. Far from it, the process has become an exercise in obfuscation, as nominees search for that all-purpose cocoon which protects them from having to defend previous views that might now be deemed controversial, while at the same time excusing them from offering any more current views on the great issues of the day.

President George W. Bush's election as president offered an important opportunity for substantive public debate on conservative issues before the Court. Each of his two presidential election victories – close as they were – carried with them Republican control of both Houses of Congress. When the president announced his first nominations for the federal bench in early 2001, he declared: "Every judge I appoint will be a person who clearly understands the role of a judge is to interpret the law, not legislate from the bench." With Republicans in control of every branch of government, perhaps the ducking and weaving strategy employed by past judicial nominees would no longer be necessary.

Yet as it turned out, Republican dominance of the federal government proved fleeting. That party's narrow control of the Senate, already hanging on by a slim thread in early 2001, was lost when Senator James Jeffords of Vermont defected from the Republican Party and agreed to caucus with the Democrats to give them control. Although Republicans regained control of both legislative houses in 2002, they soon found their Republican majorities threatened once again by the war issue early during President George W. Bush's second term.

During President Bush's first term, Senate Democrats served notice that there might be yet another tool at their disposal to undermine even those nominations that enjoyed the support of a narrow Senate majority: the filibuster. Senators had only rarely deployed filibusters in earlier judicial appointment wars. Most notably, in 1968 Lyndon Johnson withdrew Justice Abe Fortas's bid for promotion to chief justice of the United States after a vote to invoke cloture failed by a 45-43 vote. Employed so rarely against nominations of any kind, the filibuster quickly became a lightning rod for controversy in the battle to confirm President Bush's lower court nominees. During the spring of 2003, Senate Republicans tried to put the administration's more controversial nominees up for a vote on the Senate floor, only to run up against the filibuster, which required 60 votes to end debate through cloture. All Republican attempts to invoke cloture were easily defeated by the votes of 45 of the 48 Senate Democrats. Unable to break the logjam, Frist and the Senate Republican leadership began to consider more drastic solutions to the problem – namely, a Senate rules change to prevent endless filibusters on judicial nominations. Frist and his colleagues were not just thinking about lower court nominations; they feared that by allowing the tactic to work now, a precedent would be set for its use against Supreme Court nominations as well.

President Bush did not have the opportunity to fill a Supreme Court vacancy during his first term in office, when his popularity was at its peak. In fact, over a decade passed between Breyer's 1994 appointment and Sandra Day O'Connor's June 2005 announcement that she intended to retire from the Court. Though bolstered by Republican majorities in 2005, his administration labored to navigate a challenging political environment, punctuated by the flawed handling of Hurricane Katrina and the rising death toll in Iraq. With the news of Chief Justice Rehnquist's death on September 3, 2005, President Bush was afforded the opportunity to transform the Supreme Court from the top down. Would the debate over the administration's Supreme Court nominees offer the opportunity to determine whether they would in fact "interpret the law" rather than "legislate from the bench"? Would there be a larger debate over the Court's role in addressing abortion, free speech, affirmative action and other great legal issues? Or would these nominees be allowed to hunker down into the same defensive stance that had offered little new information for public debate?

If confirmation obfuscation remained the operating principle, John Roberts was the ideal conservative nominee to implement it in hearings to consider his nomination as chief justice. A court of appeals judge for just two years, Roberts' reputation as a formidable legal mind had been cultivated first in the Reagan administration's Justice Department, later in the Solicitor General's Office, and then eventually as a top-flight litigator in private practice. Other Reagan administration attorneys could vouch for Roberts' conservatism, but there was only a slim judicial paper trail for his questioners to pounce on. When attacked for positions he took as head of the EEOC, Clarence Thomas had successfully argued that as a member of the administration, he was responsible for advocating administration policy. Roberts could rely on a similar defense for any of the memos he wrote to other Justice Department officials during the 1980s, including those advocating conservative positions on social issues such as abortion.

The Roberts hearings began with the nominee's declaration that he approached the law with no agenda or platform; rather, he was like umpire in a baseball game: "My job is to call balls and strikes, not pitch or bat." With that warning issued, Roberts deftly quoted Ruth Bader Ginsburg's rule of thumb for nominees: "No hints, forecast, previews." Indeed, he repeated that guideline no less than 10 times during the first day of testimony alone. Ginsburg had used the rule to avoid uncomfortable questions about live issues; Roberts used it to fend off questions about almost any specific precedent, past or present. The nominee conceded that the 14th Amendment encompassed a right to privacy, but couched that with the qualification that "every current justice" also takes that position, lessening its impact. Under tough questioning from Senator Joseph Biden, Roberts invoked the "no hints, forecasts or previews" guideline to avoid commentary on past privacy precedents. Only reluctantly did Roberts indicate agreement with *Moore v. City of East Cleveland*, a 1969 Supreme Court opinion protecting the right of a grandmother to live with her two grandsons from different parts of her family. Considerable effort was spent debating Roberts over whether he was being more or less forthcoming than Ginsburg. Roberts remained unflappable throughout the hearings, though little new information was learned. Given the partisan tenor of the times, Roberts' 78-22 confirmation vote for chief justice could only be deemed a political non-event.

With Roberts' nomination secure, President Bush turned on October 3, 2005, to his own White House Counsel, Harriet Miers, as a replacement for O'Connor. Miers was a political novice in Washington, and was in fact little known outside of her hometown of Dallas, where she had risen to the leadership ranks of the local and state bar associations, as well as serving on the city council. Miers' positions on social issues were unknown, and conservatives were troubled by that fact. Christian fundamentalists may have been encouraged that Miers was a devout evangelical protestant, but would her religious faith influence her jurisprudence? As she had written no judicial opinions and held no high executive office where important decisions were made, there was no way to tell. Her pending Senate confirmations hearings offered both conservative and liberal Senators an opportunity to probe her views on these issues, and the Senate leadership made clear that the nominee could not duck those issues as Roberts had.

Rather than subject herself to the kind of open-ended confirmation process that might embarrass the administration, Miers formally withdrew her nomination twenty-four days after it was forwarded to the Senate. Certainly this move satisfied conservative critics such as Pat Buchanan, George Will and Robert Bork, each of whom complained that Miers' nomination was tantamount to political cronyism, as she lacked the judicial experience of so many other candidates. From the point of view of the White House, her withdrawal accomplished a far more important goal: it short-circuited a broad ranging debate on issues before the Supreme Court that would occupy the administration's attention for weeks, and which would likely result in an embarrassing defeat.

The subsequent nomination of Judge Samuel Alito to be associate justice presented an altogether different set of challenges. With over a decade of service on the U.S. Court of Appeals for the Third Circuit, Alito was the opposite of Miers on paper: as a judge he had specifically weighed in on abortion and the Establishment Clause, among other hot-button issues. Alito's 1984 job application to the Reagan Administration's Justice Department professed his commitment to overturn *Roe*, which could be a source of discussion as well. But those who prepared Alito for his hearings had the Roberts hearings fresh in their mind. Before the Senate Judiciary Committee, Alito made frequent reference to the importance of engaging in the "judicial process" to decide questions. Like Roberts he refused to engage in analysis on any past precedents. As for his controversial job application, Alito reminded Democratic Senators that it was written more than two decades earlier, and that he would have to look at *Roe v. Wade* and all other precedents with an open mind if they ever came before the Court. The combination of conservative jurisprudence and forthright statements in his job application convinced many Democratic Senators that Alito would be a conservative judge in the mold of Scalia and Thomas. But the confirmation hearings gave away nothing, whether to the Senators or to the public. Alito was confirmed much more narrowly than Roberts, by a 58-42 vote. Despite the unwillingness to engage on issues, Alito's confirmation – bolstered by his own obfuscation tactics – was never really in doubt.

7. CONCLUSION

The nominations of Samuel Alito and John Roberts to the United States Supreme Court promised to advance the conservative agenda on the High Court as it was defined by President George W. Bush during the course of two successful presidential campaigns, and then as rearticulated by the president when he announced the nominations during the summer and autumn of 2005. Among other objectives, President Bush hoped their respective appointments would bring "judicial modesty" to the bench, helping to return such issues as abortion and school prayer to the proper control of state and local legislatures. Even more important, he hoped they would offer a more expansive view of the constitution's conception of executive power, hoping it would afford his office greater discretion in prosecuting his administration's war on terrorism. The Senate confirmation hearings for President Bush's two nominees offered the potential for a rich and substantive debate on these and other issues before the public. Unfortunately, the confirmation hearings for each nominee produced instead a game of stealth, with each man carefully avoiding taking a position on any issues deemed important enough to matter.

The public's access to confirmation hearings in the modern era has provided a unique (if somewhat infrequent) opportunity to foster a true dialogue about the Court and its role in our democracy. This type of dialogue is warranted by the intense stakes nearly all Supreme Court appointments have assumed in the modern era. If the Supreme Court served as the "brake" on the body politic during the late 19th and early 20th centuries, by the middle of the 20th century it had become the accelerator pedal. With that shifting role came accusations that the Warren Court in particular had become a "super legislature," relying on judicial activism to issue rulings not justified by text, history or logic. Social conservatives speak of returning the Court its more traditional conservative moorings.

Unfortunately, whatever educational moment might have been available has so far been lost amid a charade of obfuscation by Supreme Court nominees, aided and abetted by Senators from both sides of the political aisle who do not hold nominees accountable for their opinions. Lost in the process is the bond that links future justices to the entire body politic, rather than just to their appointing presidents and their partisan stalwarts.

NOTES

1. In one 2003 poll, 60% were able to comment positively or negatively about Clarence Thomas, as compared to 39% who said they had "not heard enough about him" to comment either way. By contrast, 43% said they had not heard enough to comment about Sandra Day O'Connor, the first female justice in the history of the Supreme Court, and 46% said they had not heard enough to comment about Chief Justice Rehnquist. Meanwhile, these three individuals had incredibly high name recognition as compared to Justice David Souter (68% said they had not heard enough to comment), Justice John Paul Stevens (74%) and Justice Steven Breyer (75%) (*Survey by Quinnipiac University Polling Institute*, February 26–March 3, 2003. Retrieved April 18, 2007 from the iPOLL Databank, The Roper Center for Public Opinion Research, University of Connecticut).

ACKNOWLEDGMENTS

This chapter benefited immensely from the contributions of two individuals who I seem to come back to again and again for advice and good counsel whenever I embark on a work of scholarship on law and courts matters: Patrick D. Schmidt and Joel B. Grossman. Special thanks as well to the anonymous reviewers who made excellent suggestions to improve this chapter, as well as to the editor of this volume, Austin Sarat, who showed endless patience with me as I labored to improve my argument.

REFERENCES

Bell, L. (2002). *Warring factions: Interest groups, money, and the new politics of Senate confirmation.* Columbus: Ohio State University Press.

Blasi, V. (1983). *The Burger Court: The counterrevolution that wasn't.* New Haven: Yale University Press.

Bronner, E. (1989). *Battle for justice: How the Bork nomination shook America.* New York: W.W. Norton.

Burbank, S. (2002). Politics, privilege and power: The Senate's role in the appointment of federal judges. *Judicature* (July–August), 28–33.

Carp, R., Manning, K., & Stidham, R. (2004). The decisionmaking behavior of George W. Bush's judicial appointees. *Judicature* (July—August), 20–28.

Carter, S. (1994). *The confirmation mess.* New York: Basic Books.

Casper, J. (1976). The Supreme Court and national policymaking. *American Political Science Review, 70*, 50–66.

Comiskey, M. (1993). Can the Senate examine the constitutional philosophies of Supreme Court nominees? *PS: Political Science and Politics, 26*, 495–500.

Comiskey, M. (2004). *Seeking justices: The judging of Supreme Court nominees.* Lawrence, Kansas: University Press of Kansas.

Dahl, R. (1957). Decision-making in a democracy: The Supreme Court as a national policy-maker. *Journal of Public Law, 6,* 279–295.

Danelski, D. (1987). Ideology as a ground for the rejection of the Bork nomination. *Northwestern University Law Review, 81,* 900–920.

Denning, B. (2002). The Judicial Confirmation Process and the Blue Slip. *Judicature* (March–April), 220–222.

Funston, R. (1975). The Supreme Court and critical elections. *American Political Science Review, 69,* 795–811.

Gerhardt, M. (2000). *The federal appointment process.* Durham, NC: Duke University Press.

Gillman, H. (2006). Party politics and constitutional change: The political origins of liberal judicial activism. In: R. Kahn & K. Kersch (Eds), *The Supreme Court & American political development* (pp. 138–168). Lawrence: University Press of Kansas.

Hearings on the Nomination of Antonin Scalia to be Associate Justice of the Supreme Court of the United States. United States Senate, 99th Congress, 2nd session, 1986.

Hearings on the Nomination of Clarence Thomas to be Associate Justice of the Supreme Court of the United States. United States Senate, 102nd Congress, 1st session, 1991.

Hearings on the Nomination of Robert H. Bork to be Associate Justice of the Supreme Court of the United States. United States Senate, 100th Congress, 1st Session, September 15–19, 21–23, 25, 28–30, 1987.

Lewis, N. (2003). Conservatives Furious Over Court's Decision. *New York Times,* June 27, p. 19.

Maltese, J. (1995). *The selling of Supreme Court nominees.* Baltimore: Johns Hopkins University Press.

Robertson, T. (2003). Historic ruling/U.S. reaction: Gays, lesbians praise decision; others compare it to *Roe v. Wade. The Boston Globe,* June 27, p. A28.

Schwartz, H. (1988). *Packing the courts: The conservative campaign to rewrite the constitution.* New York: Charles Scribner's Sons.

Shogan, R. (1996). The confirmation wars: How politicians, interest groups and the press shape the presidential appointment process. In: Twentieth Century Fund Task Force, obstacle course: The report of the Twentieth Century Fund Task Force on the presidential appointment process (pp. 87–218). New York: The Twentieth Century Fund Press.

Sulfridge, W. (1980). Ideology as a factor in Senate consideration of Supreme Court nominations. *Journal of Politics, 42,* 560–567.

Tushnet, M. (2006). The Supreme Court and the national political order: Collaboration and confrontation. In: R. Kahn & K. Kersch (Eds), *The Supreme Court & American political development* (pp. 117–137). Lawrence: University Press of Kansas.

Watson, G., & Stookey, J. (1988). The Supreme Court confirmation hearings: A view from the Senate. *Judicature, 71,* 186–196.

Watson, G., & Stookey, J. (1995). *Shaping America: The politics of Supreme Court appointments.* New York: Harper-Collins.

Wittes, B. (2006). *Confirmation warriors: Preserving independent courts in angry times.* Lanham, MD: Rowman & Littlefield.

Yalof, D. (1999). *Pursuit of Justices: Presidential politics and the selection of Supreme Court nominees.* Chicago: University of Chicago Press.

WHY DOES A MODERATE/ CONSERVATIVE SUPREME COURT IN A CONSERVATIVE AGE EXPAND GAY RIGHTS?: *LAWRENCE V. TEXAS* (2003) IN LEGAL AND POLITICAL TIME[☆]

Ronald Kahn

ABSTRACT

Legalists and social scientists have not been able to explain the expansion of gay rights in a conservative age because they refuse to respect the special qualities of judicial decision making. These qualities require the Supreme Court to look simultaneously at the past, present, and future, and, most importantly, to determine questions of individual rights through a consideration of how citizens are to live under a continuing rights regime. Unless scholars understand how and why Supreme Court decision making differs from that of more directly politically accountable institutions we can expect no greater success in explaining or predicting individual rights in the future.

☆ Research assistance was provided by Brian Holbrook, Oberlin '09.

Special Issue: Constitutional Politics in a Conservative Era
Studies in Law, Politics, and Society, Volume 44, 173–217
Copyright © 2008 by Emerald Group Publishing Limited
All rights of reproduction in any form reserved
ISSN: 1059-4337/doi:10.1016/S1059-4337(08)00806-5

INTRODUCTION

Why does a conservative/moderate Supreme Court in a conservative political age expand implied fundamental rights to sexual intimacy for gays and sustain the fundamental right of women to choose whether to have an abortion? One would expect the Supreme Court in the late 20th and 21st centuries to be quite conservative. Since 1969, when President Nixon named Warren Burger as Chief Justice, and 2005, when Republican President George Bush appointed Chief Justice Roberts, thirteen appointments have been made to the Supreme Court. Eleven of those appointees were made by Republican Presidents.[1]

The Supreme Court has not overturned any of the major individual rights cases from the progressive Warren Court era (1954–1969). Moreover, during the years under Chief Justice Warren Burger, 1969–1986, the Supreme Court expanded individual rights in significant ways. It decided that there was a right under the Constitution to abortion choice in *Roe v. Wade* (1973); that gender classifications under the law would be subject to heightened judicial scrutiny in *Craig v. Boren* (1976); and that race can be one factor among many in the admission of students to colleges and universities in *Regents of the University of California v. Bakke* (1978).

During the Rehnquist Court, the Supreme Court has reaffirmed the right to abortion choice in *Planned Parenthood of Southeastern Pennsylvania v. Casey* (1992)[2] and the principle that race can play a role in university admissions in *Grutter v. Bollinger* (2003). Even with the addition to the Court of Chief Justice Roberts and Justice Alito, the Supreme Court refused to say that race cannot be a factor in attempts by school boards to diversify public schools.[3] Most significantly, in *Lawrence v. Texas* (2003), the Supreme Court overturned *Bowers v. Hardwick* (1986) and extended the implied fundamental rights of privacy and personhood to homosexuals.

Moreover, the Supreme Court has reaffirmed and expanded implied fundamental rights and equal protection under the law during a period of dominance of social conservatives, evangelical Christians, and others, who view the protection of their definition of "family values" as a central mission of government. These social conservatives hoped that Republican appointees to the Supreme Court would roll back abortion rights, gay rights, affirmative action policies, and constitutional separation of church and state. However, in these doctrinal areas, the Supreme Court has either sustained doctrine in opposition to the core values of the base of the Republican Party, or actually has expanded rights in these doctrinal areas.

In the first section of this chapter, I argue that this conservative-moderate Supreme Court in a conservative age has expanded implied fundamental rights for gays and sustained the right of abortion choice because of the non-originalist justices' reliance on what I will call principled bi-directional Supreme Court decision making (PBD). The Court's decision making is principled because of the importance of rights and polity (institutional) principles; it is bi-directional because of the key relationship between the internal Court decision-making process and the social and political world outside the Court.

In the second section of this chapter, I explore why so many law school scholars, political scientists, and historians have failed to explain, much less predict, the expansion of implied fundamental rights by the Supreme Court in the late 20th and early 21st centuries. While focusing on Cass Sunstein's theory of judicial minimalism, I argue that because both law school scholars and social scientists seek to explain doctrinal change based on phenomena external to the Court, they fail to understand why a conservative Court in a conservative era expands implied fundamental rights; they fail to recognize that at the core of Supreme Court decision making is a mutual construction process, in which both internal institutional norms and principles and external phenomenon are central. Moreover, the external world important to the Court is not simply or primarily a concern about interest group and legal advocacy politics; it is a concern for lives as lived by citizens under a rights regime.

In the final section of the chapter, I explore the political effects of non-originalist Supreme Court justices' accepting PBD, and originalist justices rejecting it. I argue that PBD leads to a legal secularity, a form of objectivity that increases the relative autonomy of the Supreme Court from direct influence of politics. This objectivity also raises questions in the wider society about the legitimacy of the Supreme Court's power to define implied fundamental rights. This questioning of Court legitimacy has become a defining fissure in American politics and among constitutional scholars of quite different political stripes. However, even with the legitimacy of PBD becoming a key fissure in American politics, I argue that the Supreme Court has continued to be a motor for social change in this conservative age.

I conclude the chapter with a brief discussion of the implications of PBD with regard to how we should study the Supreme Court as an institution in a wider process of American political development. I argue that because of the unique qualities of Supreme Court decision making, as evidenced by the PBD, and the nature of what I call legal time, the Court, unlike more directly politically accountable institutions, like the Presidency, does not suffer from what Stephen Skowronek has called the waning of political time.[4]

Finally, the special qualities of Supreme Court decision making, when compared to decision making in more directly politically accountable institutions, explain why a moderate-conservative Supreme Court in a conservative political era expands implied fundamental rights and why in the future a Supreme Court in a liberal era will not simply be liberal in its decision making.[5] Moreover, because PBD take rights principles seriously, along with their social construction through application to the lives of our nation's citizens, we can understand that, although the Supreme Court is not democratic in formal process terms, it is expansive substantively, in policy terms, with regard to widening rights protections under the Constitution for minorities.[6]

PLANNED PARENTHOOD OF SOUTHEASTERN PENNSYLVANIA V. CASEY (1992) AND LAWRENCE V. TEXAS (2003): PRINCIPLED BI-DIRECTIONAL SUPREME COURT DECISION MAKING

We can witness the core elements of PBD and why implied fundamental rights have been sustained and expanded in a conservative political era through an analysis of *Planned Parenthood of Southeastern Pennsylvania v. Casey* (1992), the case in which the Supreme Court reaffirmed the right of abortion choice, and *Lawrence v. Texas* (2003), the case in which the Supreme Court overturned *Bowers v. Hardwick* (1986) and extended the implied fundamental rights of privacy and personhood to homosexuals. These include: (1) a determination of what rights principles are at issue in a case, and whether these principles have expanded or contracted over the decades; (2) a crucial social construction process, in which there is a consideration, through a process of analogy of what rights and social constructions should be made by the Court in the case before it, in light of previously defined rights and social constructions; (3) a linking of what might be called the "empirical" elements of past and present social constructions – that is the applications of rights principles to lives as lived by individuals – with "normative" visions of what constitutes justice as central to that right, through what I will call the "interpretive turn"(Kahn, 2006a, pp. 69–70).[7]

There also is a crucial fourth element in PBD, in which there is a consideration of polity principles by the justices, as to the role of the Court compared to more directly political venues, such as the legislative or executive branches of government, as to where constitutional choices should be made in the case before it. Of particular concern is whether the Supreme Court should act in response to periods of high levels of political controversy, interest group politics, or differences as evidenced by public opinion.

PBD is the means through which the Court applies polity (political institutional) and rights principles, in light of the lives of citizens as they have lived them under the privacy rights regime, as the complexity and the diversity of the nation's society, economy, and politics increase. Through a process of analogy, the Court considers whether a legal concept, such as liberty, should be extended to a group that heretofore had been denied such rights, as was the case in *Lawrence* with regard to gay rights.

It is important to note that the bi-directional mutual construction process may be viewed as a general and regular feature of Supreme Court decision making. However, the degree of bi-directionality and the range of the social construction process will differ by doctrinal area. For example, I would expect that there are more limits on the social construction process in First Amendment jurisprudence, in speech and religion cases, because of a concern among justices and constitutional scholars, for the development of universal principles, in which one religion is not treated differently than other religions and a speaker is not treated differently based on the content of her speech. Moreover, because the process is cumulative in each doctrinal area, one would expect the breadth and nature of the social construction process, as well as the degree of bi-directionality to be similar within a doctrinal area and different across doctrinal areas. For me it is counter-intuitive to the premise that the Court follows politics that the highest degree of social construction and bi-directionality occurs between the Supreme Court and the lives of gays as constructed by Rehnquist era Court. Moreover, it is significant that the difference between originalists and non-originalists (not simply between liberals and conservatives) on the Court is the dividing line as to how robust the social construction is to be.

Finally, viewing Supreme Court decision making as including rights and polity principles past and present, social constructions past and present, bi-directionality, through the process of analogy, will allow scholars to study how non-originalists and originalists in different Court eras define rights and polity principles and engage in the social construction process to make constitutional choices. Through such study we can see whether there is any built-in, cumulative aspect to Court decision making. In saying this I am not arguing that all rights decisions are necessarily progressive from prior rights definitions. I am suggesting that today's conservative non-originalists and today's originalists may be different in important ways from those of prior generations.

Planned Parenthood of Southeastern Pennsylvania v. Casey (1992)

In deciding whether *Roe* should be overturned, the *Casey* Court pinpoints the ways in which *Roe* differs from *Plessy* and *Lochner* with regard to its application of factors at the core of PBD: "Because neither the factual underpinnings of *Roe*'s central holding nor our understanding of it has changed (and because no other indication of weakened precedent has been shown), the Court could not pretend to be reexamining the prior law with any justification beyond a present doctrinal disposition to come out differently from the Court of 1973."[8]

The rights principles and the social constructions that link these principles to the lives of citizens not only made it difficult for the Court to overturn *Roe*; they also forced the Court to discuss the right of abortion choice in *Casey* as one of personhood, a far more expansive social construction than that of privacy. Women and their families had grown to rely on the existence of rights of abortion choice, and that reliance provided the Court additional reasons for its acceptance of the right of abortion choice as fundamental.[9] This expanded concept of personhood in *Casey* was a result of the mutual construction of legal precedents that increasingly recognized the active place of women in society, and rights principles that were extended as a reflection of that expanded role. It also is attributable to timing and the fading of vigorous critiques of substantive due process.[10]

In *Casey*, the Supreme Court realized that the factual underpinnings of the right of abortion choice were moving in the same direction as expanding interpretations of the right of privacy between 1973 and 1992. For this reason, the *Casey* Court concluded that if it were to overturn *Roe*, it could not be based on a determination by the Court that the rights at issue in *Roe* were no longer valid in light of the experiences of our nation's citizens. Moreover, to decide otherwise would be giving in to political pressure, a concession not in the institutional interests of the Court or the rule of law.

Lawrence v. Texas (2003)

When changes in society and in rights principles and doctrine are symbiotic, landmark cases will not be overruled; when social constructions in prior landmark cases are no longer tenable, landmark cases are ripe for serious modification or outright overturning.[11] The willingness of the Supreme Court in *Lawrence* to look at the expansion of rights of personhood since *Roe* and *Bowers'* failure to engage in PBD are the major reasons why that case was overturned in *Lawrence* (Kahn, 2006a, p. 72).

One can see the *Lawrence* Court saying that a major problem in *Bowers* was the Court's failure to engage in PBD when it argues that the *Bowers* Court erred by not looking at precedents. It treated the issue as whether one had a constitutional right to engage in a particular sexual act, when in fact broader rights were at stake. At the heart of *Bowers* was a question about individual rights – the same rights that had formed the basis for the privacy protections established in such cases as *Griswold v. Connecticut* (1965),[12] *Eisenstadt v. Baird* (1972),[13] and *Roe v. Wade* (1973).[14] When the *Lawrence* Court did engage in PBD, it did not simply overturn *Bowers*; it eviscerated it, rejecting many of its premises root and branch (Kahn, 2006a, p. 72).[15]

The Court emphasizes that the *Bowers* Court construed the issue too narrowly, as merely involving the right to engage in certain sexual conduct. "The laws involved in *Bowers* and here ... have more far-reaching consequences, touching upon the most private human conduct, sexual behavior, and in the most private of places, the home ... When sexuality finds overt expression in intimate conduct with another person, the conduct can be but one element in a personal bond that is more enduring. The liberty protected by the Constitution allows homosexual persons the right to make that choice."[16]

One also can see PBD in action when the *Lawrence* Court considers the validity of *Bowers* (1986) in light of two subsequent cases, *Casey* (1992) and *Romer v. Evans* (1996),[17] and finds that they "cast [the *Bowers*] holding into even more doubt."[18] "The foundations of *Bowers* have sustained serious erosion from our recent decisions in *Casey* and *Romer*. When our precedent has been thus weakened, criticism from other sources is of greater significance."[19] Because PBD is a continuing process, the *Casey* decision is especially significant. There is a shift in *Casey* toward recognition of abortion rights issues as involving the right of personhood, a far more forceful statement about liberty interests than the passive notion of privacy found in *Roe v. Wade* (1973). The *Lawrence* Court specifically refers to this critical social construction regarding the depth of women's right to abortion choice in *Casey*:

> These matters, involving the most intimate and personal choices a person may make in a lifetime, choices central to personal dignity and autonomy, are central to the

liberty protected by the Fourteenth Amendment. At the heart of liberty is the right to
define one's own concept of existence, of meaning, of the universe, and of the mystery of
human life. Beliefs about these matters could not define the attributes of personhood
were they formed under compulsion of the State.[20]

There is a specific reaffirmation in *Lawrence* of the *Casey* conditions
that must be present in order for the Court to overturn landmark
decisions (Kahn, 2006a, p. 77). These conditions required the
Lawrence Court to consider both substantive components (principles and
prior social constructions) of what privacy meant prior in *Bowers* and what
personhood meant in *Casey* as well as what "pure animus" meant in
Romer.[21]

One also sees PBD at work as the Court considers the continued validity
of *Bowers* in light of *Romer v. Evans* (1996). The *Lawrence* Court writes,
"*Romer* invalidated an amendment to Colorado's Constitution, which
named as a solitary class persons who were homosexuals, lesbians, or
bisexual either by 'orientation, conduct, practices or relationships,' "[22] and
noted that in *Romer* the Supreme Court had concluded that the amendment
violated the Equal Protection Clause because it was "born of animosity
toward the class of persons affected,"[23] The Court viewed the Colorado
amendment as based on pure animus.

As in *Casey*, the *Lawrence* Court had to consider what letting *Bowers*
stand would do to key institutional norms that inform the Court's
legitimacy. More specifically, the importance of PBD, in which rights
principles are applied in light of the lived of persons, can be seen in
Lawrence when the Court discusses why it does not simply follow the will of
the majority, as expressed by state legislatures or the history of majority
animus against homosexuals. In so doing, the Supreme Court draws on its
institutional norms that are quite distinct from those of political institutions.
We see this when the Court explains why it cannot simply make decisions on
a finding that there has been a moral condemnation of homosexual acts over
the years by a majority of citizens, or the state legislature. Justice Kennedy,
relying on *Casey*, notes that the Court's "obligation is to define the liberty of
all, not to mandate our own moral code."[24]

[T]he Court in *Bowers* was making the broader point that for centuries there have been
powerful voices to condemn homosexual conduct as immoral ... These considerations do
not answer the question before us, however. The issue is whether the majority may use
the power of the State to enforce these views on the whole society through operation of
the criminal law.[25]

Supreme Court decision making does not start and stop at the founding. "[H]istory and tradition are the starting point but not in all cases the ending point of the substantive due process inquiry."[26] It is through the lens of PBD, looking both backward and forward, that the Court articulates what liberty means. Through PBD, there is an application of concepts of emerging awareness, reliance, and workability, as used in *Casey*, becomes critical to understanding the *Lawrence* Court's decision to overturn *Bowers*. Reliance is defined at the level of individuals, rather than at the level of political institutions.

The Court directly confronts the important question of whether "the fact that the governing majority in a State has traditionally viewed a particular practice as immoral is sufficient reason for upholding a law prohibiting the practice."[27] In doing so, it affirms the importance of a continuous and continuing PBD when the Court interprets the Constitution.

> Had those who drew and ratified the Due Process Clauses of the Fifth Amendment or the Fourteenth Amendment known the components of liberty in its manifold possibilities, they might have been more specific. They did not presume to have this insight. They knew times can blind us to certain truths and later generations can see that laws once thought necessary and proper in fact serve only to oppress. As the Constitution endures, persons in every generation can invoke its principles in their own search for greater freedom.[28]

Justice O'Connor's *Lawrence* concurrence also features a robust PBD. O'Connor rejects traditional norms as a sufficient basis for disadvantaging groups of citizens: "Moral disapproval of a group cannot be a legitimate governmental interest under the Equal Protection Clause because legal classifications must not be 'drawn for the purpose of disadvantaging the group burdened by the law.' "[29] Moreover, O'Connor specifically alludes to the importance of the liberty interests at stake in the case: "We have been most likely to apply rational basis review to hold a law unconstitutional under the Equal Protection Clause where, as here, the challenged legislation inhibits personal relationships."[30]

Even though O'Connor wants a more toned down response to *Bowers*, one based on the Equal Protection Clause and the substantive elements in *Romer*, an analysis of her PBD reveals broad agreement with many of the majority's substantive conclusions.[31] There are far more similarities between O'Connor's views and the non-originalist Justices in the majority, than there are between O'Connor and the originalists in dissent.[32]

Fighting over the Legitimacy of Principled Bi-Directional Supreme Court Decision Making

The vehement opposition to the non-originalist PBD by Justice Scalia and the other originalists on the Court, Justices Thomas and Rehnquist, provides the most persuasive evidence for the importance of non-originalist PBD in contemporary Supreme Court decision making. It is quite clear that Justice Scalia here and in other cases is trying to stop PBD employed by non-originalists. It is also quite clear that Justice Scalia understands the political implications of engaging in PBD. For example, in *Romer*, Scalia predicted the broad outlines of expanded rights for gays that are found in the *Lawrence* decision. In *Romer*, he argued that if the Court engages in a decision-making process with the characteristics of what I have called PBD, then *Romer* and *Bowers* could not stand together – as they did not in *Lawrence*.[33] Nor are Scalia and the non-originalists simply discussing forms of argumentation, or syntax, as they advocate quite different processes of Supreme Court decision making.[34]

In *Lawrence*, Scalia continues to attack the conditions laid down in *Casey* under which the Supreme Court is to overturn landmark decisions,[35] the very same conditions that are at the core of PBD. Scalia's conception of history and tradition is in marked contrast to that of the Justices in the *Lawrence* majority. Scalia emphasizes that "fundamental rights" must be "so rooted in the traditions and conscience of our people as to be ranked as fundamental."[36] This is quite different from Kennedy's approach in *Lawrence*: "[H]istory and tradition are the starting point but not in all cases the ending point of the substantive due process inquiry."[37]

Thus, we see the bases for Scalia's opposition to the *Lawrence* Court's finding that there is "an emerging awareness that liberty gives substantial protection to adult persons in deciding how to conduct their private lives in matters pertaining to sex."[38] For him, an "emerging awareness" as defined by the non-originalists does not establish a "fundamental right" (Kahn, 2006a, p. 72). For Scalia, the continued presence of state laws against homosexual sodomy offer clear evidence that the protection of such acts is not "deeply rooted in the nation's history and traditions."[39]

Scalia recognizes that PBD is central to the *Lawrence* decision and its antecedents when he argues that one should not "believe" the *Lawrence* majority's disclaimer that its reasoning will not lead to legal recognition of same-sex marriage.[40] Scalia writes,

> If moral disapprobation of homosexual conduct is "no legitimate state interest" for purposes of proscribing that conduct; and if, as the Court coos (casting aside all pretense of neutrality) "[w]hen sexuality finds overt expression in intimate conduct with another person, the conduct can be but one element in a personal bond that is more enduring;" what justification could there possibly be for denying the benefits of marriage to homosexual couples exercising "[t]he liberty protected by the Constitution"?[41]

For Scalia, the *Lawrence* decision builds on an illegitimate social construction process which, if allowed to continue, will lead to a constitutional right to same-sex marriage. As in *Romer*, where Scalia predicted that *Bowers* and *Romer* could not stand together[42], Scalia is predicting here that, if the PBD that began in *Griswold* and persisted all the way through *Lawrence* is allowed to continue, establishing a right to same-sex marriage under the Constitution is just a matter of time.

Thus, Scalia's rejection of a robust PBD as central to his approach to interpreting the Constitution means that his notion of what constitutes the mandate of history and tradition is dramatically different from the non-originalists (Kahn, 2006a, p. 83). In rejecting the emerging awareness and reliance arguments used in *Casey* and *Lawrence* as simply result-oriented[43], Scalia opposes rights which evolve and are defined and redefined under non-originalist PBD. One sees this when he seeks the narrowest reading of the *Lawrence* decision, and refuses to admit that *Casey* expanded the basis of abortion choice from a right of privacy to personhood, and when he refuses to accept the view that a rule of law can include a changing definition by the Supreme Court of what constitutes liberty under the Constitution (Kahn, 2006a, pp. 83–84). Most importantly, he refuses to accept the *Lawrence* majority view that simple moral opposition is not sufficient justification for upholding a law under rational basis review.

Rejection of Political Contestation as a Basis for Determining Individual Rights

The Supreme Court sustains and expands individual rights, even gay rights, because, as explored above, majority and concurring Justices in *Casey* and *Lawrence* strongly reject political contestation and majoritarian opinion as reasons on which to decide implied fundamental rights cases. When the *Casey* and *Lawrence* Courts engaged in PBD, they considered whether the rights at issue in these cases, privacy and personhood, are still important and expanding and whether citizens have accepted these rights in their lives.

Non-originalist Justices accept the idea that because the Supreme Court is supposed to be a counter-majoritarian institution, it should not make constitutional choices on the same bases as more directly political accountable institutions.

For example, the *Casey* Court stresses that the politically controversial nature of *Plessy* and *Lochner* is what links these cases with *Roe*. The Court describes these cases as of "comparable dimension," because all three cases "responded to national controversies and take on the impress of the controversies addressed."[44] The Justices discuss overruling under conditions of "intensely divisive controversy," and find that when such cases are decided, there is a "dimension present whenever the Court's interpretation of the Constitution calls the contending sides of a national controversy to end their national division by accepting a common mandate rooted in the Constitution."[45] In such situations, the Court emphasizes that it must ensure that its decisions are not perceived as giving into political pressure if the Court wants to retain its legitimacy. Decisions must be "sufficiently plausible"; decisions viewed as "compromises with social and political pressures" lack plausibility because they are viewed as unprincipled, and place the Court in the position of being viewed simply as a political body, and thus illegitimate.[46] For non-originalists, PBD adds to the plausibility of their decisions, and thus to the Court's legitimacy as an institution which is called upon to follow the rule of law, not politics. The Court highlights its institutional legitimacy concerns, specifically at issue if it were to overturn *Roe*:

> Whether or not a new social consensus is developing on [the abortion] issue, its divisiveness is no less today than in 1973, and pressure to overrule the decision, like pressure to retain it, has grown only more intense. A decision to overrule *Roe*'s essential holding under the existing circumstances would address error, if error there was, at the cost of both profound and unnecessary damage to the Court's legitimacy, and to the Nation's commitment to the rule of law. It is therefore imperative to adhere to the essence of *Roe*'s original decision, and we do so today.[47]

Expanding Gay Rights in a Conservative Political Age

Understanding the key components of non-originalist Supreme Court decision making helps explain why a conservative Court in a conservative age chooses to expand the rights to abortion choice and homosexual privacy and personhood. The Supreme Court sustains the right of abortion choice and expands gay rights because of the institutional effects of the Supreme

Court accepting and engaging in PBD. PBD causes the Supreme Court to be simultaneously empirical and normative and inward and outward looking in its decision making. It results in the mutual construction of the internal and external through a process I will call the "interpretive turn."

The fact that PBD is both empirical and normative means that the Court must ask whether the acts of citizens or groups, compared to others who have such acts protected, in light of governing principles, such as equal protection and rights of privacy and personhood, should be given similar legal protections. It is empirical because justices engage in the application of legal concepts through a consideration of the day-in and day-out lives of citizens and classes of citizens, both those who have and those who have not been granted constitutional protections in the past. Social constructs are informed by adduced social "facts," but they are not the social facts themselves.[48] Social facts gain meaning in constitutional law cases through the process of social construction; they gain resonance in light of definitions of polity and rights principles, social constructions in prior decisions, and the lives of citizens.[49]

The process is also normative. The empirical only gains meaning through application of core evaluative standards derived from what justice, liberty, and equality have meant in the past and present, with a concern for what rights and justice might mean in the future. This was demonstrated in *Casey* and *Lawrence* when all Justices engaged in a decision-making process which was simultaneously normative and empirical. The fact that it is simultaneously empirical and normative means that justices must look at issues of gay rights in terms of questions of fairness and equality.

Supreme Court decision making has a second important quality; it is simultaneously internal ("inward looking") and external ("outward looking"). Internal influences are such things as (1) the "law itself" (whether in the form of the Constitution, statutes, or settled legal doctrine in the form of precedent) and (2) "judicial norms and procedures" – including "the norm that judges be apolitical, a norm reinforced by the requirement that judges craft their legal rulings according to a 'legal grammar' in which some forms of argument (historical, textual, structural, prudential, and doctrinal) are considered legitimate and others (whim, personal policy preference) are not" (Kahn & Kersch, 2006b, pp. 17–18).

The process is also external or outward looking to social, political, institutional, cultural, historical, and intellectual forces. Here we focus in more direct terms on the lives of individuals and groups in the world outside the Court, as the Court engages in a mutual construction of the external with the internal. I note that the external also comes into the law as part of social constructions developed in prior cases, and the external is opened up again when the Court decides a case and engages in a new process of social construction.[50] Thus, there is a past, present, and future aspect to the consideration of gay rights.

At the core of Supreme Court decision making, is an "interpretive turn," in which the normative and empirical are mutually constructed, through a consideration of the "internal" legal and "external" lives of citizens as lived under a rights regime. The interpretive turn in the Supreme Court "locates the ground of (Court) objectivity as internal, rather than external to interpretation."[51] This means that the process produces an objectivity and separateness from the direct effect of either the internal legal or the external lives of individuals. This quality is distinctive to the Supreme Court, and is crucial to understanding its decision making and place in American political development.

The mutual construction of the legal and empirical through the interpretive turn means that the process occurs through the simultaneous consideration of the normative and empirical, as applied within the contemporary social matrix.[52] The empirical is looked at through the prism of rights principles, notions of liberty and equality in the law. It centers on the Court's construction of the social, political, and economic world outside the Court, in light of rights and polity principles, precedent, and the social constructions that have been developed over the decades by prior Courts.

SOCIAL SCIENTISTS AND LEGAL SCHOLARS FAILED TO EXPLAIN (MUCH LESS PREDICT) THE EXPANSION OF GAY RIGHTS

Historians and Political Scientists

The unique qualities of the dual mutual construction process and the Supreme Court's autonomy from the direct effects of other political institutions have important ramifications for how we study the Supreme Court as an actor in American political development and the politics that surround the Court. In "system" terms, the unique qualities of the mutual construction process inform the boundary conditions of the Supreme Court. To view Supreme Court decision making as primarily internal or narrowly legalist is to proceed according to a faulty assumption – that the process is simply about rights as norms mechanically applied. However, few scholars now view Supreme Court decision making in such narrowly legalist terms. The greater problem in contemporary scholarship is not a belief in legalism, but the notion that Supreme Court decision making can be explained only by factors external to the Court.

Both social scientists and legal scholars seek to explain doctrinal change based on phenomena outside the Court. This is because all such externalist approaches are built on expectations of correlations of Court action with factors outside the Court, whether they are public opinion, international events such as the embarrassment during the cold war with the denial of equal rights to African-Americans,[53] critical elections,[54] or the policy view of Presidents and those they appoint to the Court.[55] Correlations do not explain Court actions. They are one-dimensional; they only explore the external, and do not link them to the internal legal. Both social scientists and legalists fail to recognize that at the core of Supreme Court decision making is a mutual construction process, in which both internal institutional norms and principles and external phenomena, such as their view of the lives of our nation's citizens are taken into account. This bi-directional mutual construction process has unique qualities which are different from more directly politically accountable institutions.

The first indication of the problems inherent to standard historical and social science approaches to explaining doctrinal change is the willingness of all too many scholars to view the motor of doctrinal change as one of law versus politics, with law and politics segmented as internal and external elements, and the place of law as secondary to politics in such accounts.

The nature of the social construction process provides clear evidence that the "law" versus "politics" dispute that has dominated much of the academic debate over the nature of Supreme Court decision making is misguided. This debate is better conceptualized as being about the respective influences of internal and external factors on Supreme Court decision making, with "law" being an important potential internal influence and electoral "politics" being a significant potential external influence (though elections do not comprise the whole of potential external influences). The complex interplay of these factors is distinctive to courts as institutions, and it is crucial to understanding them as such. It is because of this dynamic perpetually playing itself out in courts that courts are not "little legislatures." The interplay of the internal and external taking place in courts also gives them a special place in accounts of American political development. As seen above, the Court links or bridges the internal to the external in its decision making, through what I have called a mutual construction process.

Because Supreme Court decision making cannot be segmented into internal and external elements, since such elements are bi-directional in ways we have explored, analyses explaining doctrinal change and the Court as an institution in the process of American political development that are based on a problematic of "Law" versus "Politics" are lacking and unpersuasive.[56]

Historians and historically oriented social scientists have tried to make a link directly between specific historical events, such as a critical election or the "growth of the administrative state," and Court decision making – with little success.[57] They have argued Court decisions result from "revolutions" in the nation, such as the Founding, the passage of the Civil War amendments, and the New Deal. Although recently some of these historians have begun to reconsider the revolutions thesis, historians in and out of the legal academy, such as William J. Novak, G. Edward White, and Barry Cushman, have argued that change in doctrine is the result of historical events such as the New Deal revolution and critical elections. Some legal scholars have adopted the historians' external stance by arguing a revolutions theory. These include the preeminent "revolutions" constitutional scholar of our age, Bruce Ackerman, who argues that periods of normal politics are punctuated by periods of constitutional revolutions, such as the Founding period, the passage of Civil War Amendments, and the New Deal. With regard to the New Deal era, Ackerman argues that critical elections and the growth of the administrative state caused the Supreme Court to decide the *West Coast Hotel* case, and produce a revolution in jurisprudence with its rejection of *Lochner* era polity and rights principles.

Too many historians fail to emphasize the incremental, but constant nature of change in the law, because they center their analysis only on landmark cases, asking whether they can be explained by specific historical events, rather than looking at the evolution of doctrine over the decades. Landmark cases, whether they overturn prior cases or not, tend to be products of a long-term process during which rights principles and their supporting social, economic, and political constructions have been under attack.[58]

Attitudinalism, a popular political science approach to explaining doctrinal change that seeks to explain Supreme Court decision making based on the attitudes that Justices have to government policies, clearly demonstrates the problem with simply externalist analyses of Supreme Court decision making.[59] This is because of the importance of institutional norms and processes on the Supreme Court; these severely restrict Justices from making decisions on attitudinal grounds.[60] The presence of constituting institutional norms and practices means that Supreme Court rulings have objectivity and are independent of individual subjective policy opinions held by each participant in a majority opinion.[61] The collective nature of decision making acts as a constraint on individual preferences. Preexisting institutional norms and expectations of behavior limit the effect of a priori policy choices on judicial decision making. Because of this, Supreme Court decision making is not reducible to the sum total of individual private preferences of Justices, in contrast to what the attitudinalists argue. Because of the dual mutual construction process (normative and empirical and internal and external), the act of decision making is also not reducible to historical and political events external to the Court.

The attitudinal model may be viewed as external because the policy wants of justices are viewed by attitudinalists as policy positions or ideologies in the minds of justices prior to the case itself. Graber argues that the scholar should not preload her analysis by the emphasis on internal "legal" arguments, or external strategic and policy preferences. Graber argues that "no decision can be explained entirely as a sincere or sophisticated effort to secure policy preferences," – a view that attitudinalists fail to acknowledge.[62] While Justices do have attitudes about policy, law, precedent, and external strategic concerns limit the application of simple policy wants. While law does not compel a specific action by the Court, for Graber a clear line of precedents with regard to Court action does produce a boundedness of action in Court decision making, to a far greater degree than scholars of external strategic causation are willing to admit.

Another behavioral explanation for Court decision making that also does not take seriously the importance of the mutual construction process are those that emphasize that Justices act strategically to further the institutional interests of the Court. The operation of the mutual construction process in implied fundamental rights cases provides additional evidence for why the Supreme Court is not simply or primarily "strategic" in its decision making.[63] In *Casey*, the Court provided a detailed explanation of the conditions under which landmark decisions are to be overturned, argued for a robust PBD, and specifically rejected political contestation and the votes of legislatures and the wider public as central to its determination of the implied fundamental rights. In *Romer*, the Court relied on the *Casey* conditions, and its support of a robust PBD, to find unconstitutional an amendment to the Colorado Constitution that would have denied gays the use of regular legislative, executive, and state court means to protect their rights. Finally, in *Lawrence*, the Court reaffirmed *Casey*'s conditions for overturning landmark decisions, and engaged in PBD that resulted not simply in overturning *Bowers* on minimalist equal protection grounds, but in an expansive opinion extending rights of personhood and liberty to gays, one that did not preclude the Court from deciding that gays have a right to same-sex marriage under the Constitution.

If the Supreme Court chose to be strategic with regard to its institutional needs, in *Casey* and *Lawrence*, it would be far more concerned about the political reactions by Congress, the states, and the people. Strategic factors as explanations for Court action in *Casey* and *Lawrence* are submerged because Justices accept institutional norms that ask them to consider substantive constitutional questions as to what constitutes privacy, personhood, and liberty through the mutual construction process as described above. The Court does not focus on its strategic institutional interests; it engages in the process to decide whether rights have been violated by government, in comparison to what rights have been protected in the past.

This does not mean that Justices never think strategically. Rather, they rarely think in solely strategic terms.[64] There are indications of strategic considerations in *Casey* and *Lawrence*. This seems particularly so in O'Connor's concurrence in *Lawrence*, where she specifically decides to leave for another day the question of the constitutionality of laws that outlaw sodomy for both heterosexuals and homosexuals, trusting that state legislatures will not pursue such laws given the *Lawrence* decision. As much as one might want to argue that O'Connor is thinking strategically, when she chooses not to overturn *Bowers* or invoke due process principles as the basis for her decision, it would be unwise to interpret her concurring opinion as primarily or simply strategic. If strategic institutional concerns of the Court with regard to political reaction to a decision on gay rights were central to her thinking, why did she engage in an expansive social construction of gay rights in her equal protection analysis?

Justice Scalia critiques O'Connor's position in *Lawrence* by arguing that O'Connor cannot have it both ways. She cannot set up a social construction of rights that limit government from being able to say simply that a state's belief that homosexual sodomy is immoral is permissible (even under the rational basis, or minimal scrutiny test), and then argue that the very same PBD will not lead to increased homosexual rights, even, perhaps, the right to marry. Scalia is arguing that the dynamics of PBD as described in *Casey*, continued in *Romer*, and reaffirmed in *Lawrence*, are present in her non-originalist concurrence; that to accept her concurrence has left the fox in the chicken coop with regard to future increases in implied fundamental rights, including the rights of homosexuals.

One could say that O'Connor chose to respect institutional concerns by not overturning *Bower*, and by using an equal protection basis to simply invalidate the Texas anti-sodomy law. However, even if this is accurate (and there is talk of trusting legislatures to do the right thing in O'Connor's concurrence), the nature of O'Connor's definition of the rights involved, and her respect for PBD as outlined in *Casey*, continue to be important to the future of implied fundamental rights. Rarely are cases only about strategic-institutional concerns, even, as Graber has demonstrated, in times when Presidents are brought to the Court for abuses of power during times of war.[65]

Moreover, strategic approaches do not work because the separation of the analysis of Supreme Court decision making into the legal, institutional-strategic, and attitudinal cannot adequately explain the reasons for doctrinal change. Graber finds that there is an intermingling of the legal, strategic, and attitudinal in Supreme Court decision making:

> Legal and strategic explanations both rely as much on interpretation as logic. Any finite series of decisions can be described without logical contradiction as good faith efforts to interpret the law or as sophisticated efforts to realize policy preferences ... The extent to which any judicial decision was motivated by legal or strategic factors, at bottom, depends on contestable theories about what constitutes good legal and strategic practice. (Graber, 2006, p. 45)

He concludes, "The most fruitful investigations will explore the ways in which legal, strategic, and attitudinal factors interact when justices make decisions, and not engage in fruitless contests to determine which single factor explains the most" (Graber, 2006, p. 60).

Cass Sunstein's Theory of Judicial Minimalism

Pragmatic legalists, law school scholars such as Cass Sunstein, also would have led us not to expect the *Lawrence* decision due to their faith in judicial minimalism as the primary jurisprudential strategy for the mature Rehnquist Court. Ironically, support for judicial minimalism in the past was favored by conservative scholars and jurists, but now has become a central idea in the scholarship of progressives such as Cass Sunstein and Mark Tushnet.[66]

Sunstein and other pragmatic legalists, like behavioral political scientists, have rejected the presence and the importance of the social construction process within Supreme Court decision making, and seem to be siding with behavioral political scientists in looking primarily to external rather than jurisprudential guideposts for Court decision making.[67] Sunstein failed to predict the depth and breadth of the rights of homosexual rights of privacy and sexual intimacy in *Lawrence v. Texas* (2003) because "judicial minimalism" as a statement of what Supreme Court decision making is or should be distorts the nature of Supreme Court decision making. This distortion has at its base a pragmatic and ends-oriented conception of Supreme Court decision making, in contrast to Sunstein's prior model of Court decision making which had as its central premise that the Supreme Court was not to accept the status quo as neutral. This concept, that the Court should not accept the status quo as neutral, essentially depends on the presence of the social construction process.

One could ask why the Court did not simply overturn the anti-sodomy statute based on an argument of desuetude, as Sunstein favored, rather than eviscerating *Bowers* and employing a maximalist mode of decision making in *Lawrence*.[68] As we saw above, the answer lies in the fact that the Court's failure to engage in the social construction process in *Bowers* would rob principles and social constructions in cases before and after *Bowers* of their precedential value, thus undermining rights important to a majority of the Court. It also would undercut non-originalist principles in *Casey* as to the nature of the social construction process, further adding to a critique of the non-originalist view of the rule of law and the Supreme Court's role as the arbiter of the Constitution.

Allowing *Bowers* to stand or deciding the case on equal protection grounds, or even on a more minimalist basis, would have undermined moral propositions that were already in the law that were important to six members of the Court, including O'Connor.[69]

It is quite clear that even though O'Connor wants a more minimalist response to *Bowers*, based on the Equal Protection Clause and the substantive elements in *Romer*, an analysis of her social construction process provides evidence that she agrees with many of the substantive conclusions that are at the core of the majority's opinion. However, of importance to our consideration of Sunstein's minimalism, O'Connor is not minimalist in her analysis, only in her decision to utilize an equal protection rather than a substantive due process rationale. That is, O'Connor engages in a social construction process that does not shy away from key elements of the *Bowers* decision, including the notion that moral disapproval of gays cannot be a rational basis for denying rights, and that *Bowers*, and the Texas law itself rested on the imputation of inferiority of gays by the state.

It is also quite clear that the reason why so many scholars failed to predict that *Bowers* would be overturned, and why even fewer scholars predicted that it would be eviscerated to the point of *Lawrence* raising questions about the possibility of a right to marry, was because of their acceptance of judicial minimalism as a strategy for Court action. This strategy is not an adequate explanation of the process of Supreme Court decisions, with institutional rules that favor the application of past polity and rights principles through a process of social construction, a process the *Bowers* Court avoided. Had *Bowers* been viewed in light of other landmark cases that were overturned, such as *Plessy* and *Lochner*, and in light of *Casey*, a case in which the Court chose not to overturn *Roe v. Wade*, the *Lawrence* decision would not have been unexpected.

There are implications of these findings for future constitutional theory. If any theory redefining the rights of subordinated groups is to have legitimacy in the interpretive community and wider society, it must be meaningful to people as to the nature of the world they see about them, and how the world should look in the future. For example, Lessig raises important questions about concepts of meaning in Ackerman's theory. He demonstrates that Ackerman's work centers on "the modalities of social meaning."[70] Lessig argues that fear of faction leads Ackerman to resist Mark Tushnet's call for plasticity in the process of constitutional change, with the result that major constitutional moments are rare and hard to achieve. Fear of faction also leads Ackerman to give the Supreme Court a major role in putting new constitutional values into effect, by the synthesis of inter-generational constitutional values in the process of deciding cases.

There is a similar problem in Sunstein's constitutional theory. Any transformative theory of constitutional change must involve a concern for changes in meanings as to what constitutes structural inequalities and how they should be linked to definitions of what constitute denials of equal protection of the law. Through case analysis we can identify new social constructs that have validity because there is broad agreement on them over time. Moreover, there is a linkage between the definition of social constructs and whether legal classifications that refer to specific subordinated groups are to be subjected to close Court scrutiny. Again, social constructs are not simply facts from social scientists – nor do social constructs necessarily change when social reality changes, as in the case of *Lochner*. Social constructs have within them images of superordination and subordination that become constitutionally recognized as precedent: concepts of the average women accepted in pre-*Reed* cases and rejected post-*Reed* and *Craig*; children as subject to psychological coercion in *Lee v. Weisman*; and the relationship between women and their spouses in *Casey* with regard to spousal notification. As these social constructs change so do our visions of the denial of equal protection of the law, and what constitutes public and private action.[71]

In critiquing Bruce Ackerman's vision of constitutional change, Lessig argues that Ackerman favors too much plasticity in the translation by the

Supreme Court and lesser courts of the meaning of alterations of the Constitution. He believes that high levels of plasticity in the translation process undercut the moral meaning of structural change and the values of Constitution. However, when one looks at rights of privacy and sexual intimacy, the social construction process in *Lawrence* demonstrates a tighter fit with polity and rights principles and precedent than in *Bowers*. This suggests an appropriate level of plasticity, in Lessig's terms, in the definition of rights of personhood for homosexuals. Thus, *Lawrence* increases the legitimacy of the Court among legal scholars and other members of the interpretive community.

However, through case analysis that considers the construction of social, economic, and political world outside the Court, we can identify when the Court is changing the translation of constitutional principles to take in the new realities of life. Definitions of intimate relations, privacy, and state power over private space become so meaningful to the nation that to deny them to some groups just because they are disfavored is seen as unjust. It is the important difference in the meaning of the rights of citizens before the law that is at the core of the process of change in the rights of subordinated groups. Differences in constitutional principles, of due process versus equal protection, can tell us much about the meaning and legitimacy of the acts which are looked at, as Sunstein has emphasized.[72] However, in Sunstein's concept of judicial minimalism, the advocacy of polity principles over rights principles, and the lack of emphasis on the way the Court constructs the world outside itself, mischaracterizes how the Supreme Court makes its decisions and therefore is not a cogent model for understanding that process.

Sunstein's theory also fails to account for how the Court deals with subordinated groups in the equal protection and implied fundamental rights contexts. *Casey*'s intellectual relationship to *Lawrence* goes beyond its employment of PBD, as discussed above, and also includes ideas about pregnant women's relationships to society and to their families and partners. Similar types of choices must be made by courts when they must decide questions of the rights of subordinated groups, such as homosexuals, because the landscape is somewhat similar, though not identical, to that of a pregnant woman in private and public space. The Court must ask what is to remain private and what must be public, with regard to what the more powerful can do to the less powerful.

A constitutional theory of subordinated groups requires that choices to be made on the basis of past traditions of oppression, as to which classifications in the law should be suspect. However, if one determines which groups are to be suspect in a fashion discussed by Sunstein, one still has a decision to make as to which conditions or situations need to be compared. In the suspect classification system, once we decide who is in (gender, religion, and race, but not sexual preference and size of body, for example) then we can look at all such classifications and scrutinize what level of argument in support of the classification the state must give to allow it to exist.

But the analysis cannot stop there, and this may be why Sunstein is misguided in his analysis. The meaning of race, religion, and sexual orientation is not the same in all contexts. With regard to sexual orientation classifications, a court must decide whether a majority's view of sexual orientation is to be the basis for permitting or denying some fundamental right or interest. To make this decision, we have to consider questions other than whether a majority of Americans favor homosexuals engaging in some right or interest. To make a decision on pure animus by the majority, as we saw in *Romer*, is not permissible, because the Court is about defining rights, not simply following politics. The social construction process is how rights are defined.

Therefore, a new theory on the rights of subordinated groups must be more questioning about politics and the fairness of the political system than Sunstein's concept of judicial minimalism. Moreover, it must recognize that trusting courts should be valued over trusting politics, because not to take such a stance undermines the fundamental rights in the Constitution. Understanding the process of social construction is the key to developing a theory of the rights of subordinated groups.

We need to ask whether Sunstein's minimalism and his constitutional theory based on polity principles with rights principles in the background, can best conceptualize how the rights of subordinated groups are determined, especially in light of the more complex causes and manifestations of the subordination of minorities. Finally, in our search for a theory of the rights of subordinated groups, we must ask the following basic questions about the relationship among constitutional theory, practice, and liberalism: Are the problems found in Sunstein's concept of judicial minimalism caused by his acceptance of central premises in liberal theories of the state, society, and law? Is the problem of establishing a theory of subordinated groups a problem of American exceptionalism, with a too unitary theory of American political thought? These questions are for another day.[73]

The major problem with Sunstein's concept of judicial minimalism is his failure to continue to call on the Supreme Court to reject the status quo as neutral. The process through which the Supreme Court decides whether or not to reject the neutrality of the status quo provides an argument for the importance of the role of the Court's construction of the social, economic, and political world outside the Court in the process of its decision making. A process of construction, but not the specific process of construction that is advocated by Sunstein, is central to Supreme Court decision making. As Alschuler demonstrates, the Court engaged in such constructions well before the age of judicial realism.[74] Moreover, the construction of the social, economic, and political world outside the Court is mandatory if polity and rights principles are to continue to have meaning in our changing society. Again, I am not advocating acceptance of the specific way in which Sunstein asks the Court to construct the social, political, and economic world outside the Court.

These concerns become more apparent when we ask whether Cass Sunstein's *One Case at a Time* does justice to the complexities of constitutive Supreme Court decision making. First, there is no discussion of the social construction of rights or polity principles; nor is there discussion of the necessity that the Supreme Court reject the status quo as neutral. Sunstein also does not offer a discussion about the relationship of polity and rights principles in Supreme Court decision making, even though he does admit that the Court rejects an all-rights or all polity-based constitutional theory. Nor is there a discussion about whether and when minimalism may not be warranted in a line of cases. For example, while the reasonableness test, and not maximalism, may have been warranted in *Reed v. Reed* (1971) to encourage government action on gender discrimination, one can ask whether maximalism may be warranted later in the development of principles protecting against gender discrimination. Perhaps more importantly, there is no discussion of when maximalism may be an appropriate strategy to protect individual rights.

Might there be minimalist and maximalist ages and, if there are, when do they occur? Is minimalism usually and always in order? Is this a time-bound argument about the Court now? Or does the lack of minimalism in the Warren and Burger Court constitute a criticism of those Court eras? What historical, institutional, political culture, legal, and political factors inform the presence of minimalism and maximalism? Perhaps this book should be read as a primer on how to get progressive legal change in this conservative post-Reagan era. One can ask what effect minimalism may have on the degree to which individual rights principles will be viewed as foundational in the future.

One Case at a Time can be read as a more complex polity malfunction justification for Supreme Court decision making than that offered by John Hart Ely (Ely, 1980). Sunstein's vision of a properly running Madisonian

Republic is far more demanding than Ely's because the political system is to deliberate on public-regarding values, not simply keep a numerical majority from being unfair to a discrete and insular minority. Also, while Sunstein's minimalism eschews natural rights, such rights are part of the background of his deliberative democracy to a degree not found in Ely's constitutional theory. The reason for this is that rights talk undermines the Supreme Court and political institutions in the process of solving constitutional problems because jurists disagree on the basis for such actions. This is a pragmatic argument for retail rights protection, rather than for the wholesale, maximalist change.[75]

Viewing fundamental rights principles as secondary to polity norms as Sunstein does in his concept of judicial minimalism will result in less protection of individual rights, because Sunstein's trust of political institutions that is at the core of his judicial minimalism is unwarranted; and the Court in many areas of doctrine, such as privacy rights, has said it is unwarranted. Without maximalist decisions, states and the national government would just stonewall to limit minimalist privacy rights, as they did on racial segregation. Is there evidence that political institutions will take cues for increased rights protection should the Court make minimalist decisions? Would they not cave in to the naked preferences of whatever group has power in a state or the national government to stop the protection of rights?

I also question whether it is best for the Supreme Court to have a minimalist approach in an argument for a right. While it is true that minimalism may foster a decision for a new right because Justices can agree on the right for different reasons, the minimalist approach may not be best for the development of constitutional law, the contribution of the interpretive community to that development, and to the clarification of what rights and government powers the nation can expect. Minimalism may stifle a full discussion of legal arguments in later cases. Institutional values like deliberation and political and social stability in the short run seem more important to Sunstein than a clear definition of individual rights. This may sacrifice the needs of subordinated groups.

THE LEGITIMACY OF PBD: A DEFINING FISSURE ON AND OFF THE SUPREME COURT

There are two primary effects of non-originalist PBD.[76] The first effect is an objectivity, or universalism, in the way the Court thinks about legal questions. The second effect is an autonomy (relative) of the Supreme Court from the direct influence of politics and more directly politically accountable institutions, such as the Presidency and Congress. These effects constitute important differences between the Supreme Court and political institutions and lead to defining fissures on and off the Supreme Court.

The importance of the objectivity of the legal process cannot be overemphasized. Here objectivity does not refer to the objectivity of facts. Supreme Court decision making is objective because the Court engages in an analogical process in deciding whether a right defined in prior cases should apply in the case before the Court. In defining what equal protection or liberty means, objectivity is gained because the Court is asked to compare behaviors, rather than evaluate how society views those behaviors.[77] To decide what constitutes equal protection or liberty, to remain objective and autonomous, the Court must focus on actions, not actors; comparison with contexts of actions that have been protected in the past play a principal role in determining whether previously unprotected groups should come under the umbrella of constitutional protection.

This process produces a legal secularism which is a defining characteristic of the Supreme Court, most legal institutions, and of the rule of law itself. We see legal objectivity in *Roe* when the Court respects the differences among and between the religious and non-religious as to their views about when life begins. We see it in *Lawrence* as well, when the Court considers whether it is appropriate for the Supreme Court to decide questions of rights on the basis of a society's Judeo-Christian values, and castigates former Chief Justice Warren Burger for his concurrence in *Bowers* which justified the constitutionality of anti-homosexual sodomy laws on the premise that sodomy violated Judeo-Christian values.[78] Deciding *Bowers* on such a consideration disregarded basic (non-originalist) institutional norms as to how individual rights are determined. As the *Lawrence* Court illustrates, it is not legitimate for the Supreme Court to decide questions of individual rights in general, and gay rights in particular, either on the premise that homosexual sodomy is a violation of Judeo-Christian values or on the basis that state legislatures, or the people themselves, think certain conduct is simply immoral; such decisions must be made after the Court *first* engages in PBD.

The legal objectivity or secularism of the non-originalist PBD and the attendant Court autonomy are politically significant. The legal objectivity of PBD also helps explain why a conservative Court in a conservative political era not only expands the jurisprudential basis for the right of abortion choice – moving from a concept of privacy to one of personhood, but also why personhood rights under the Constitution were extended to homo-sexuals, in the dramatic and unexpected expansionist decision in *Lawrence v. Texas* (2003).[79]

First it results in the core difference on the Rehnquist and Roberts Courts being between non-originalists and originalists, rather than between conservatives, moderates, and liberals. Non-originalism is not simply the converse of originalism; nor is it disrespectful of foundational polity and rights principles that are at the core of the Constitution, as originalists would argue. The political implications of this are enormous for the future of homosexual rights (Goldford, 2005).

For non-originalists accepting the components of PBD is the basis for claims of Court legitimacy and its uniqueness among governmental institutions; for originalists accepting the components of PBD is the basis for criticizing the legitimacy of the Supreme Court as a forum to define implied fundamental rights.

In the framework of a mutual construction process with robust PBD, disagreements between originalists and non-originalists regarding how the Constitution should be interpreted become clearer. In this context, we can explain the response by Justice Scalia to the substance of *Casey* and its rules or conditions under which the Supreme Court may overturn landmark decisions. We also can better understand Justice Scalia's opposition to the acceptance of these conditions in both the *Lawrence* majority opinion and his even more heated response to Justice O'Connor's concurring decision. The doctrinal implications of her acceptance of a robust PBD with regard to future implied fundamental rights are what most concerned Justice Scalia. This also helps us understand why he viewed O'Connor as disingenuous when she argued that one should not fear that her invalidation of the Texas sodomy law on equal protection grounds might lead to a constitutional right to same-sex marriage.

All Justices, originalists, and non-originalist alike, agree to follow precedent, consider polity and rights principles in making constitutional choices, and engage in analogical reasoning. All see themselves as dealing with the normative and empirical in ways that are special to courts. All see themselves as engaging in a process of interpretation. Both originalists and non-originalists acknowledge that Supreme Court decision making has normative and empirical elements, and that it is both inward and outward looking.

Where they differ primarily pertains to what should be included in the process of social construction. The conflict between the originalists and non-originalists is over the relationship between the internal and external (and the normative and empirical). The "external" reference point for most originalists is the narrow time frame of founding periods. Originalists reject the permissibility of the external in Court decision making moving beyond the founding periods of the Constitution and its amendments. For Scalia, and most originalists, the manner in which privacy, personhood, and homosexual rights have developed is not principled because those doctrines reflect rights principles that are defined in terms of the lives of individuals well past the founding of the Constitution and the Civil War Amendments.

Originalists oppose consideration of the rights of gays in terms of looking at their lives, through the normative and empirical PBD, because the normative bases of these rights come from implied fundamental rights which were established by an expansive notion of the empirical. The rights do not derive from the "original intent" of the Constitution – they are not tied directly to the words of the Constitution or its amendments. Scalia refuses to accept PBD and all rights based on that process, if that process moves beyond intentions derived from founding periods. Thus, *Roe*, *Casey*, *Romer*, and *Lawrence* are all illegitimate claims of "Constitutional" law. This suggests that a primary fissure on the mature Rehnquist Court, with regard to, among other things, the treatment of implied fundamental rights, is between originalists and non-originalists, rather than between conservatives, moderates, and liberals, and at the core of such differences is the legitimacy of a robust PBD.[80] Many scholars argue that all Justices, originalists as well as non-originalists, engage in the interpretive turn through a process of construction, and one is not more objective than the other in terms of the bases on which they make constitutional choices.[81] They are correct. However, the attack by the originalists on a core element of the non-originalist decision making, PBD's application of principles to the lives of citizens, is tantamount to a rejection of the validity and legitimacy of the process itself, and thus of much of contemporary constitutional law.

The legitimacy of an expansive PBD and the nature of its components is not simply the defining fissure within the mature Rehnquist Court: it has become a core conflict within the interpretive community, and, more generally within contemporary American politics. This was evident in 2005, as the Senate considered the "nuclear option" to get rid of long-standing institutional rules that require sixty votes, rather than a simple majority, to close debate, and thus to stop a filibuster for nominations to the federal courts. It was also evident in the Senate's consideration of President George W. Bush's nominee, Judge John Roberts, to replace Justice O'Connor on the Supreme Court, when questions centered on whether he would honor precedents.

The legal objectivity or secularism witnessed in PBD in *Casey* and *Lawrence* is exactly what the religious right and social or cultural conservatives off the Court also oppose, and their secularist opposition admire. Thus, there is a feedback effect between differences on the Court over the legitimacy of a robust PBD, and the cases that result from such differences, to American politics, one which portends to be with us for many years. These differences are not simply over controversial Court decisions, such as *Roe*, *Casey*, and *Lawrence*, they are over the nature of Court decision-making process and the place of the Court in American political development.

The key issue in this debate is whether a social construction process is to occur in the future. The question debated today is not whether a conservative, moderate, or liberal will be appointed to the Court, but rather will the nominee will be a non-originalist or an originalist. Criticism from cultural conservatives now focuses on Justices Kennedy and O'Connor, not because they are liberal; they are not. Rather, they are criticized for the *Casey* and *Lawrence* decisions and their view of Court role. They are criticized because they accept the components of a Court decision making process whose rules allow the continuation of implied fundamental rights of privacy and personhood, and their application to the rights of homosexuals. The central question has become whether appointees will honor precedents that employ the main components of that process and, most importantly, engage in PBD in the future, with the possible result that implied fundamental rights will be expanded, as they were in the past, in *Casey*, *Romer*, and *Lawrence*.[82]

PBD as a Motor for Social Change

Social constructions become "pictures in precedents" of the rights principles of liberty, privacy, and personhood.[83] As these pictures grow, new groups are viewed as possible candidates for protection under them. These core elements of objectivity and autonomy represent an invitation, a hope, to groups not currently afforded equal protection of law – that they also might partake in the protection of basic rights like liberty, privacy, and personhood. When these new groups step up to bat, they argue to court that they also deserve protection, and the mutual construction process, which links the normative and the empirical, makes it increasingly more difficult for courts to say no. The rights development process gains a persona of its own, on the Supreme Court, in the legal-interpretive community of law professors and social scientists, and the wider interpretive community of legal advocacy groups, journalists, bloggers, and the informed public. With such hopes, there continues to be an important role for legal advocacy groups and members of the wider interpretive community in American political development.[84]

However, the heated debate that abounds today over the place of the Supreme Court in our system of governance is caused in part by the effects of its objectivity and autonomy. Controversy is greatest as the Court engages in PBD that applies principles, such as privacy and personhood, to groups in the society which do not have such rights. The objectivity of non-originalist decision making and the institutional norms of PBD which lead to judicial autonomy from pressures of majoritarian politics infuriate the religious right and other cultural conservatives. The exercise of this legal secularism becomes politically charged and controversial especially when it brings new minority groups under the protection of law. This objectivism may not be understood, or appreciated, by the wider public, and the politicians they elect. It is an anathema to citizens and groups who hold strong moral positions as to what constitutes proper behaviors and lifestyle, and who seek government support of them. For these citizens, the Court's mandate to be legally objective appears as a legal secularism that does not respect their moral and ethical values, that is, their sectarianism.

One can ask: Why should views and votes of the people of Kansas on questions of gay rights and the right to abortion choice be trumped by the Supreme Court?[85] One response is that its decision-making process, institutional norms, and place in American political development call on the Supreme Court to decide questions of individual rights, and do so in ways peculiar to it as a legal, not political, institution. The social construction process, interpretive turn, consideration of internal-legal and external-social factors at the level of lives of citizens, and the cumulative nature of the comparison of principles and past social constructions, through a process of analogy, lead the Court to the *Casey* and *Lawrence* decisions, that is to landmark decisions which are at loggerheads with the majority coalition.

The Supreme Court and the Non-Waning of "Legal Time"

In such a setting, PBD is closely linked to the place of the Supreme Court in American political development. There has been a feedback effect from conflicts over the legitimacy of PBD to general American politics (Keck, 2006).

This suggests that the bi-directionality between the internal Court and the world outside occurs at several levels, at the level of a consideration of the lives of citizens, as the Court makes decisions about rights of privacy and personhood, and at the level of politics itself. However institutional norms lead the Court to reject the politics from outside, as it continues to respect core elements of PBD and expand rights.

These unique qualities of Supreme Court decision making also mean that the "legal time" of the Supreme Court is quite different from the "political time" of directly "political" institutions such as the Presidency, as are the resulting path trajectories of the Supreme Court in American political development.[86]

Stephen Skowronek argues that throughout the history of our nation there has been "a waning of political time" in which each president can meet his commitments, due in part to the "thickening" of political institutions. Ever-increasing expectations of political change through Presidential action are met with less time in which to meet such demands – even though resources of the Office of the President have increased through the decades. This problem is most evident in presidents elected in periods of reconstructive politics. Presidents Lincoln, Roosevelt, and Reagan each had shorter time periods in which to carry out programs of reconstruction.

The universalism and objectivity of PBD, basic norms of what the rule of law means, and the place of the Supreme Court today as the final arbiter of the Constitution, lead to a far greater autonomy of the Supreme Court from other governmental institutions than is found in the Presidency – making the Supreme Court less subject to the sort of thickening that Skowronek describes in political institutions. The processes of increasing returns are weaker on the Court, and the Court's autonomy means that, a large extent, the "reconstruction" of the law is in the hands of the Court. It is usually the end point of incremental moves in prior cases that pinpoint the anachronistic nature of past social constructions in support of individual rights, and thus the rights themselves. Thus, the Supreme Court is able to make constitutional choices in opposition to the primary commitments of the majority coalition, and the major political institutions that it may control, over a longer time frame than the President, who is more subject to the effects of the thickening of government with each passing decade.

Also, the Supreme Court may not be as change resistant as political institutions, and as change resistant as is assumed by Pierson's concept of path dependence, that is based on increasing returns. There may be fewer start-up and switching costs to develop new social understandings, than in political institutions (Pierson, 2000, pp. 260–261). The Supreme Court has mechanisms to change the direction of the law, by overturning landmark cases, when principles and social constructions of them become anachronistic. The Court can distinguish prior decisions, and reinterpret what the underlying social facts mean, if the rights at issue are not so out of kilter with the world outside the Court. This may sound ironic to those who view stare decisis as if it were a narrowly legalistic, mechanical process – but it is true.[87] The autonomy, universalism, and objectivity of PBD results in the Supreme Court viewing its relationship with political institutions as less threatening to it than are political institutions to each other.

The basic constitutional theories of the "rule of law" over government, and constitutional law as a means to limit the abuse of government power, provide the Supreme Court with additional institutional incentives to question the action of political institutions, rather than accept them.

The Supreme Court is subject to fewer "switching costs" for changing paths because it tends to hear cases and issues over which lower courts and society are in conflict; institutions outside the Court are not sure what the law is or what the Constitution requires, and in many cases are demanding an answer from the Supreme Court, in order to secure stability. In other words, cases are not heard unless "reversals of course" or a change in the path of the law is a real possibility. The hypothetical alternatives, of changing paths, that political institutions are supposed to abhor under increasing returns path dependence, constitute the regular business of the Supreme Court. While the "cost of exit" from paths for political institutions is high, the cost of exit and change for the Supreme Court is not as great.

CONCLUSION

Legalists and social scientists have not been able to explain the expansion of gay rights in a conservative age because they refuse to respect the importance of the special qualities of judicial decision making. These qualities require the Supreme Court to look simultaneously at the past, present, and future and to consider what individual rights should be in terms of the lives of the nation's citizens, not simply their political desires. Unless political scientists, historians, and legal theorists respect the complexities of the Court's internal decision process and how the outside world is brought into the Court – in ways quite different from more directly politically accountable institutions – they will not have any greater success in the future in predicting or explaining the expansion of individual rights.

NOTES

1. President Nixon appointed Chief Justice Burger (1969) and Justice Blackmun (1970), and Justices Powell and Rehnquist, both in 1972. President Ford appointed John Paul Stevens (1975). Democratic President Carter had no appointees to the Supreme Court. President Reagan appointed Sandra Day O'Connor (1981), reappointed Justice William Rehnquist as Chief Justice and Justice Scalia in 1986, and Justice Kennedy (1988). President George Herbert Walker Bush appointed Justices David Souter (1990) and Clarence Thomas (1991). Only two appointees to the Supreme Court were made by a Democratic President, Bill Clinton, who appointed Justices Ruth Bader Ginsburg (1993) and Stephen Breyer (1994). It was not until 2005, eleven years later that additional appointments would be made to the Supreme Court. In 2005, Republican President George W. Bush appointed John Roberts as Chief Justice and in 2006 Samuel Alito as an Associate Justice to the Supreme Court.

2. Some scholars of quite different political persuasions have argued that *Casey* only upheld *Roe* technically. They emphasize that the *Casey* Court, under its "undue burden test" allowed Pennsylvania to institute a 24-hour wait period before an abortion, a rule requiring doctors to discuss with patients the growth of the fetus and alternatives to abortions, and state record keeping on abortions, while not allowing states to require spousal notification, even with a bypass provision.

To ascertain whether or not *Casey* simply upheld *Roe* technically or was rights expansive, one must do more than an analysis in policy terms of whether the Pennsylvania abortion law has made it harder or easier in the short run to get an abortion; one would have to explore whether the right itself is more or less fundamental when you compare the Court decisions. In this regard the *Casey* decision upheld the fundamental right to choose an abortion, and in important ways made the right more fundamental. The jettisoning of the trimester framework in *Casey* was a significant step in expanding the right of abortion choice because it did away with medical science as the ground on which the right to choose rested. *Casey* got rid of the collision course, as O'Connor described it, which would undermine the right to choose as medical science now allows fetuses to be kept alive, albeit with scientific aids, closer to conception and women to have safe abortions closer to term.

See *Gonzales v. Carhart*, No. 05–380 (2007), the most recent Supreme Court "partial birth abortion" case, in which the fundamentality of the right to choose is evident, along with its trumping of the protection of the potential life when Justice Kennedy openly states the constitutionality of lethal injections for fetuses rather than allow certain abortion procedures. Kennedy writes, "Some doctors, especially later in the second trimester, may kill the fetus a day or two before performing the surgical evacuation. They inject digoxin or potassium chloride into the fetus, the umbilical cord, or the amniotic fluid. Fetal demise may cause contractions and make greater dilation possible. Once dead, moreover, the fetus' body will soften, and its removal will be easier." Moreover, based on *Roe* and *Casey* a state could pass a law today which would permit women to choose an abortion up to term, as long as it met standards of humanity as described in *Gonzales v. Carhart*.

3. See *Parents Involved in Community Schools v. Seattle School District No. 1.*, 05–908 (2007), a Supreme Court case which did limit the discretion of schools boards to use race as a factor in the placement of students in public schools; however, in that case a majority of the Roberts Court allows race to be one factor among others in the assignment of students to schools.

4. See Skowronek (1997, pp. 407–464) for a discussion of the waning of political time, which is the increasingly narrow window during which each subsequent president can make reforms that are demanded by the majority coalition that elected him. The notion that most windows for change are narrow in American politics is evident in numerous works on American politics (Baumgartner & Jones, 1993; Kingdon, 2003).

5. See Kahn (1994) for an analysis of the Warren and Burger Courts in this regard.

6. In discussing contemporary non-originalist Supreme Court decision making, I am not invoking John Hart Ely's notion that the Court's role is to keep the pluralist political system open procedurally for discrete and insular minorities. Rather, I am arguing here that the Court's application of past rights principles and social constructions through a process of analogy to the new case it is to decide means that substantive issues of justice are considered. As Lawrence Tribe has argued (Tribe, 1980) and the *Lawrence* Court affirms, rights questions have never been simply procedural, even though many scholars wish to perceive them as such. There must be substantive questions of justice that trigger and inform choices about rights, even ones that center on procedural fairness.

See Kahn (2006a, pp. 78–81) for the view that both Justice Kennedy, in the Lawrence majority opinion that rests on due process grounds, and Justice O'Connor, in a concurring opinion that rests on equal protection grounds, demonstrate that there are substantive non-procedural fairness elements in making their constitutional choices.

7. In emphasizing that PBD is central to doctrinal change, I recognize that the Court is besieged by a large number and wide range of analogies to prior cases and suggestions for argumentation as found in the many competing briefs it receives and oral arguments it hears. However, because many cases come before the Supreme Court because of conflicting decisions in lower federal courts and state courts and because of the importance and complexity of the issues raised in such cases, rarely can a Court's decision be viewed as primarily due to the number, intensity, and the content of briefs and oral arguments.

8. *Planned Parenthood of Southeastern Pennsylvania v. Casey*, 505 U.S. 833, 864 (1992).

9. See Kahn (1994, pp. 257–258) and Kahn (1999a, 1999b), for details of the Court moving from a privacy to a personhood basis for the right of abortion choice.

10. *Lawrence*'s rights analysis can also be read as an overt rejection of Scalia's substantive due process methodology articulated in his plurality opinion in *Michael H. v. Gerald D.*, 491 U.S. 110 (1989), a case which involved the question whether a father of a child that resulted from an adulterous affair has any rights with regard to that child. In this case, Scalia invoked *Bowers v. Hardwick* for the proposition that the Court should not recognize as fundamental rights that do not have a deep and

specific common law reference. Concurring Justices O'Connor, Kennedy, Stevens and dissenting Justices Brennan, Marshal, and Blackmun refused to accept this proposition.

11. Many times there are Supreme Court decisions that signal the possibility of a landmark case being overturned, such as the cases involving segregation in higher education prior to *Brown*. Also, in many Lochner era cases the right of contract and liberty under the Due Process Clauses did not trump the police powers of government. See Kahn (1999b, pp. 50–59) for the place of the social construction process in death penalty cases, one which has resulted in recent years in Supreme Court cases which limit the circumstances in which the death penalty is permitted. Perhaps, the Court will reconsider its failure to socially construct a relationship between government institutions, race, and death penalty conviction rates in *McCleskey v. Kemp*, 481 U.S. 279 (1987). This is a case ripe for modification or even overturning.

12. *Griswold v. Connecticut*, 381 U.S. 479 (1965).

13. *Eisenstadt v. Baird*, 405 U.S. 438 (1972).

14. *Roe v. Wade*, 410 U.S. 113 (1973).

15. Rather than basing its decision on due process rights of privacy and personhood grounds, the *Lawrence* Court could have found the Texas law banning homosexual sodomy unconstitutional on equal protection grounds, or on more minimalist grounds, such as desuetude, as advocated by Cass Sunstein, in Sunstein (2003). Acceptance of the social construction process, in which rights principles and social constructions, past and present, are compared through a process of analogy, means that considerations by justices as to whether to be minimalist or maximalist in their decision making are not their first or primary concern. For a full and detailed critique of Sunstein's theory judicial minimalism as applied to *Casey* and *Lawrence*, see Kahn (2005).

16. *Lawrence v. Texas,* 539 U.S. 558, 567 (2003).

17. *Romer v. Evans*, 517 U.S. 620 (1996).

18. *Lawrence v. Texas*, 539 U.S. 558, 573 (2003).

19. *Ibid.* at 576. The Court here refers to criticism in the interpretive community, drawing on work by Charles Fried and Richard Posner. Moreover, the courts of five states have declined to follow *Bowers* in interpreting provisions in their own state constitutions parallel to the Due Process Clause of the Fourteenth Amendment. In *Bowers*, one cannot see the level of settled expectations in the interpretive community and among jurists that sustains its constitutional validity.

20. *Ibid.* at 574 (quoting *Casey*, 505 U.S. 833, 851).

21. *Lawrence v. Texas*, 539 U.S. 558, at 574 (2003) (quoting *Romer*, 517 U.S. 620, at 624). In this chapter I focus on the most controversial implied fundamental rights, the right of sexual intimacy and the possibility of the right to marry for gays and the right of abortion choice for women. However, to fully understand why such rights have expanded in a conservative age and to understand the crucial role played by the acceptance of PBD by non-originalist, whether liberal, moderate, or conservative, I need to explore the controversy as to whether such rights are to be found in the Due Process Clauses of the 14th and 5th Amendment or the Equal Protection Clause of the 14th Amendment. Moreover, we see in both the doctrinal areas of due process and equal protection, the Supreme Court has opposed strict tiered analysis and

favored a more robust consideration of substantive rights and procedural considerations.

22. *Ibid.* at 574 (quoting *Romer*, 517 U.S. 620, 624).

23. *Ibid.* (quoting *Romer*, 517 U.S.., 620, 634).

24. *Ibid.* at 571 (quoting *Casey*, 505 U.S. 833, 850).

25. *Ibid.*

26. *Ibid.* at 572 (quoting *County of Sacramento v. Lewis*, 523 U.S. 833, at 857 (1998), Kennedy, J. (concurring)).

27. *Ibid.* at 577.

28. *Ibid.* at 578–579.

29. *Ibid.* at 583 (quoting *Romer*, 517 U.S. 620, 633).

30. *Ibid.* at 580. This phrase, "the challenged legislation inhibits personal relationships" implies that Justice O'Connor, like the *Lawrence* majority, is concerned about due process liberty interests of homosexuals.

31. O'Connor is not minimalist in her analysis of the substantive rights at issue in *Lawrence*. She is a minimalist only in her conclusion to base this decision on the equal protection rather than due process grounds. That is, O'Connor engaged in PBD which did not shy away from criticizing key substantive elements of the *Bowers* decision, including its key premise that moral disapproval of gays by government is a rational basis for denying rights. Contrast this with Sunstein's theory that minimalist justices think primarily in pragmatic terms.

32. The depth of O'Connor's social construction of rights at issue in the anti-sodomy law raises questions about the argument that we can view O'Connor simply as a centrist justice because of her views about judicial role, as lucidly explored by Keck (2004). This view speaks only to minimalist outcomes, i.e., that O'Connor chose not to overturn *Bowers* and rested her argument on equal protection grounds. It does not speak to the impact and implications of her reasoning including social constructions on future constitutional law.

33. *Romer v. Evans*, 517 U.S. 620, 620–644 (1996).

34. Scholars who view Supreme Court decision making as simply patterns of argumentation, rather than processes through which Justices decide cases, the answers to which are not known prior to the process itself, understate the degree to which Justices view Court decision making as a constitutive process, rather than one in which Justices make arguments in support of a preconceived policy desire. Moreover, one can see PBD at work in the cases, with justices discussing the nature of the process, as we see in *Casey* and in other cases as well. When Justice Scalia vehemently criticizes Justice O'Connor for engaging in PBD in *Casey*, it is part of a running debate in numerous abortion rights cases. For example, see *Webster v. Reproductive Services*, 492 U.S. 490, 529 (1989), where O'Connor in concurrence opposes the trimester framework in *Roe*, and *Scalia*, concurring at 532–537, excoriates O'Connor, and other non-originalists on the Court for engaging in what I have called a PBD. Justice Scalia opposes the non-originalists for making constitutional choices that respect the bi-directionality between rights principles and individuals in society under a rights regime created by the Court, as well as the importance of the cumulative nature of principles and social constructions.

There are important similarities among the non-originalist justices, whether conservative, moderate, or liberal, with regard to how they engage in constitutional interpretation, and, most importantly, with regard to their rejecting, as binding on them, the principles and social constructions present at the founding of the Constitution and the Civil War Amendments. They also disagree with the originalists that the Court should continue to follow 18th and 19th century polity principles as to the power of the Supreme Court to make robust constitutional choices.

Finally, it is not simply the vehemence and the bellicosity of Justice Scalia's response to non-originalist PBD that suggest the importance of PBD to contemporary Court decision making, but also the number and depth of the arguments used by both originalists and non-originalists in debating the canons of what constitute legitimate constitutional interpretation. There is a relationship between acceptance and rejection of PBD, and the components of that process, to actual Court choices. The Justices are not simply discussing a colleague's trope or logic, given the fact that this debate has occurred at numerous times within the Burger and Rehnquist Court eras, and builds on debates about Court decision making and institutional role in the Warren Court era.

Moreover, because Court decision making is not simply an individual act by a Justice, but rather is part of a continuing written discussion among the justices, studying patterns of written opinions allows scholars access to the decision-making process itself. When one sees arguments and antagonisms reappear over many cases, and we can document changes in the opinions by justices, one can conclude there are significant differences among the justices with regard to how they view Supreme Court decision making, and the components of that process that they view as legitimate. For example, Justice Potter Stewart dissents in *Griswold v. Connecticut*, 381 U.S. 479, 529–531 (1965) finding that there is no right to privacy in the Constitution that allows married couples to decide whether to use contraceptives. In *Roe v. Wade*, 410 U.S. 113, 169 (1973), we see Justice Stewart concurring, and supporting the right of abortion choice because *Griswold* and later cases such as *Eisenstadt v. Baird*, 405 U.S. 438 (1972) "make clear that freedom of personal choice in matters of marriage and family life is one of the liberties protected by the Due Process Clause of the Fourteenth Amendment." In mentioning this example I am not saying that PBD is simply the institutional norm that Justices follow precedent. It is a much more active, constitutive process, as is evident in the reason Justice Stewart gives for recognizing the right of abortion choice for women.

35. *Lawrence v. Texas*, 539 U.S. 558, at 586–592 (Scalia, J., dissenting).

36. *Ibid.* at 593 (2003).

37. *Ibid.* at 572 (quoting *County of Sacramento v. Lewis*, 523 U.S. 833, 857 (1998), Kennedy, J. (concurring)).

38. *Lawrence v. Texas*, 539 U.S. 558, 590 (2003).

39. *Ibid.* at 594.

40. *Ibid.* at 604. (quoting Kennedy's majority opinion at 578). For the argument that *Bowers* and *Romer* cannot stand together, see Scalia's dissent in *Romer v. Evans*, 517 U.S. 620, 640–644.

41. *Ibid.* at 604–605(quoting Kennedy majority opinion at 574, 578, and 567).

42. *Romer v. Evans*, 517 U.S. 620, 620–644 (1996).

43. Part of the opposition by Scalia and the other originalists on the Court to the *Casey* decision, and now to the *Lawrence* decision, is that the right to privacy itself is not found in the Constitution. For them *Griswold*'s right of privacy was a

misinterpretation of the Constitution, as was *Roe*. Therefore, the right of homosexual sodomy as part of the right of privacy is not a right protected in the Constitution and thus any PBD which follows *Roe*, including the PBD process as outlined in *Casey*, is illegitimate. Originalists refuse to consider the impact of such rights of changes in the social, economic, and political world outside the Court since *Griswold* in 1965 and *Roe* in 1973. The attack by originalists on the non-originalist PBD takes quite direct forms. Scalia cannot rest his case against homosexual rights on the view that all rights not specifically stated in the Constitution cannot be fundamental rights. Thus, Scalia leaves the door ajar, conceptually, for the Court at times to define implied fundamental rights when government is very abusive of its citizens.

44. *Planned Parenthood of Southeastern Pennsylvania v. Casey,* 505 U.S. 833, 861 (1992).

45. *Ibid.* at 866–867.

46. *Ibid.* at 865–866.

47. *Ibid.* at 869.

48. The analysis of PBD is not centered simply or primarily on the question of whether the Supreme Court uses, misuses, or misinterprets social science data or social, economic, and political facts, in a single case. Erickson Rosemary J. and Rita J. Simon (1998, pp. 149) find that the Supreme Court gives far more weight to the decisions in prior cases or precedents, rather than the quality of the social science data used in precedents. Few citations are made to social science data when discussing precedents. This suggests that what are considered in later cases are not social facts or data, but rather the social constructions derived from the social facts. I would suspect that issues of the quality of data may be more central in other areas of law than constitutional law, such as environmental law and torts.

49. See Hirsch (1992, pp. 115–193), for a lucid critique of the Supreme Court for disregarding social facts, when defining liberty interests under the Constitution. Here, I argue that it is through the social construction process that the Court extends rights to groups previously unprotected.

50. This is to be expected because Supreme Court decision making in the area of American constitutional law always has had significant common law roots, in which legal principles were applied in light of the economic, social, and political world outside the Court (see Strauss (1996); One can see it in Kahn (2002) and Levi (1949).

51. See Goldford (2005 p. 186).

52. See Hacking (1999, pp. 7–37) for the argument: "Ideas do not exist in a vacuum. They inhabit a social setting. Let us call that the *matrix* within which an idea, a concept or kind, is formed." One can see this process at work when Justices must determine whether a right has been violated.

53. See Dudziak (2000).

54. For a theory of doctrinal change which focuses on periods of "higher lawmaking" versus normal times, and the impact of critical elections in the 1930s, resulting in the formation of the post-Lochner era activist Supreme Court, see Ackerman (1991, 1998).

55. See Comiskey (2004, Chapter 7), for a fascinating review of the difficulties that Presidents have had in attempting to pack the Supreme Court; also see Silverstein and Haltom (1996) with regard to Clinton's Ginsburg and Breyer nominations to the Supreme Court.

56. See Kahn and Kersch (2006b, pp. 3–6), for the analytic limitations of the "law against politics" debate.

57. For the most comprehensive critique of arguments made by historians that external political events can explain *West Coast Hotel*, and the judicial "revolution" of 1937, see Cushman (1998). For an insightful discussion of the debate in the early 20th century over whether the Constitution should be changed by evolution through interpretation or by amendment, see Gillman (1997). However, in this discussion, Gillman continues the traditional reification by externalist scholars of the importance of 1937 as the key dividing line between the Court following originalist thinking and one in which the Constitution is to be defined as a "living" document. Also, see Kahn (2002) for an argument that 1937 is not an important dividing line as to the Constitution as a living document.

58. See Klarman (2004, 2005) and Welke (2001) for recent works by historians which do not have these limitations.

59. See Segal and Spaeth (1993, 2002) for classic statements of the attitudinal approach. See also Spaeth and Segal (1999) for the view that, when Justices disagree with the establishment of a precedent, they rarely shift from their previously stated positions in later cases. The analysis is in terms of end product policy, not in terms of a consideration of the principles and social constructions in prior cases, influencing how the Justices engage in the interpretive turn in later cases.

60. See Goldford (2005, p. 334).

61. *Ibid.* 348. Thus, the Constitution, in principle (and as constitutive practice) is distinct from whatever anyone says about it, including the founders. The Constitution can be invoked as a critical standard against current practices which are alleged to be unconstitutional.

62. See Graber (2006, p. 35).

63. See Kahn (2006a, pp. 75–81) for an extended analysis of why Justices in *Casey* and *Lawrence* were not acting strategically.

64. Political scientists need not accept the externalist stance of behavioralists, nor legalist pragmatism. See Graber (1997, p. 802) for the argument that "If the right to abortion and the right to engage in homosexual sodomy both follow logically from a more general right of privacy, then a society whose constitution is interpreted as protecting that general right of privacy should not keep abortion legal and ban homosexual sodomy. At the very least, Supreme Court justices in gay rights cases should not reject general constitutional rights to privacy without explaining why they are still protecting abortion."

65. All political signals indicated that maximalist decisions in *Casey*, *Romer*, and *Lawrence* would trigger negative political reactions, and they did. If the Court simply had strategic concerns, it is difficult to understand why the Court in both *Casey* and *Lawrence* specifically rejects the importance of the presence of controversy and growing political contestation and controversy over abortion choice and gay rights, at a time when a centerpiece of the governing majority, and the administration that it elected, was its opposition to the right of abortion choice and expanded gay rights.

66. See Sunstein (1999) and Tushnet (1999). Tushnet is even more trusting of politics and more dedicated to a minimalist role for the Supreme Court than is Sunstein. See Graber (2000) for a superb analysis of this book. See Kahn (2006b),

for the argument that Tushnet's popular constitutionalism is another externalist theory of constitutional change, with many similarities to Sunstein's minimalism.

67. See Sunstein (2003).

68. See Sunstein (1999, p. 200).

69. See Kahn (2006a, pp. 78–81). In recent decades, Justices of all stripes have moved away from a mechanistic three-tiered formula for applying equal protection principles. This has increased the presence of substantive as opposed to procedural denial of access to the political system bases for invoking equal protection principles. Primary examples of this can be found in *City of Cleburne v. Cleburne Living Center,* 473 U.S. 432 (1985), a case granting heightened Court scrutiny for the disabled, and *United States v. Virginia,* 518 U.S. 515 (1996), a case finding the Virginia Military Institute in violation of the equal protection principles because it was a male-only state university.

70. See Lessig (1989) for the place of what I call social constructions in what Lessig describes as context in the "process of translation" in Supreme Court decision making. Also, see Lessig (1995) "The Regulation of Social Meaning," *The University of Chicago Law Review* 62 (1995): 943–1045.

71. The social construction component of PBD forces Justices to apply past rights principles and social constructions to the case before them through a process of analogy that forces them to ask whether the aspects of individuals' lives for which a right to be left alone has been requested is similar to the aspects of individuals' lives that have been protected from government intrusion in prior cases. And they must do with concern for what is just, not simply popular. This process is quite different from how more directly politically accountable institutions make decisions.

72. See Sunstein (1988) for Sunstein's view of the relationship between due process and equal protection which the Supreme Court rejected in *Lawrence.*

73. See Kahn (1999c) and Smith (1997) for the important argument that the American liberal tradition is built on multiple traditions which are less supportive of the needs of subordinated groups.

74. See Alschuler (2000) for the argument that judges were deciding cases with a strong regard to the nature of the world outside the court well before the period of Holmes and judicial realism. Pragmatists over-emphasize the degree to which courts before the 1920s simply applied principles when deciding cases.

75. A similar strategy of minimalism in the more general political system in the post-Reagan age might be President Clinton's pursuit of piecemeal healthcare reform after his universal healthcare proposal was rejected.

76. See Kahn (2006a) for a fuller discussion of these characteristics of the contemporary Supreme Court.

77. The old adage "If it looks like a duck, walks like a duck, and quacks like a duck, then it must be a duck" is apropos here, given the importance of the process of analogy in legal thinking.

78. *Lawrence v. Texas,* 539 U.S. 558, 571 (2003).

79. See Kahn (1994, pp. 257–258, 1999a) for details of the Court moving from a privacy to a personhood basis for the right of abortion choice.

80. See Kahn (2006a, pp. 90–92) for an expanded analysis of the basic components of PBD.

81. See Goldford (2005, p. 186): "Originalist intent itself ... is not discovered, but rather constructed by interpretation, and thus cannot be the ground of objectivity in the sense in which originalism understands it." Thus, he finds originalism is not the obverse of non-originalism.

82. In making this argument, I am not arguing for a Whiggish view of history, i.e., that all change is progress, and progress is preordained by PBD. I am arguing that the rate of social change by the Supreme Court, and its pattern of change, will be different from those of other institutions in the wider political system. I am also arguing that non-originalist PBD makes it easier for legal advocacy groups to define injustices that have not yet received a level of visibility and concern that would produce action by the wider political system. See Kersch (2006), for a superb argument against viewing constitutional change through Supreme Court decision making in Whiggish terms. Moreover, an interesting question arises as to whether a PBD with a robust social construction process could lead to a retrenching of individual rights. I think not. When the Court has overturned landmark decisions, such as in *Brown* and *Loving*, it has made more robust, complex, and filigreed social constructions to expand rights. This is an interesting issue for future study, for one could ask is this what is happening presently with regard to affirmative action. However, in this regard, it is not clear that the Court has ever been robust in the PBD surrounding affirmative action. Finally, as David Strauss has argued in Strauss (1989), the Supreme Court has taken the least progressive of possible paths from *Brown*, but the overall political system may have taken an even more conservative path on overcoming the affects on racial segregation and discrimination.

83. See Kahn (2006a, p. 94) for an extended analysis of this process.

84. For evidence of the bi-directionality of influence between the Supreme Court and interpretive community, particularly with regard to the role of legal advocacy groups, see Kersch (2006), Nackenoff (2006), Novkov (2006), and Keck (2006), and the other contributions to Kahn and Kersch (2006a).

85. For an anecdotal account of the conservative movement in Kansas's distain for liberals and liberalism in general and homosexuals in particular, see Frank (2004). It seems that an important dimension in Kansas is not simply opposition to liberal social policies, but also disdain for the legal objectivity (secularism) of the Supreme Court and its institutional autonomy. The Terri Schiavo case, which involved a conflict over whether courts or Congress should make the decision whether she was to stay on life support systems, is an example of contemporary social conservative thinking which rejects legal objectivity for politics that will support their moral choices.

86. See Skowronek (1997, pp. 407–464), for a discussion of "political time" with regard to presidencies through time.

87. This does not mean that the Court always engages in a (re)construction process, and always seeks to interpret the Constitution in light of change outside the Court. Polity and rights principles and the social constructions on which they are built may become static. However, this is not the usual process of Supreme Court decision making and doctrinal change.

REFERENCES

Ackerman, B. (1991). *We the people 1: Foundations*. Cambridge: Harvard University Press.

Ackerman, B. (1998). *We the people 2: Transformations*. Cambridge: Harvard University Press.

Alschuler, A. W. (2000). *Law without values: The life, work, and legacy of Justice Holmes*. Chicago: University of Chicago Press.

Baumgartner, F. R., & Jones, B. D. (1993). *Agendas and instability in American politics*. Chicago: University of Chicago Press.

Comiskey, M. (2004). *Seeking justices: The judging of Supreme Court nominees*. Lawrence: University Press of Kansas.

Cushman, B. (1998). *Rethinking the New Deal court: The structure of a constitutional revolution*. New York: Oxford University Press.

Dudziak, M. L. (2000). *Cold war civil rights: Race and the image of American democracy*. Princeton: Princeton University Press.

Ely, J. H. (1980). *Democracy and distrust*. Cambridge: Harvard University Press.

Frank, T. (2004). *What's the matter with Kansas? How Conservatives won the heart of America*. New York: Henry Holt and Company.

Gillman, H. (1997). The collapse of constitutional originalism and the rise of the notion of the 'living constitution' in the course of American state-building. *Studies in American Political Development, 11*, 191–247.

Goldford, D. (2005). *The American Constitution and the debate over originalism*. New York: Cambridge University Press.

Graber, M. (1997). The Clintonification of American law: Abortion welfare, and liberal constitutional theory. *Ohio State Law Journal, 58*, 731–818.

Graber, M. (2000). Commentaries on Mark Tushnet's taking the constitution away from the courts: The law professor as populist. *University of Richmond Law Review, 34*, 373–412.

Graber, M. (2006). Legal, strategic or legal strategy: Deciding to decide during the Civil War and reconstruction. In: R. Kahn & K. I. Kersch (Eds), *The Supreme Court and American political development* (pp. 33–66). Lawrence, KS: University Press of Kansas.

Grutter v. Bollinger, 539 U.S. 306 (2003).

Hacking, I. (1999). *The social construction of what?* Cambridge: Harvard University Press.

Hirsch, H. N. (1992). *A theory of liberty: The constitution and minorities*. New York: Routledge Press.

Kahn, R. (1994). *The Supreme Court and constitutional theory, 1953–1993*. Lawrence: The University Press of Kansas.

Kahn, R. (1999a). Institutional norms and Supreme Court decision making: The Rehnquist Court on privacy and religion. In: C. Cornell & H. Gillman (Eds), *Supreme Court decision making: New institutionalist approaches* (pp. 177–198). Chicago: University of Chicago Press.

Kahn, R. (1999b). Institutional norms and the historical development of Supreme Court politics: Changing 'social facts' and doctrinal development. In: G. Howard & C. W. Clayton (Eds), *The Supreme Court in American politics: New institutionalist interpretations* (pp. 43–49). Lawrence, KS: University Press of Kansas.

Kahn, R. (1999c). Liberalism, political culture, and the rights of subordinated groups: Constitutional theory and practice at a crossroads. In: D. F. Ericson & L. B. Green (Eds), *The liberal tradition in American politics: Reassessing the legacy of American liberalism* (pp. 171–197). New York: Routledge Publishing.

Kahn, R. (2002). *Marbury v. Madison* as a model for understanding contemporary judicial review. In: M. A. Graber & M. Perhac (Eds), *Marbury versus Madison: Documents and commentary* (pp. 155–180). Washington, DC: CQ Press.

Kahn, R. (2005). Why *Lawrence v. Texas* (2003) was not expected: A critique of pragmatic legalist and behavioral explanations of Supreme Court decision making. In: H. N. Hirsch (Ed.), *The future of gay rights in America* (pp. 229–264). New York: Routledge.

Kahn, R. (2006a). Social constructions, Supreme Court reversals, and American political development: *Lochner, Plessy, Bowers,* But Not *Roe.* In: R. Kahn & K. I. Kersch (Eds), *The Supreme Court and American political development* (pp. 67–113). Lawrence, KS: University Press of Kansas.

Kahn, R. (2006b). The constitution restoration act, judicial independence, and popular constitutionalism. *Case Western Reserve Law Review, 56,* 1083–1118.

Kahn, R., & Kersch, K. I. (Eds). (2006a). *The Supreme Court and American political development.* Lawrence, KS: University Press of Kansas.

Kahn, R., & Kersch, K. I. (Eds). (2006b). Introduction. In: R. Kahn & K.I. Kersch (Eds), *The Supreme Court and American political development* (pp. 1–30). Lawrence, KS: University Press of Kansas.

Keck, T. M. (2004). *The most activist Supreme Court in history.* Chicago: University of Chicago Press.

Keck, T. M. (2006). From *Bakke* to *Grutter*: The rise of rights-based conservatism. In: R. Kahn & K. I. Kersch (Eds), *The Supreme Court and American political development* (pp. 414–442). Lawrence, KS: University Press of Kansas.

Kersch, K. I. (2006). The New Deal triumph as the end of history? The judicial negotiation of labor rights and civil rights. In: K. Ronald & K. I. Kersch (Eds), *The Supreme Court and American political development* (pp. 169–226). Lawrence, KS: University Press of Kansas.

Kingdon, J. W. (2003). *Agendas, alternatives, and public policies* (2nd ed.). New York: Addison-Wesley.

Klarman, M. (2004). *From Jim Crow to Civil Rights: The Supreme Court and the struggle for racial equality.* New York: Oxford University Press.

Klarman, M. (2005). Courts, Congress and Civil Rights. In: N. Devins & K. Whittington (Eds), *Congress and the constitution* (pp. 173–197). Durham, NC: Duke University Press.

Lessig, L. (1989). Plastics: Unger and Ackerman on transformation. *Yale Law Journal, 98,* 1173–1192.

Lessig, L. (1995). The regulation of social meaning. *The University of Chicago Law Review, 62,* 943–1045.

Levi, E. H. (1949). *An introduction to legal reasoning.* Chicago: University of Chicago Press.

Nackenoff, C. (2006). Constitutionalizing terms of inclusion: Friends of the Indian and citizenship for Native Americans, 1880s–1930s. In: K. Ronald & K. I. Kersch (Eds), *The Supreme Court and American political development* (pp. 366–414). Lawrence, KS: University Press of Kansas.

Novkov, J. (2006). *Pace v. Alabama*: Interracial love, the marriage contract, and postbellum foundations of the family. In: K. Ronald & K. I. Kersch (Eds), *The Supreme Court and American political development* (pp. 329–365). Lawrence, KS: University Press of Kansas.

Pierson, P. (2000). Increasing returns, path dependence, and the study of politics. *American Political Science Review, 94,* 251–267.

Segal, J. A., & Spaeth, H. J. (1993). *The Supreme Court and the attitudinal model.* New York: Cambridge University Press.

Segal, J. A., & Spaeth, H. J. (2002). *The Supreme Court and the attitudinal model revisited.* New York: Cambridge University Press.

Silverstein, M., & Haltom, W. (1996). You can't always get what you want: Reflections on the Ginsberg and Breyer nominations. *Journal of Law and Politics, 12,* 459–479.

Skowronek, S. (1997). *The politics presidents make: Leadership from John Adams to Bill Clinton.* Cambridge: Harvard University Press.

Smith, R. (1997). *Civic ideals: Conflicting visions of citizenship in U.S. history.* Cambridge: Harvard University Press.

Spaeth, H. J., & Segal, J. A. (1999). *Majority rule or minority will: Adherence to precedent on the U.S. Supreme Court.* New York: Cambridge University Press.

Strauss, D. A. (1989). Discriminatory intent and the taming of Brown. *University of Chicago Law Review, 56,* 479–487.

Strauss, D. A. (1996). Common law constitutional interpretation. *University of Chicago Law Review, 63,* 877–935.

Sunstein, C. (1988). Sexual orientation and constitution: A note on the relationship between due process and equal protection. *University of Chicago Law Review, 55,* 1161–1179.

Sunstein, C. (1999). *One case at a time: Judicial minimalism on the Supreme Court.* Cambridge: Harvard University Press.

Sunstein, C. (2003). What Did *Lawrence* Hold? Of autonomy, desuetude, sexuality, and marriage. *The Supreme Court Review, 2003,* 27–74.

Tribe, L. (1980). The puzzling persistence of process based constitutional theories. *Yale Law Journal, 89,* 1063–1080.

Tushnet, M. (1999). *Taking the Constitution away from the courts.* Princeton, NJ: Princeton University Press.

Welke, B. Y. (2001). *Recasting American liberty: Gender, race, and the railroad revolution, 1865–1920.* New York: Cambridge University Press.

CASES CITED

Bowers v. Hardwick, 478 U.S. 186 (1986).

City of Cleburne v. Cleburne Living Center, 473 U.S. 432 (1985).

County of Sacramento v. Lewis, 523 U.S. 833 (1998).

Eisenstadt v. Baird, 405 U.S. 438 (1972).

Gonzales v. Carhart, Supreme Court No. 05-380 (Decided April 18, 2007).

Griswold v. Connecticut, 381 U.S. 479 (1965).

Lawrence v. Texas, 539 U.S. 558 (2003).

Lochner v. New York, 198 U.S. 45 (1905).

Loving v. Virginia, 388 U.S. 1 (1967).

Marbury v. Madison, 5 U.S. (1 Cranch) 137 (1803).

McCleskey v. Kemp, 481 U.S. 279 (1987).

Michael H. v. Gerald D, 491 U.S. 110 (1989).

Parents Involved in Community Schools v. Seattle School District No. 1., Supreme Court No. 05-908 (Decided June 28, 2007).

Planned Parenthood of Southeastern Pennsylvania v. Casey, 505 U.S. 833 (1992).

Plessy v. Ferguson, 163 U.S. 537 (1896).
Reed v. Reed, 404 U.S. 71 (1971).
Regents of the University of California v. Bakke, 438 U.S. 265 (1978).
Roe v. Wade, 410 U.S. 113 (1973).
Romer v. Evans, 517 U.S. 620 (1996).
United States v. Virginia, 518 U.S. 515 (1996).
Webster v. Reproductive Services, 492 U.S. 490 (1989).
West Coast Hotel v. Parrish, 300 U.S. 379 (1937).